# Cases in Educational Psychology

## A CANADIAN PERSPECTIVE

**John F. Durkin**

University of Victoria

Prentice Hall

Toronto

**National Library of Canada Cataloguing in Publication Data**

Durkin, John F. (John Frederick), 1944–
      Cases in educational psychology : a Canadian perspective

ISBN 0-13-091419-3

    1. Educational psychology—Case studies. I Title.

LB1051.D87 2003         370.15        C2001-903435-0

---

ISBN 0-13-091419-3

Vice President, Editorial Director: Michael J. Young
Acquisitions Editor: Lori Will
Marketing Manager: Christine Cozens
Developmental Editor: Laura Paterson Forbes
Production Editor: Cheryl Jackson
Copy Editor: Jennifer Howse
Production Coordinator: Peggy Brown
Page Layout: Heidi Palfrey
Creative Director: Mary Opper
Cover Design: Sarah Battersby
Cover Image: Photo Disc

1 2 3 4 5  06 05 04 03 02

Printed and bound in Canada

# Brief Contents

# Contents

## Chapter 11  Cognitive Learning Theories  124

# PART 5  APPROACHES TO INSTRUCTION  134

## Chapter 12  Mastery, Direct, and Constructivist Approaches  134

## Chapter 13  Differentiated Instruction, Group/Cooperative Learning, and Brain-Based Approaches  146

## PART 6    CLASSROOM MANAGEMENT    159

### Chapter 14    Emotions, Stress, and Motivation    159

### Chapter 15    Learning Environments and Learned Difficulties    171

## Chapter 16   Classroom Management   183

# PART 7   ASSESSMENT   198

## Chapter 17   Assessment and Evaluation   198

## PART 8  CONTROVERSIES    211

### Chapter 18  Controversies    211

## PART 9  ALTERNATIVE, DISTANCE, AND ELECTRONIC EDUCATION    223

### Chapter 19  Alternative Schools and Organizations    223

# Preface

*Cases in Educational Psychology: A Canadian Perspective* grew from my experience teaching educational psychology to a variety of students. It is designed for students in the faculties of education, child and youth care, and social work, as well as other students who will be working with young people. It can be used as a stand-alone text or in conjunction with more traditional educational psychology textbooks. No prerequisite to this information is assumed. The cases are based on my experiences and situations discussed in my classes, as well as on interviews with professional year students, teachers-on-call (TOC), and teachers in the first couple of years of their careers.

Invariably there have been times when students appeared to take notes in a robotic fashion. My attempts to engage the students in discussions usually resulted in a few students interacting while others quietly waited, often with looks of impatience. This feeling of lethargy disappeared, however, when I offered students the opportunity to discuss actual situations among themselves before we discussed them in class or before they made small group presentations.

Even before I started using case studies as an important part of my teaching approach, student evaluations of my classes were high and their comments usually were positive; the limited opportunity I provided to apply knowledge to real situations often was mentioned as a positive feature of the class. This evaluation did not correspond to my own rating of my teaching however. I found the situation in my class to be quite frustrating and the teaching process to be more exhausting than it should have been. Since a fundamental aspect of my approach to teaching and counselling involves accepting responsibility for personal actions, I decided to examine my own thoughts about teaching and how these thoughts manifested in my classes. This examination revealed a bind implicit in most approaches to educational psychology: Teachers in training need to learn the theoretical basis of psychology and education, but many students today choose to learn only what they see as meaningful and useful now. Students realize that additional information is available upon demand.

During my assessment of the teaching approach I had been using, I checked to see how much material students remembered from my previous courses. I found that they had forgotten almost all of the material and only recalled some story or incident related to the topic. It was demoralizing to realize that many of my students were unable to answer basic application questions on a quiz after I had spent hours teaching the material to them.

Over the years I have discovered the solution to this disheartening bind, which is to increase and expand student involvement in my class. In doing so, I trust students will have meaningful and relevant comments to make and accept, with some trepidation, that forgetting the details of some theory is not the end of the world. I recognize that I cannot force students to learn material when they do not want to, and focus on a case method approach instead.

The gradual implementation of the case method and the use of exercises has proven to be a successful approach to teaching educational psychology. The cases in this text are preceded by basic coverage of the theoretical issues developed in the cases, and students are encouraged to discuss the cases in terms of theoretical underpinnings rather than as episodes. Assessment weighting for quizzes has been reduced — although not eliminated — and the majority of the marks are now focussed on projects requiring the analysis of both short and more complex cases. Students have to develop the skills to analyse the case using appropriate theoretical models.

Some of the impetus for my changes came from *The Courage to Teach* (Palmer, 1998). Palmer pointed out that "good teachers possess a capacity for connectedness" (p. 11). Palmer felt that failure to maintain this connectedness was due to fear on the part of both teachers and students. Teachers maintained or reverted to a presentation of theories and facts, while students silently copied these down and returned them on quizzes or papers. This absence of classroom interaction provided a stagnant learning environment, preventing students from achieving the greatest understanding of the material.

## KEY FEATURES OF THE TEXT

### Approach

**Case Approach to Learning**    The *Introduction to the Case Method* section of the book discusses and illustrates the case study approach to learning. A method for preparing cases is presented and some common problems students encounter are discussed.

**Modular Approach**    The modular approach used in this text allows instructors to vary the order in which topics are introduced to students. Instructors can increase or decrease emphasis in particular areas or change the relationship of topics without being concerned that crucial information in another chapter is required.

# Content

**Special Needs**   The cases cover a wide range of situations a Canadian teacher might encounter, including special needs, gender, ESL, and cultural issues.

**Added Emphasis**   The text places more emphasis on issues related to the brain and teaching, as well as new approaches to education, including electronic education, than many other educational psychology texts.

**Diversity of Students**   The cases and concepts involve a mix of elementary-level, secondary-level, and general community situations. The principles in each case usually apply to several contexts.

# Cases

**'Real Life' Cases**   The ideas for cases are drawn from the experiences of education students, apprentice and experienced teachers, and others working with young people. Composites of these experiences are used as the foundation for developing stories that generalize the incidents both in terms of the people involved and the incident, as well as illustrating a basic principle.

**In-Class Cases**   The shorter cases can be used in a regular class at the end of a lecture. They are structured so that the issue involved is quite clear and students can read the case in a few minutes. Questions are designed to quickly draw students' attention to the principal points of the case. Students should be able to complete the case in 20 minutes and be ready to report their views to the rest of the class in that time.

**Presentation and Report Cases**   The longer cases are more fully developed and include background details that must be considered to understand the case. These cases will involve much more preparation. Students will not get the basic issues by quickly skimming the case. These cases can be used for either individual or group work requiring preparation outside of class. Students will have to use a proper case preparation method such as the one given at the beginning of the text in order to fully develop these cases.

**Advanced Cases**   Four complex cases involving several key issues can be found at the back of the book. These can be used for a final assessment based on group or individual presentations or reports.

**Variety of Formats**   Students can demonstrate their understanding of the issues in a case using a variety of formats ranging from the traditional written report to group presentations, dramatizations, and various multi-media formats.

# Pedagogy

**Questions and Activities**   Each case is followed by questions that are meant to help draw attention to the key features of the case. The cases and questions create activities that allow students to access and construct their own knowledge in multiple formats.

**Exercises**   Most chapters contain short exercises that will help students deepen their understanding of the issues being discussed.

**Summary**   Each chapter begins with a point form summary of the theory related to the cases that follow it. These summaries are extensive enough to provide a review of the basic theoretical information and a vocabulary for classroom discussion, but allow students to focus on applying the theory to 'real life' case studies.

## INTRODUCTION TO THE CASE METHOD

Students are encouraged to use the case method (outlined in the *Introduction to the Case Method*) to analyse the cases. While the stories are interesting in themselves and lead to discussions about what someone should have done or could do, these comments often are only quickly formed opinions. Much deeper learning results from using a common vocabulary to illustrate the general principles in the case and how they could apply to other situations or to our own teaching. Discussions of teaching, learning, and management strategies are best done based on theory rather than as a replacement for theory.

The *Introduction to Case Method* section also contains information about how students can develop cases from their own experience. Students are encouraged to develop cases based on general principles rather than extreme examples of teacher/classroom behaviours that are incident-specific and do not lead to general understanding, keeping in mind the need for confidentiality and sensitivity towards others.

### Students As Decision Makers

The case method puts students in the role of decision maker. Students are faced with situations similar to those they will encounter in their first few years of teaching. Facts are not presented in some fixed pedagogical order; sometimes they are not even distinguished from opinions. While principles are involved and demonstrated, there is no one answer for the more complex cases. Students are challenged to develop their own concepts and insights through inquiry, questioning, and self-directed learning. This prepares students for their transition to a classroom environment. Instructors are freed to stimulate development of principles, rather than presenting material that students may not find relevant.

## REFERENCES

Palmer, P.J. (1998). The courage to teach: Exploring the inner landscape of a teacher's life. San Francisco: Jossey-Bass Publishers.

## ACKNOWLEDGMENTS

The approach and cases in this book arose from interactions with students, clients, teachers, and other professionals over more than three decades. Many of these interactions resulted in a slow evolution of my approach to teaching and learning; others were revolutionary leading to an examination of my whole approach. Sometimes the changes were pleasant; sometimes they were upsetting. I am thankful for both.

I feel a special sense of gratitude to my wife, Dianne, who has been such an important part of my work with young people. Her encouragement and involvement through the years has made all the difference.

# Introduction to the Case Method: Notes for Instructors and Students

The Case Method is an approach to learning that can be used in conjunction with lectures or on a stand-alone basis. The central feature of the Case Method is the involvement of students in the analyses of situations that are thought to be representative of those they might encounter in work life, and/or that might illustrate basic principles in a field to the student. Active involvement in learning, rather than passive receiving of information, is the underlying aspect of case study. If students do not see a connection between theories and actions, and do not reflect on both their own and other "real" situations, then they will react in habitual and unskilled ways when decisions have to be made.

Use of the Case Method approach involves quite substantial changes for both instructors and students. Instructors have to come to terms with their anxieties about the importance of students knowing a large body of information. Instructors have to accept that knowing information without being able to apply it is an unproductive activity. Rather, students must internalize information and reflect upon it if they are ever going to be able to use it.

Methods of assessment probably also will have to change. Exams and quizzes provide safety for instructors because they can state with quite a high degree of confidence whether the answer is correct or not. This tends to reduce student challenges to marking and the anxiety that results from these challenges. Case studies on the other hand do not have correct answers; instructors have to make judgments about students' understanding of concepts and insights to situations.

Students also may be resistant to changes in instructional approaches. They have extensive experience with, and have demonstrated their proficiency in, a relatively passive approach. It generally has only been necessary to take a relatively passive role in the class and memorize a few notes in order to be successful. Students can go for a whole year with little interaction with other students or with instructors. Case Method, on the other hand, involves the energy of concentrated attention, the effort of analysis, and the anxiety of exposure to the views of other students. Some students are very threatened by the concept that they cannot have some guarantee as to what is the right answer. Students who want to get an A+ because that is how they define themselves can be quite upset with the concept that the instructor is allowing a variety of answers as being correct.

This anxiety about being correct or about covering a certain amount of information is real and must be dealt with through discussion and through offers of support. In the end, both instructors and students must understand that in the real world of teaching there often is no immediately obvious right answer. Teachers often have to respond to situations relatively quickly without the support of detailed information. In my early years I was often anxious because I had to act but couldn't know what the outcome of my actions might be. I could apply my training and what experience I had, but the future was not written yet so there was no guaranteed answer. Even after many years of experience I find that acting in the midst of uncertainty is a fundamental challenge in my work.

The use of the Case Method also places facility challenges on an instructor. Case analysis usually involves group discussions. These discussions in turn place demands on class enrolment and physical nature of the instructional space. Rigid seating in large classrooms is a challenge. An ideal situation involves a small number of students sitting around a table — at least, I think it would be an ideal situation but I have never had it happen so I don't know for sure. I have found that the only approach is just to use what I have. In large classrooms I allow groups of students to move to any location they think would be comfortable for them. These locations have included my desk or table, the floor at the back or front, and outside the classroom. I always use a fixed time for the discussion and ask students to reconvene at a certain time. Students have met in stairwells, washrooms, janitor's closets, as well as lounges and coffee shops. While students almost always seem to be very involved in their case, the requirement that students appoint a spokesperson and give a brief account of their discussion probably serves to focus those individuals that might use the time to gossip.

The Case Method is not the answer to all learning situations. Sometimes it is necessary for students to learn both theoretical information and basic skills before they have the expertise to understand a case in other than an abstract and unrealistic manner. The use of case method approaches without basic foundations has tended to bring the whole approach into question. This is not to say that a person has to be an expert to do a case study, however. Usually a basic knowledge of vocabulary and skills is sufficient for productive case analysis. Knowledge and skill deficits quickly will be identified and can be corrected as needed.

## REPORTING CASE ANALYSIS

The first issue that needs to be considered before a case is assigned is how students are going to report their analyses. There is no need to assign a long case if students are going to give a quick summary in class. Complex cases involving statistical or financial manipulations are particularly difficult to use for class presentations. Usually the least productive form of presentation involves each student writing a long analysis for the teacher. This form means that students do not learn from each other's presentations; it also means that the instructor is left with a great deal of marking. Long written reports may be necessary, however, when there is a requirement for some type of formal assessment to demonstrate competency in complex situations.

Presentations to the class usually are the best approach, although the method for doing these presentations needs to be considered carefully. Having students make one presentation after another is not usually very helpful. By the third presentation, both the students and the instructor are so bored they don't hear a word that is said. A more successful approach is to have students make presentations over a number of days with no more than two groups presenting on a single day and then going on to other material. Another approach is to have one group make a presentation and then others are asked to come up and add anything that has not already been covered.

Group methods that do not use presentations also can be very effective. Poster sessions require each group to prepare an analysis of the case in such a way that others can understand their analysis through the use of graphs, tables, images, and bulleted summaries. Students go around and look at each other's presentations. I sometimes provide cookies and juice. Students are encouraged to discuss presentations with the groups involved. Another way to use groups without having reports or presentations is to have one person from a group going to another group and explaining their group's analysis. The audience group then responds, including any additional items they considered in their analysis. Videos, web sites, and role plays provide variety and introduce students to alternative ways of presenting information.

## SELECTING GROUP MEMBERS

Methods of establishing groups for case studies need to be given some consideration. The easiest approach is to have students work with those who are nearby. This could be appropriate for the first couple of cases. Students usually sit in the same place in class and it is helpful for them to get to know each other a bit more. Continued use of this approach, however, leads to boredom and to a serious reduction in the value of the case approach, namely the opportunity to work with other students.

There are several approaches that can be used to increase the opportunities for a student to work with others in the class. One method is to simply ask everyone to work with someone new. This will work for a couple of times but then becomes too confusing as students look for someone with whom they have not worked. Another approach is to have students choose a case they would be interested in pursuing. If too many students choose the same case, then they can be asked to choose another or break up into manageable groups. Sometimes with this approach a group of students sitting near each other will form a group and then just choose a case for convenience. Students also can be assigned to a case. This should be done in a non-personal way as for instance by having students count from 1 to 4 and then have the 1s be a group, etc. A deck of index cards with one student's name on each card also can be used. The deck is shuffled and the cards dealt to produce a group of whatever size is required.

Having instructors assign students to groups is suitable when discussion is going to take place in class but may not be suitable when there are larger case studies involving group meetings outside class. Students have many demands on their time. Many students have families and part-time jobs. Their timetable may be quite fixed and it may be quite difficult for them to meet at non-class times. Other students may feel uncomfortable about evening meetings, giving out contact information to other students, or meeting with a particular student. For case studies that involve work outside class it is probably better to allow students to choose their own groups. The number of these case studies assigned also needs to be considered. Requiring more than one or two preparations outside class time probably is not suitable for the majority of classes.

A final approach is to allow students to prepare cases on an individual basis if there is some reason that they cannot participate in a group. The case is discussed in groups in class and then a person can work alone. In this case a written presentation rather than an oral one in class probably is more suitable.

## ASSIGNMENT INSTRUCTIONS

The following is a typical handout I would give my students for a case to explain what is required for the case analysis. This case is meant to be a written report and is for 25 marks.

## (CLASS NAME)
## INSTRUCTIONS FOR CASE STUDY ASSIGNMENT

### Purpose

The purpose of this assignment is to give you an opportunity to develop and apply some of the basic principles outlined in class to a case study. You are to take some of the principles we have been discussing and apply them to the fictional but representative classroom or other location. Successful completion of this assignment will require you to move beyond the specifics of the situation and apply general principles. Anecdotal statements about characters in the assignment may be required as illustration but will not be accepted as the substance of the case.

### Components

Each case study must include the following areas:

1) **Summary of Important Facts:** Outline in a logical order the most important facts of the case. The use of headings may help you in this outline. Do not list miscellaneous facts in the order given in the case.

2) **Problem(s):** Clearly state the problem(s) that need(s) to be solved. Your statement of the main problem(s) should refer to general principles with the specifics of the case being used only for illustration.

3) **Analysis:** This is the critical segment of the case study. Organize your analysis according to the basic issues in the case. In this section please demonstrate that you understand basic principles discussed in class. An objective approach is required; little

attention should be given to simple platitudes. State clearly any assumptions you are making and any reservations you have about your analysis. Your analysis should lead clearly to your recommendations.

4) **Accommodating Individual Needs:** Your analysis and recommendations sections must demonstrate how your case study accommodates individual needs.

5) **Recommendations:** Based on your analysis and issues of individual needs, in a numbered sequence outline the steps that you think should be taken to deal with the issue(s) in the case. It is not necessary for you to restate general principles here but your recommendations should follow clearly from the application of principles in the Analysis section.

## Format of Case Study

Please use the headings in the component section above to organize your paper. The preferred length of the report is 8–10 double-spaced pages (2,000 words), not counting the title page or any appendices. You must cover all of the areas above.

Considerable care needs to be taken in the preparation of your case study. It needs to have a logical flow, be easy to read, and be free of grammatical and spelling errors. Your case study should be typed or written in a legible manner. It should be stapled; no junk covers please.

## Group Mark

Students can work alone or with a maximum of two other students. When students work together, one mark will be assigned to all members of the group. The only exception to this will be if one member of the group does not contribute to the project. In this case the non-participating member will have her/his mark prorated by the percentage of participation.

## Marking of the Case Study

To help me be more objective in my marking, I use a marking outline. Marks for the case study will be assigned as follows:

| Criteria | Possible Mark |
| --- | --- |
| Spelling/Grammar | 2 |
| Important Facts | 3 |
| Problem | 3 |
| Analysis | 10 |
| Individual Needs | 3 |
| Recommendations | 4 |
| **Total** | **25** |

The C range reflects satisfactory work; obtaining marks in the B range involves high quality work. Marks in the A range are reserved for exceptional work showing high levels of scholarship and originality.

## Copies

Students are required to submit two copies of the case study. One will be marked and returned to you; the other will be kept for course documentation.

## Due Dates

Case Study Reports are due by class time on (due date). The penalty for late assignments is 2 marks per day, i.e., 20/25 becomes 18/25. Reports will not be accepted after (one week from due date) at class time regardless of the penalty. No unauthorized exceptions.

## Class Discussion

Students should be prepared to discuss their case study with other students in the class on the due date. This will not involve a formal presentation and there are no marks for the discussion.

## ASSIGNMENT MARKING

I find it very helpful to use some type of marking guide for evaluating student work. The marking guide constantly reminds me of critical factors in the report and allows me to give students a considerable amount of feedback without writing the same comments over and over. The following marking guide is one that I developed over the years for case assignments. The categories reflect comments that were given frequently.

## (COURSE NAME)
## CASE STUDY MARKING REPORT

## Student Names: _____

| Criteria | Possible Mark | Actual Mark |
| --- | --- | --- |
| Spelling/Grammar | 2 | ____ |
| 0–1 = more than 3 spelling mistakes and/or weak grammar | | |
| 2 = less than 3 spelling mistakes and easy to read | | |
| Important Facts | 3 | ____ |
| 1 = list of "facts" from handout | | |
| 2 = relevant facts selected to support analysis | | |
| 3 = above plus method of organizing facts for analysis | | |
| Problem | 3 | ____ |
| 0–1 = no material or general statements | | |
| 2 = clear presentation of problem using principles | | |
| 3 = above plus unique definition of problem | | |

| Analysis | 10 | ____ |
|---|---|---|

0-1 = no material or general statements

2-4 = above plus assumptions and reservations

5-6 = above plus an attempt to apply basic principles

7-8 = above plus clear, over-arching statements of principles and strategies

9-10 = above plus unique contributions to the issue

| Individual Needs | 3 | ____ |
|---|---|---|

1 = a brief coverage of issue

2 = clear description of role of individual needs

3 = above plus unique understanding of individual needs

| Recommendations | 4 | ____ |
|---|---|---|

1 = general recommendations

2-3 = specific recommendations that follow from analysis and basic principles

4 = above plus unique contributions to the issue

| **Assignment Value 25** | **Your Mark** | ____ |
|---|---|---|

✓ satisfactorily completed       ◯ needs more thought

# STUDENT PRESENTATIONS

The handout for groups who are doing a presentation is somewhat different, although the same basic skills are important. Usually class presentations require a 2-page summary of the presentation for all students in the class. Students give it to me before the presentation and I use it for any additional notes I need plus comments about their presentation. About 20 percent of the mark is allowed for the organization, creativity, and interest value of the presentation itself.

## (CLASS NAME)
## GROUP PRESENTATION INFORMATION

### General Instructions

Members of the group will work together to deliver a presentation that deals with the components of the case study as outlined below. Presentations are limited to 20 minutes +/- two minutes. Marks will be deducted from presentations that do not meet time guidelines. The most important part of the presentation is, of course, your analysis but attention also should be given to the organization of your presentation, techniques to maintain interest, and creativity in presentation technique.

## Presentation

Marks for this section of the assignment are based on the way materials and experiences have been organized to help students understand the concepts involved, the degree to which the presentation is properly timed as well as clear or even memorable, and the unique contribution that the group has made to the presentation of the concepts involved.

## Components

Each case analysis presentation must include the following areas:

1) **Summary of Important Facts:** Outline in a logical order the most important facts of the case. The use of an overhead with headings may help you in this outline. Do not list miscellaneous facts in the order given in the case.

2) **Problem(s):** Clearly state the problem(s) that need(s) to be solved. Your statement of the main problem(s) should refer to general principles with the specifics of the case being used only for illustration. An overhead or a poster succinctly stating the problem(s) should be available during your presentation.

3) **Analysis:** This is the critical segment of the case study. Organize your analysis according to the basic issues in the case. In this section please demonstrate that you understand basic principles discussed in class. An objective approach is required; little attention should be given to simple platitudes. State clearly any assumptions you are making and any reservations you have about your analysis. Your analysis should lead clearly to your recommendations. Your audience will need some type of visual emphasis to follow this section of your presentation.

4) **Accommodating Individual Needs:** Your analysis and recommendations sections must demonstrate how your case study accommodates individual needs.

5) **Recommendations:** Based on your analysis and issues of individual needs, in a numbered sequence outline the steps that you think should be taken to deal with the issue(s) in the case. It is not necessary for you to re-state general principles here, but your recommendations should follow clearly from the application of principles in the analysis section. Your recommendations should be introduced to your audience in a sequential fashion. Displaying an overhead with all of them right at the beginning of this section may be confusing.

## Handout

Each presentation must include a short handout for other students summarizing your case and emphasizing the main points of your study. Two typed pages is the ideal length for the handout. A copy of the handout is to be submitted to me before the beginning of the presentation.

## Marking of Projects

To help me be more objective in my marking, I use a marking outline. Marks for each presentation will be assigned as follows:

| Criteria | Possible Mark |
|---|---|
| Presentation | 5 |
| Important Facts | 2 |
| Problem(s) | 2 |
| Analysis | 10 |
| Individual Needs | 2 |
| Recommendations | 4 |
| **Total** | **25** |

As in all grades for this course, a "C" mark indicates satisfactory performance; marks in the "B" range are given for well researched, interesting, and clearly delivered presentations, while "A" marks are reserved for exceptional presentations that show both considerable depth of knowledge and outstanding presentation skills.

## Group Mark

One mark will be assigned to all members of the group. The only exception to this will be if one member of the group does not contribute to the project. In this case the non-participating member will have her/his mark prorated by the percentage of participation.

## STUDENT APPROACHES TO CASES

Case analysis allows considerable freedom for individual thought and creativity. At the same time, students must consider the following factors when doing their analyses.

## Context

While most cases can be analysed from a number of theoretical positions, each case comes at a particular location in the class and probably is meant to be viewed in the context of information being covered in class. This is particularly true of shorter cases. Longer cases may involve the synthesis of several theoretical positions, but still should be seen as occurring in a particular context. Often instructors will provide questions that will orient students to the context.

## Overall Picture

Students should read the case through to get an overall picture of the situation. This first reading may lead students to believe they understand the situation; they need to be careful of this initial 'understanding'. Our minds usually search for the underlying meaning in a series of events, but may close too quickly based on only a cursory understanding of the situation and a large number of assumptions.

## Important Facts

Some students find a simple listing of the facts as being the best approach for them. Other students need to get an image of the overall relationships in the case and will find a web approach to be the best.

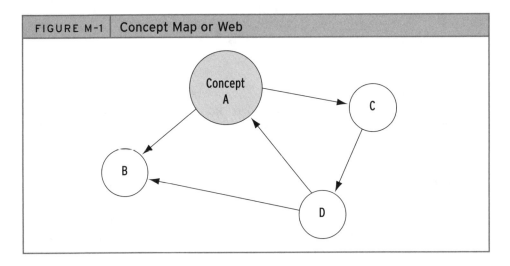

| FIGURE M-1 | Concept Map or Web |

## Problem(s)

Problem(s) should be grouped from most serious to least. Perhaps those that are least serious are so minor that their impact is being overshadowed by more serious situations, and so they do not need to be considered.

## Case Analysis

This section of the case study usually is the most important. At this point, students have to try and understand both the obvious and the not-so-obvious features of the case. An understanding of the case usually is a gradually development, often involving discussions with others. Students sometimes have difficulties in this section because they tend to just repeat the material from the case description rather than moving to a more abstract analysis using the vocabulary that is being studied. The episodes in the case are only illustrations of the issues involved.

Students need to consider the relative value of different bits of information in the case. Comments and opinions need to be separated from more factual data. The particular biases that individuals may have also need to be considered. Analysis of longer cases in particular may involve the gathering of additional information. Students may have to find out how many hours it takes to perform some activity or what are the laws related to a particular situation before they can do an effective analysis.

Sometimes students need to make assumptions about situations related to the case. Generally these assumptions are acceptable if they are clearly stated and would be the normal case in a similar situation. Assumptions requiring unusual situations usually are not acceptable. It would be normal, for instance, to assume that a teacher has a heavy work-load. On the other hand, assuming a house fire when no mention of this was made in the case study would not be acceptable.

## Accommodating Individual Needs

Teachers frequently have classes where one or more students present unique challenges. Sometimes little is known about these students' abilities, backgrounds, or difficulties. In all cases teachers have to develop their own understanding of these students from bits of data obtained from the students and their parents, from experimenting with a variety of approaches, and possibly from some type of formal testing.

## Recommendations

Recommendations should follow from analysis and should be supported by reference to particular models or underlying principles. They also should be feasible in the context of the problem. When students are making recommendations they should include the costs as well as the benefits of a particular approach. In general, there are no solutions to problems that completely solve them, and almost any solutions also have a downside. Students need to support the argument that their recommendations are the best given the context.

## WRITING OR PRESENTING A CASE

Presentation of cases involves conciseness and precision. Long, rambling stories usually will not convey the depth of students' analyses or the value of their recommendations. In class discussions students should be prepared to make their points concisely and then be prepared to listen to other points of view. The ability to listen to other points of view, incorporate them if they seem useful, and leave them out if they don't seem to be strong positions without being offensive, are skills that develop with practice; they are important skills in working with other people.

Although there are no sets of 'right answers' to the cases in this book, this does not mean that *any* case report is satisfactory. Some case studies clearly show a greater understanding of theoretical principles and insights to the actual situation of the case than do others.

## NATURE OF CASES IN THIS BOOK

The cases in this book come from a large number of locations and contexts in Canada. Information about location and context is given when it is relevant. Otherwise students should not make assumptions related to location, ethnic grouping, gender, etc. People in different contexts deal with the same issues although the extent of problems and the resources available may vary. All cases are fictional with any similarity to actual situations being unintended.

The nature of this book involves the presentation of problems. Teaching often is the continuous solving of problems, and so the book is a realistic from that point of view. However, major difficulties probably occur less frequently than is implied by their presence in this text.

## STUDENT-DEVELOPED CASES

Instructors may chose to have students develop their own case studies from the students' experiences. In this case students are encouraged to develop cases based on general principles rather than extreme examples of behaviours that are incident-specific and do not lead to general understanding. Students also have to be aware of ethical concerns. These concerns arise where a student describes a situation and does not protect the privacy of the people involved. Changing names, for instance, is not enough if members of the group are familiar with the situation being discussed.

Students also have to be careful about biases and stereotypes. Our society, particularly our educational institutions, sensitizes us to recognize some prejudices, but accepts or encourages others. For now at least, this phenomenon is called political correctness; history may chose to use other labels and evaluations of the situation.

## MODEL CASE ANALYSIS

The following case has been chosen for demonstration because of its ambiguous nature and its brevity. Ambiguous cases are both more interesting and more difficult than those with a clear-cut issue. They also reflect situations those working with young people often encounter. The analysis of the case represents one approach to reporting a case. Instructors may require or accept other approaches from students.

## CASE METHOD-1: JANE

Jane is a very quiet and withdrawn 15-year-old student who makes very little contact with other students and adults. She performs adequately at most routine work, but has difficulties when analysis or synthesis is required. Jane appears not to like any class activities that involve performance or social interaction. She does not take part in any music or drama programs and does not attend any of the noon hour activities.

Jane speaks so quietly that it is often difficult for other students to understand her. There have been some well-meaning attempts by the other girls to bring her into the mainstream social life of the class, but Jane rejects these. The teacher has tried some suggestions from the school counsellor, without success so far. The teacher briefly talked to Jane's mother about Jane's lack of friends and was told that her parents did not see it as a problem. "Jane spends most of her time with us," her mother said. "We think she is young yet to be involved in many social activities."

Although Jane is thought to be 'kinda weird' by the other students, she finds and obviously enjoys some acceptance on the basis of her computer skills; she practises these at home. She is of normal stature and build for her age, but manages to find excuses for not taking part in games or PE most of the time, an exception being distance running.

Little is known about Jane's past school history since she came from a private school in another province. Her mother visited the school on the first day of classes, but neither parent has come to any parent-teacher meetings. The only communications so far have been through report cards and two brief phone calls by the teacher. Invariably Jane is driven to and from school by one of her parents.

# CASE ANALYSIS REPORT

## Summary of Important Facts

- Jane performs adequately at the knowledge and comprehension levels for her grade but seems to have difficulty at higher levels of cognitive functioning.
- For some reason Jane shows great reluctance to participate in group and performance activities.
- Jane is good with computers; this skill is a source of interaction with other students.
- Other students do not reject Jane; indeed, they have made efforts to involve her.
- Jane has appropriate fine and gross motor skills as she types and runs well.
- Jane's parents are satisfied with her social behaviour.
- Jane's parents do not have much contact with the school although her parents drive her to and from school.

## Problem(s)

The problem(s) in this case revolve around two questions:

1. Does Jane have a cognitive problem, a social problem, or some combination or interaction?
2. Should the teacher try to deal with any perceived problem, or should the teacher accept that Jane's parents do not see any difficulty with Jane's behaviour?

## Analysis

This case illustrates that the essential issue in any interaction with humans is not usually easy or obvious. Most situations in our lives and in the lives of others are the result of a combination of forces all acting at the same time. At this point it is impossible to tell if Jane has any cognitive challenges since we don't know whether her problems with analysis and synthesis arise from an inability to answer questions, or a hesitancy to do so.

Jane does seem to have some social challenges. She would like to have friends but seems to be most successful in her social interactions in a situation where she has some control and where the nature of the interaction is relatively fixed. When the situation is less controlled, she is quite hesitant. Jane also is new to the school and does not interact with other students in the evening or on the way to and from school. This may be her choice, or it may reflect other social constraints in her life such as her parents' opinions and behaviours.

Jane's case is an example of the situation where it is difficult to separate the components of the situation and say for sure what is causing what. On the assumption that the best place to start with any unclear situation involving a student is the one that involves the least amount of "clinical" intervention, labeling, or problem discussion, the teacher should start by looking at ways that could increase Jane's feelings of safety and decrease any potential concerns she may have about participating in class.

## Accommodating Individual Needs

While the nature and extent of Jane's difficulties are not clear, she does need some basic interventions. Treating her in the same manner as other students in the class will not improve her performance and indeed, may cause her problems to worsen. At this point Jane requires support in problem-solving and social interaction. The results of these interventions, combined with information obtained from other sources, will determine if any extensive changes in content or teaching approach related to her are required.

## Recommendations

1. It is recommended that the teacher remark from time to time about Jane's strengths with computers and running;

2. that the teacher reduce the perceived penalty of making a mistake, encouraging all students to take chances in situations where they are not completely sure of the answer;

3. that the teacher structure more group activities involving class content so that Jane and other students have an issue around which to structure their interactions;

4. that if the above approaches seem to lead to an improvement in both Jane's social and cognitive levels, the teacher speak to her parents about the possibility of involving Jane in structured community programs such as church youth groups, guides or scouts, etc.;

5. that if Jane's cognitive skills do not improve as she becomes more comfortable in the class, the teacher slowly begin the process of deciding whether any intervention is required and if this intervention would be helpful.

## REFERENCES

Barnes, L.B., Christensen, R. C., & Hansen, A.J. (1994). *Teaching and the case method: Text, cases, and readings*. (3rd Ed.). Boston, Massachusetts: Harvard Business School Press.

Silverman, R., Welty, W.M., & Lyon, S. (1996). *Case studies for teacher problem solving*. (2nd Ed). New York: The McGraw-Hill Companies, Inc.

# chapter one

# Education and Psychology

## DEFINITIONS

Educational psychology texts do not always define either education or psychology. When definitions are given, they are often basic and somewhat mechanistic. Two examples are given below.

- Education is the field that deals with knowledge and behaviours related to teaching and learning.
- Psychology is the science that examines behaviour and thinking, especially that of humans.

| Exercise 1–1 | Root Meanings |
| --- | --- |

*The Oxford English Dictionary* gives the following root meanings to the two words:

**Education**: To rear or bring up a person or animal. Related to word to lead out.

**Psychology**: Study of the psyche, mind, or soul.

1. How does an understanding of the roots of the two words influence

your understanding of education and psychology?

2. What are your emotional reactions to the root meanings of the two words?

3. In what ways do the root meanings expand the concepts beyond the simple mechanistic concepts in usual definitions?

The debate that underlies the difference between basic definitions of education and psychology in North America and their meanings drawn from their word roots is one that has been central to both fields from the beginning. It continues today, although many don't recognize the debate in the words themselves.

## YOKE

Education ——————————— Psychology

Education and psychology are yoked together like a team of horses. Any movement by one means that the other has to go in somewhat the same direction. It doesn't mean, however, that they both want to go the same way or at the same pace. Indeed, it is usually a case of one moving a little and the other following. For instance, the increase in individualism in modern psychology has a corresponding increase in child-centred approaches to education.

---

### Exercise 1–2 | Advances

1. List advances in psychology that have influenced our understanding of children.

2. List advances in psychology that have influenced education.

3. Outline some possible changes in psychology — particularly social

psychology — that might occur in the next decade, and discuss how these might affect education.

4. List the contributions of teachers to our understanding of children and education.

---

## HISTORY OF EDUCATIONAL PSYCHOLOGY

Outlining the history of broad fields such as education and psychology is a bit like trying to stuff an elephant into a sack. Where do you start? Peoples of all times and geographic areas have concepts about what represents the best way to educate someone. Both oral and written literatures for thousands of years have recorded these ideas. Modern educators still support many of these concepts.

| Exercise 1–3 | **Centuries Past** |
| --- | --- |
| Look up references to education or teaching by individuals or organizations | from hundreds of years ago. Do you agree with their views? |

*Talks to Teachers*, a series of lectures William James gave in the early 1890s, probably launched educational psychology as a specific field of study. John Dewey established the first laboratory in North America involving the application of psychology to education in 1894. James' and Dewey's views on education are still current and often are studied on their own or used to form the basis for other writings on education. The main components of their approaches are given below.

## William James

- Pragmatism, or the belief that the ultimate test of a concept was its practical consequences, was James' underlying philosophy.
- James emphasized the importance of the individual.
- Researchers need to observe teaching in practice to improve education.
- Students need to be challenged for mental growth.

## John Dewey

- Dewey developed the Chicago School of Pragmatism.
- Learning is a process of inquiry involving thinking and doing.
- Learning should involve the whole child, not just academic subjects.
- Teachers should be guides and coworkers with students.
- All children deserve an education.

You might want to look up early female writers on education or writers from other cultures.

## MODELS

When we try to communicate our understanding of almost any issue to another person, we need to use some way of explaining a great many details in a few words. For instance, we might use the word *kitchen* to mean a sort of generic kitchen. The details might vary from situation to situation, but we would expect all kitchens to have a stove, a table, some type of dish cupboard, etc. When we use the word kitchen in a generic way, we are relying on the fact that we all have approximately the same mental image of a kitchen. Another name for this mental image or mental map is a **model**.

Models arise when someone attempts to use a word, phrase, or graphic to indicate a complex reality. Having to describe the details of this reality every time we communicate would be too time-consuming and, in many cases, would not be feasible. Models can be very general in the sense that they signify a loose grouping of characteristics.

An example would be the word *child*. At first it would seem that everyone knows what *child* means, but when we ask people what they mean by the phrase we find that there is a lot of variation in understanding of the concept. A more specific example of a model would be a 2-year-old. If you tell almost anyone with experience dealing with young children that you have a 2-year-old, they will almost all have the same sense of the types of rewards and difficulties you are experiencing.

In the same way, psychology is really the study of a series of models. Freud's model is very different from Skinner's, for instance. These models are a shorthand method to describe the results of observations and/or experimentation related to human behaviour and thinking. Sometimes even the researchers themselves get confused and think their models are reality. They fail to realize that models are tools to help us understand particular behaviours, or to predict the outcomes of certain situations. Many models are useful depending on the situation encountered. I can't really imagine how Freud's model is going to help me train my dog, but at the same time, I have serious reservations about Skinner being able to help me with an abused child. Teachers tend to be pragmatic in their use of models: if it works, use it.

One of the most interesting aspects of models occurs when we try to analyse the models that are currently the most influential. Some models get to be so accepted that many take them to be the only explanation for events. They use the model to explain events and justify actions. Indeed, most will not even realize they are using a model. Any critical examination of the model results in condemnation with name-calling, attempts to silence, and even punishment. Social institutions, including schools and the courts, will come to support the accepted model. Any data that challenges the position is ignored or explained away through some type of verbal contortion. Of course, we can all see the models of the past and may even make fun of them, dismissing them as unsophisticated or using some similar label to put them down. We tend to think we have grown beyond those models and have reached a more enlightened state.

| Exercise 1–4 | **Models** |
|---|---|

1. List the advantages and disadvantages of models.
2. List some models that were common in the last 500 years.
3. Describe two or three of the models that are operative today.
4. Imagine how these models will be viewed in 100 years.

## Models of Schools in the Past and Today

School buildings, organization, and curriculum represent the concrete expression of a culture's models. Sometimes these models become obsolete when social and economic conditions change.

| Exercise 1–5 | Model of Schools |
| --- | --- |

1. What is the model for the school today? Think of fixed times for activities, buzzers to signal changes, and a hierarchical structure.

2. Why are schools closed in the summer?

3. Why do schools stop early in the afternoon?

4. How are cooperative learning activities partially a reflection of demands by some members of society?

## HISTORY OF SCHOOLS

Schools for the general public are a relatively recent development. In that short time there have been quite dramatic changes in how schools are viewed and structured.

### Two Hundred Years Ago

- Few people went to school.
- Churches developed many of the schools and had an important role in determining the curriculum.
- Apprenticeship rather than school-based programs was the main source of employment certification for most people.

### Turn of the Century

- The 3 R's of reading, (w)riting, and (a)rithmetic were the foundation of educational programs.
- Most students completed their formal studies at the end of elementary school. This was particularly true in rural areas where high schools often were unavailable unless the student lived with relatives in a nearby town or city.
- At least at the elementary level, teaching was not seen as a career requiring much expertise or training.

### Today

- A discussion of the nature of schools today is covered under the topic of models and approaches to teaching earlier in this chapter.
- Teaching is regarded as a professional career, involving significant education.
- Conflicts between stakeholders regarding the mission and goals of the school appear to be increasing.
- Information technologies are beginning to produce fundamental changes in concepts of school and education.

## APPROACHES TO TEACHING

Provinces, school districts and teachers all have approaches to teaching they feel are the most effective and valid. A somewhat arbitrary division of these approaches is classical, curriculum, and child-centred.

### Classical

- Classical approaches to teaching employ a traditional academic education combined with mandatory arts, leadership, and sports programs.
- The goal is to produce graduates who have a well-rounded education and an expectation of leadership service in the community.

### Curriculum

- Curriculum-based approaches to teaching emphasize a standardized curriculum developed by a province or school district.
- The goal is to ensure that the majority of students meet the requirements outlined in the curriculum.

### Child-Centred Approaches

- Child-centred approaches to teaching emphasize the child's interests and abilities; a new curriculum is developed for each child.
- The goal is for each student to develop a strong sense of self-determination.

| Exercise 1–6 | **Three Approaches** |
|---|---|
| In groups of three or four debate the advantages and disadvantages of each of the three approaches to education. | Decide which approach or combination of approaches best exemplifies your views of teaching. |

## TEACHER EXPECTATIONS AND RESPONSIBILITY

### Expectations

- Teachers should expect slow improvement in their students rather than looking for some dramatic intervention that will produce immediate results.
- Teachers need to be patient as students learn and grow.
- Teachers need to have the same expectations of slow improvement for themselves as they do for their students.

## Responsibility

- The whole question of teacher responsibility and accountability is quite complex Even if teachers say their responsibility is only to the child, it is hard to know what that means in times of challenge.
- Sometimes teachers find it hard to deal with the fact that they are paid by taxpayers who may not have much choice as to where their children go to school.

## EVERYONE IS AN EXPERT

If you were to ask an adult without specialized education in chemistry to explain how a dull gray metallic element such as sodium and a light green poisonous gas such as chlorine combine to form a white crystal of tremendous importance to human health, they probably would claim that they don't know how this happens. If you asked the same adult to analyse an educational or psychological issue, chances are that they would not hesitate but rather, would speak with quite a bit of confidence about what should be done. The explanation for the difference is often given in terms of everyone having experience with school and psychological issues. The same is true with salt, however!

This analogy actually can be explored in greater depth when it is realized that the above paragraph contains a logical fallacy. The issue of salt refers to a fundamental process in chemistry while the education/psychology issue refers to more everyday experiences. People know a great deal about salt if we ask them questions related to their experience. People also know a great deal about education and psychology based on their experience. Difficulties in both cases revolve around knowing whether information thought to be correct in particular cases is the best information available, and whether it can be generalized to other situations.

Responses to any questioning of the truth of some opinion usually revolve around claims that the present approach works well. The fact that something appears to work in individual cases is not proof that the principle is the best approach, or even that it is true. Many people claim that they received a good education in very authoritarian environments where they were forced to learn material that had little relevance to their lives. There is a great deal of both anecdotal and experimental evidence, however, that this type of learning environment does not work well for many students. There also is the issue of what the students who could perform in this environment actually did learn. Maybe the learning was more of an attitude and a particular type of willful approach to life that could be quite unhealthy.

Both psychology and education are in the difficult position of either demonstrating that the obvious is true, or that the obvious is at least not completely true and providing a better explanation. In either case, the public response may be less than enthusiastic.

## GOOD AND BAD TEACHERS

The listing of factors that characterize good and bad teachers is one of the standbys in educational psychology texts.

| Exercise 1–7 | **Teacher Influences** |
|---|---|
| 1. Think of one or more teachers who inspired you in school. What were the characteristics of these teachers? | 2. Think of one or more teachers who had negative influences on your education. What were the characteristics of these teachers? |

This exercise produces a useful but somewhat predictable list of characteristics. It totally ignores the fact that teachers exist in particular contexts. For instance, students often find some subjects inherently more interesting than others. Some classes are much easier to teach than others. Teachers have personal lives that may be influencing their teaching.

| Exercise 1–7 | **Teacher Influences** (continued) |
|---|---|
| 1. Why did the teacher(s) who had a negative influence on you behave the way they did? | 2. Did your class help or hinder the teacher? <br> 3. What should happen to a teacher who is having difficulties? |

Sometimes when we do this exercise our ageism, sexism, and lack of charity amaze us. We fail to recognize the fundamental principle that almost all teachers who are having difficulty with their classes would like to be able to do better.

| Exercise 1–7 | **Teacher Influences** (continued) |
|---|---|
| 1. What are your fears about your teaching career? | 2. What kind of help would you hope to get from your principal and fellow teachers? |

## CASE 1-1: INDIVIDUALISM VS. COLLECTIVISM

All the rhetoric about accountability in schools made Christine Guyden livid. She had been a teacher for 23 years and knew that each child developed at a different rate. Assuming that a province-wide test could give any true indication of what was happening in the schools was a fundamental fallacy. Indeed, the whole issue of assessment — even for reporting to parents — was somewhat offensive to her. Children had the right to progress at their own rate, without being measured against some external standard. She also felt that children had the right to be engaged in learning activities that were meaningful to them, rather than being forced to study some imposed curriculum. Christine remembered the battle it had been to get beyond the fixed structure of the 1950s. "All those booklets and worksheets," she scoffed. "What did they have to do with the needs of each child?"

The 1970s and 1980s were years of wonderful progress, with children being allowed to explore areas of interest to them and to express themselves in their own unique ways. Now this progress was being threatened by the new 'corporate agenda,' as the change had come to be known among some of Christine's colleagues. Students were being prepared just for work in the corporate machine. Politicians everywhere seemed to be pushing for provincial testing in what they called core subjects. Christine noted that creativity and personal expression were never considered to be part of these core areas. Indeed, budget restrictions were often used as a reason to reduce funding to Arts programs.

## Discussion Questions

1. What are the two conflicting views of teaching in the above case?
2. What are the conflicting views of the role of schools in the above case?

## CASE 1-2: HOW BIG IS THE SUN?

"I seem to feel the past more and more," said Peter as he turned to the man sitting next to him. "Actually it's the little incidents I remember — the smells, the sounds, the colours."

"How old are you, Peter?" the man asked.

"I'm 83," Peter said proudly. "And I don't feel a day over 80." This brought a burst of laughter from both of them. Peter had been noticing that he found more things funny these days — not just jokes, but unexpected words and sights.

The two older men's conversation followed its usual path to the lives of their childhood. They both were raised on small farms and had many stories about times when farm work was done by hand or with horses. Somehow the difficulties of the past faded and the pleasures increased with time.

"I do have regrets though," mused Peter. "I can't think of my father, for instance, without feeling sad."

"Why?" asked his friend. "He lived a long life and usually seemed to be quite satisfied with his life."

"I just feel that I never got to know him," said Peter. "Actually, I can remember the incident that sort of separated us."

"Tell me about it," said his friend. He was always interested in a good story and it looked like Peter had one.

"I was eight or nine," started Peter, and he was soon back on the farm. "It was late October or the first part of November. I got off the bus and came up the lane. Dad was going across the yard with a pail and he stopped to speak to me. He asked me what I had learned that day. He often did that, although he didn't seem to pay much attention when I told him. That day I told him that I had just learned that the sun was much bigger than the earth and that the earth went around the sun. I found the whole concept just amazing. I remember the look on my father's face."

"Who told you such nonsense?" he demanded.

"The teacher," I answered.

"She did not," responded my father. "She wouldn't tell you such a lie. You probably just didn't hear her right."

"No, that's what the teacher told me," I persisted. "She had diagrams in a book and everything."

"Well, it's not true," huffed my father. "Any damn fool can see that the sun is smaller than the earth and that it goes around the earth."

"I didn't know how to respond," Peter continued. "I felt something break between me and my father at that moment. I think he did too. Things were never quite the same afterwards."

"Oh, you can't be serious," said Peter's friend. "I knew your father well. He was a really smart man. You couldn't put anything over on him."

"I know," said Peter. "He never really went to school, Grade 3 or something, but he could read and always seemed to know what was going on. He used to listen to the radio a lot and he talked to everybody. I guess he just missed that little thing about the sun and the earth somehow."

"I think he knew he was wrong as soon as he saw my reaction and he probably checked it out later. We just never could get over that incident, however. Somehow we both knew then that I was never going to be a farmer. That in some way what I learned in school was going to be more important to me than what he could teach me. I guess the problem is that now I'm not so sure school did have more to teach me. At least I wish I could have learned it without having to leave his world."

## Discussion Questions

1. What does this case show about models?
2. What does this case demonstrate about the nature of education in terms of social changes?

## CASE 1-3: EVERYONE IS AN EXPERT

"I can come in Thursday afternoons and help you Ms. Rau," said Ms. Jorgenson. "You seem to have so many demands with all these different students and I am available. Besides, it would be nice to see how my son Mathew is doing."

Nancy Rau had been teaching for two years, three months, and eight days. Usually she was alone in the classroom with children who all seemed to want her at the same time. Even when she had scheduled activities for students to do at their desks, a few would come to see her about something or other. In addition, there were the students who needed special help. There just wasn't a chance to catch her breath. Ms. Jorgenson's offer of volunteer help was very enticing. Nancy was a little concerned about having a parent in the classroom on a regular basis, but the thought of the additional help overcame her resistance.

"That would be great," said Nancy. "How about coming in next Thursday at noon so we can go over what you could do? We'll give it a try for awhile to see how we both like it. I sure could use some help."

"Fantastic! I'll be here on Thursday for sure. I always wanted to work with kids."

For the first couple of Thursdays Ms. Jorgenson helped organize materials and straightened the reading area. The presence of another adult in the classroom seemed to quiet all the children. Mathew had gone to his mother three or four times on the first day, but only looked her way a few times on the second day. It looked like he would soon forget she was in the classroom. At the end of class on Thursdays the two women chatted for a few minutes. Usually these chats were simple check-ins. After a few weeks, however, Ms. Jorgenson brought up the issue of reading.

"I could do reading with a couple of the kids," she said. "You know, just sitting and help them read."

Again Nancy had a little twinge of hesitation, but so many of the students needed help with reading that she responded, "Sounds like a great idea. I'll leave out some books for you to use. George and Allison particularly could use some help."

Next Thursday after class Ms. Jorgenson mentioned that she had seen some type of reading program that would really help Allison and that she would bring it in next week. Nancy was preoccupied and responded with a nod. Ms. Jorgenson quickly developed a reading program for the students who were having difficulties. It was a relief to Nancy to have some of the students involved in the program. After the program had been going for about three weeks, Nancy sat down nearby to see what was going on.

"No, that's not right," she heard Ms. Jorgenson say to Allison. "You don't pay attention when you read. You will have to keep reading it until you get it right."

This comment upset Nancy. She wanted all her students to like Language Arts and felt students should be rewarded for their effort, not punished if they didn't get everything right. She knew she would have to speak to Ms. Jorgenson but decided to leave it until classes were over.

"I heard you talking to Allison," she opened the conversation. "I really don't think it is a good idea to increase stress on children when they are trying to read. Try to encourage them by rewarding what they do."

"Well, Allison is always so scattered. She just doesn't pay attention and I think she has to learn to pay attention."

"I agree that Allison has some problems in that area but I don't think embarrassing her will help."

"Well, I know that my sister had a reading problem and the only thing that worked was the teacher forcing her to read in front of the class. My sister hated it, but boy did she try to learn to read."

"Actually I think you are too easy on a lot of the kids," continued Ms. Jorgenson. "They are out of their seats so much and seem to be talking among themselves all the time instead of you teaching them."

This attack made Nancy quite angry but she managed to respond reasonably, explaining her philosophy of education and what research had shown regarding how kids learn best.

"I just know what I know works," responded Ms. Jorgenson. "I see all that stuff coming out of the universities and from the teachers. Kids just aren't learning anything these days. Parents want their kids to learn and that's what they pay teachers for."

Nancy realized at that point that the situation with Ms. Jorgenson was becoming very difficult. She wished she had spent much more time talking to Ms. Jorgenson before she started volunteering. She was unclear about what steps she should take to correct the situation.

## Discussion Questions

1.  What should Nancy have discussed with Ms. Jorgenson before she allowed her to volunteer in the classroom?

2.  What should she do now?

3.  Why did Ms. Jorgenson feel comfortable with arguing about teaching philosophy, even though she had no training?

## CASE 1-4: THE GOOD TEACHER

"Twenty five years. Seems like a long time sometimes," mused Mr. Hunt, a middle-aged teacher, from his chair—and you had better not sit there—in the staff lounge. "Into the breech again, I guess."

Nathan didn't even smile. He hated teachers with attitudes like Mr. Hunt. They didn't seem to have any enthusiasm for their work. Probably did the same thing year after year. The military metaphor certainly didn't help. "Boy, I'd leave and go some place else if I thought like that. How can his students learn anything? They probably are bored out of their minds," he thought.

This was Nathan's first year of teaching his own classes. He had been a teacher-on-call (TOC) for a couple of years, but hadn't had an opportunity to really develop his own ideas about teaching. Now was his chance. He had tons of activities and challenges for the students. He really felt that it was necessary to keep the students involved in their education. The secret of good teaching was interesting activities *for* the kids, rather than talking *at* the kids. If the kids were interested, there would not be many discipline problems.

Students appeared to love Nathan's classes. They constantly complimented him on how much fun his classes were. They stopped him in the halls to talk about things that were going on in the school and community.

"You seem to have a great rapport with your students," observed the principal, Ms. Siegler. "I haven't seen them so interested in that subject for quite a few years." The fact that Ms. Siegler made the comment in the staff room in front of the other teachers caused Nathan some embarrassment, but he was pleased to say the least.

A week or so later, Ms. Siegler knocked on the door and came into his classroom when classes had just ended. "Hi, Nathan. Hearing great things about you still."

"Thanks, Ms. Siegler. I really enjoy the students."

"Be sure to let me know if you are having any problems Nathan. Best to nip them in the bud you know," the principal continued.

"No problems at all. Everything seems to be going great."

"You know that there is that cross-class test in about two weeks," said Ms. Siegler. "Your students should be up to about page 100 in the text or so by now I guess."

"Well, we're a little behind in the text," explained Nathan. "Sometimes the students really get interested in something and I don't want to dampen their enthusiasm."

"I know all about that," sympathized Ms. Siegler. "It was one of the main difficulties I had when I first started to teach. Actually Mr. Hunt helped me learn to pace my lessons. He is great at it. Always done on time with room to spare for other activities. You know, he was here when I started to teach. Sometimes it seems funny to now be his boss. Perhaps you should talk to him about moving your students along."

Nathan was stunned. He was surprised that the principal put so much emphasis on getting through the material. Surely it was more important that the students enjoy what they were doing. What really disturbed him however was that the principal had asked him to go to Mr. Hunt for help.

## Discussion Questions

1. What is a good teacher?
2. What is the difference between a good teacher and a popular teacher?
3. What kinds of biases did Nathan show in his judgment of Mr. Hunt?

## REFERENCES

Hunt, M. (1993). *The story of Psychology*. New York: Doubleday.

# chapter two

# The Nature of Evidence

There are many ways of looking at a statement. One way is to decide whether it is a belief, a fact, or an opinion.

- A **belief** is trust or confidence in, and acceptance of, a theology or understanding of an ultimate reality.
- An **opinion** is comprised of thoughts and feelings about a particular issue or question. Opinions may be casual or informed.
- A **fact** is something that is known to be true or to have occurred.

Beliefs are outside the nature of the issues being discussed in this text. The whole issue of evidence to support beliefs, or even whether beliefs need evidence, is complex and is its own field of study.

## FACT VS. OPINION

- While it would appear at first that facts and opinions are mutually exclusive, a more useful way to look at them is to think of them as being on a continuum:

Fact ——————— Opinion

- The more evidence there is for some statement, the closer it is to a fact.
- There never is complete certainty that something is a fact, but the evidence is much stronger for some statements than for others.
- Teachers have a responsibility to base their actions on the strongest evidence available.

| Exercise 2–1 | Fact or Opinion? |
|---|---|
| 1. Collect newspaper articles that report facts — scientific, medical, economic, etc. | 2. Where on the continuum between facts and opinions would you place the articles? |

Fact    1    2    3    4    5    6    7    Opinion

## TRUTH

What does it mean to say that something is true? Students now are deeply mistrustful of the idea of there being truth, or even that the concept of searching for truth is necessarily good (Grenz, 1996). While many students may not know anything about postmodernism beyond recognizing the term, they do understand that truth is not necessarily rational, objective, or devoid of context. They also question the concepts that knowledge solves problems, that knowledge is objective data, and that knowledge is true in all contexts.

In the postmodern world knowledge can come from intuition and emotions as well as intellect. Students understand that knowing more about a problem will not necessarily solve it, and that any explanation of a situation owes as much — or more — to the person doing the observing or analysis as it does to the situation involved. Truth often becomes a personal, or more likely a group, construct. Some take a very hard position and claim that there is no truth, or that truth is impossible to know. They don't seem to realize that the hard position of stating there is no truth is in itself a statement of a believed truth: it is true that there is no truth.

The result is a quandary of the type shown in the following statement:

## I AM A LIAR

The result of this hard position is a social and moral relativism that can lead to personal tragedy or even to extensive damage to others if the person with the belief system is in a position to influence others. A softer position might be might be a statement such as, "I believe this to be true, or at least it is my best understanding of the situation. I am willing to change my position if I receive new evidence."

Perhaps a better way to look at the statement, data, or other evidence is in terms of confidence.

Little Confidence ——————————— Lots of Confidence

Then we can look at where we might place a particular concept or model on this line. However, this does not really resolve the situation because the question then becomes: upon what do we base our confidence? While teachers can talk about the credentials of people claiming something is true or provide supporting data from several sources, most of us tend to be suspicious of the idea of credentials and only tend to give increased confidence to those data that support the beliefs we already have.

Another approach that is somewhat more successful is to think in terms of responsibility. Presumably, the less our ideas and actions influence either others or ourselves, the less important it is to question the truth of the ideas. I probably can think the moon is made of green cheese and that the trips to the moon really were just illusions manufactured in military installations if I have little authority over others. This opinion quickly becomes a problem though if I am the science teacher in a high school, or somehow am involved in funding science programs. Generally, we realize that the more our welfare or that of others depends on our actions, the more we should make an effort to examine any available data related to a concept. This often is not done, however, and indeed the demand for some kind of evidence is sometimes put down as an example of paternalism, or whatever happens to be the politically correct derogatory statement of the day.

---

| Exercise 2–2 | Fads |
|---|---|

Examine education books over the last 50 years to see what enthusiasms were thought to be the future of education, but later were found to be fads or even hindrances to education. Pick one of these and see if there was any evidence to support its use — not just comments from supporters, but actual demonstrations of how the new approach improved education in some significant manner.

---

## CORRELATION VS. CAUSATION

- A **Correlation** is a measure of the degree of relationship or association between two or more factors.
  - This association may be positive in that when one gets bigger or smaller, the other does the same. It may be negative in the sense that when one gets bigger or smaller the other does the opposite.
- **Causation** occurs when one condition produces or results in another.
  - There is no way to prove causation completely, since an alternative explanation for results may become obvious at a later time.

## EXPERIMENTAL METHOD

Over the last few hundred years, the concept of a **true experiment** has developed to try and distinguish between correlation and causation, or at least to increase confidence that one condition causes another. A diagram of the simplest true experiment is as follows:

| Sample 1 | No Treatment | Sample 1 |
| Sample 1 | Treatment | Sample 2 |

In this case, the experimenter starts with two identical samples formed by random selection from a population. One sample is treated and the other is not. The sample that is not treated is called the **control group** while the other sample is called the **experimental group**. Otherwise the two samples are managed identically. If Sample 2 is different from Sample 1 after the treatment, then there can be considerable confidence that this was the result of the treatment.

Such simple true experiments probably only are possible with inanimate objects in inert environments. In all other cases, time alone will produce a change and so there will be a change in both the control and experimental samples.

In most experiments the situation looks like:

| Sample 1 | No Treatment | Sample 2 |
| Sample 1 | Treatment | Sample 3 |

While every effort may have been made to keep conditions the same between the control and experimental groups, at the end of a time period the Control Group will have changed to Sample 2. The Experimental Group will have changed to Sample 3. The degree to which Sample 2 and Sample 3 are different may be attributed with some confidence to the treatment.

With human beings in particular, it is hard to get two samples that are identical to begin with. While there are statistical techniques for accounting for any initial differences, these approaches inspire less confidence than starting with two identical samples. In addition, it is hard to keep conditions the same for control and experimental groups of humans, especially if the research occurs over a longer length of time. However, the extent to which the experimenter(s) have tried to duplicate a true experiment should increase our confidence in the results.

Doing research with living organisms brings in two additional terms.

- In a **double blind** study, neither the experimenter(s) nor the subject(s) know who is receiving treatment and who is receiving the placebo.

- A **placebo** is a treatment procedure that mimics the experimental procedure, but lacks the active ingredient or process being studied.

While much is made of the use of double blind conditions in experiments, often the subjects and experimenters come to know who is receiving the treatment because of the treatment's effects. It may be difficult to determine the effect of this knowledge on the result.

## FIELD OBSERVATION

Many important issues in education and psychology do not lend themselves to the use of the experimental method, however. Processes may be so long and/or complex that field observation is the only way to begin to understand the factors involved. For instance, field observation helps us learn some of the factors that may be involved in a child learning to read. Later it may be possible to look at these processes in a more experimental setting. The results of field observation rightly may involve more skepticism than those from experiments, although caution is needed in both cases. We should have far more confidence in either though, than in someone just stating their opinion no matter how elegantly it is argued.

## LYING WITH STATISTICS

Some wag claimed that there were "lies, damn lies, and statistics." As with all lies, the most interesting form of statistical misrepresentation occurs when the author misleads rather than actually presents an untruth. A group that goes from 10 to 20 members could be the fastest growing group in the country as they have experienced a 100 percent increase in the year. Another group in the same area might grow from 100,000 to 125,000 and only experience a growth of 25 percent. The smaller group might claim that they were growing 4 times as fast as the bigger group.

In another case, a report from an investment company might have a graph that appears to show a rapid increase in return on one of the company's funds. The company might start the graph with a Y-axis of 6 percent rather than zero. As a result, an increase from 6 percent to 6.5 percent could be made to look quite large, even though it would appear much smaller if the Y-axis had started at zero.

The use of the three different forms of an average — mode, median, mean — is another favourite way of abusing statistics. Mean temperature, for instance, would be a poor way of picking what is generally the warmest city in Canada year round.

---

| Exercise 2–3 | **Misleading Statistics** |
| --- | --- |

1. Find examples of misleading statistics in the newspaper or in any other media outlet. Show how the author has deliberately or inadvertently tried to use statistics to mislead.

2. Take some data that you are familiar with and present it in such a manner as to mislead. For example, if you watch TV for 3 hours in the evening, then you spend only 12.5 percent of your day watching TV. This seems much less daunting than stating that you spend 75 percent of your free time (3 of 4 hours) watching TV.

3. Explain the potential problems with data about life expectancy, average salary, and average numbers of tranquilizers consumed.

---

## CASE 2-1: WELL, IT'S MY OPINION

"Well, it's my opinion," stated the somewhat miffed student. "I have as much right to my opinion as you do to yours."

"But I'm not telling you my opinion, Cheryl," claimed Ms. Simpson. "It's what the research has found."

"So research can be wrong," countered Cheryl. "Who knows, I might be right. In any case, I am entitled to my opinion."

The exchange happened last week in class and Ms. Simpson was still thinking about it. It seemed that so many students were unable or unwilling to give up their opinions when confronted by evidence to the contrary. Indeed, some seemed to believe that anything could be true. Facts were viewed with a great deal of cynicism. Feelings and thoughts were seen as having the same or more weight than any scientific data.

"I understand their cynicism," Ms. Simpson said to a colleague. "I know that many of the so-called facts of the past now are known to untrue or at least incomplete, and that many so-called studies really are just propaganda for special interest groups."

"I have experienced the same thing," said Ms. Lee. "I actually have gone about the whole issue from the other side. I start by looking at science frauds. Actually it's quite a lot of fun. It teaches the students about science and also allows them to see that I share some of their caution about its so called data."

"Frauds", exclaimed Ms. Simpson. "Sounds like a great idea. Do you have any examples?"

"Well, two that students may be familiar with are the Piltdown Hoax and Crop Circles. The Piltdown Hoax had scientists confused from about 1911 to 1953. A few scientists also went into long explanations for the cause of crop circles before the perpetrators confessed," said Ms. Lee. "Indeed, there still are people who believe in crop circles. I just read about them in the paper a couple of months ago. Students will be able to find a whole bunch of hoaxes if they just check the library or the Internet."

"Actually there seems to be more and more information about fraudulent research," continued Ms. Lee. "I've seen stuff about supposed cancer cures where the researcher made up data, and some research on violence where data was left out. Students have a right to be concerned."

Ms. Simpson felt that the issue of scientific frauds would help her students understand how the scientific method was supposed to work. She also recognized that it would reinforce their skepticism of science in general. For her though, skepticism was not the issue. Rather, it was her students' failure to understand that there even was a difference between a belief, an opinion, and a fact.

## Discussion Questions

1. What are 3 examples of scientific fraud exposed in the last 50 years?
2. How were these frauds detected?
3. Why might it be suitable for a student to have an opinion about the best music group, and not an opinion about how to teach reading in a school system?
4. What are some examples of new teaching concepts that were introduced largely based on opinion? What happened to them?
5. When are researchers being fraudulent rather than incorrect?

## CASE 2-2: THE CURE

Karl knew even before he looked in the mirror what he would find. There they were, the constellation of zits on his chin. "Why today or all days?" he whined. "I have to get up and make that report. Everyone will just be looking at my acne."

His parents were no help. They responded with their usual, "Everyone gets them, dear. They're just part of growing up. You can't really see them. Don't worry, they'll go away." They didn't even realize that their comments were contradictory.

Karl was sick and tired of the pimples and zits of acne interfering with his life. He had enough to worry about without being betrayed by his face. Surely science had developed some cure for this scourge. That evening he planned to check the Internet to see what was available.

He was amazed to get 695 873 hits when he typed in acne. Many of these sites offered various creams and lotions that supposedly cured acne. Most of the sites had before-and-after pictures showing tremendous results from the use of a particular product. Some of the sites even had the results of experiments that proved the effectiveness of a particular cure. It was not clear exactly who had done the studies, other than that they were leading dermatologists. Most of the products seemed quite expensive, especially when compared with a couple of the creams he had bought at the local drugstore. The creams hadn't been particularly effective, however, and some of these more expensive products might help.

## Discussion Questions

1. What are some ways Karl could increase his confidence in making a decision related to the products being advertised?
2. What concerns should we have about anonymous 'experts'?

## REFERENCES

Grenz, S.J. (1996). *A primer on Postmodernism*. Grand Rapids, Michigan: William B. Eerdmans Publishing Company.

# chapter three

# Genetics, Evolutionary Psychology, and Environment

## GENETICS

### General Nature

The structure and functioning of all living organisms are determined by a **genetic code** that is passed from one generation to the next. The nature of this code is specific for particular organisms, but all organisms share the same basic components.

- Humans have 46 **chromosomes** or chains of code arranged in 23 pairs.
- One member of the pair comes from each parent.
- Each chromosome contains **DNA** (deoxyribonucleic acid) shaped as a double helix.
- The genetic code starts and controls process of development from conception.
- Some characteristics are determined by one or a small number of chromosomal sites. Usually these are biological characteristics such as hair or skin colour.
- Other characteristics are shaped by the interactions of many sites. Examples of these would be the genetic components of personality and intelligence.
- While inheritance comes from both parents, children may have characteristics that neither parent exhibits.

■ For some characteristics, genes are a necessary but not sufficient condition for the actual development of the characteristic. Environmental factors also must be present. For instance, if children are going to speak they have to hear the spoken word.

■ The role of our genes does not end at birth — our genes are important contributors to maturation and other processes later in life.

■ Development varies from person to person and usually occurs in a discontinuous, rather than continuous, manner.

## Genetic Defects

■ **Genetic defect** refers to damage or change to one or more chromosomal sites or loci. Examples of damage to one locus include cystic fibrosis and hemophilia.

■ The exact genetic components of other genetic defects are more difficult to isolate. Examples include the genetic components of schizophrenia, major depression, and autism.

■ **Mutation** is probably a better word than defect since many defects seem to be accompanied by benefits. For instance, having a defect for sickle cell anemia on one chromosome leads to increased resistance to malaria.

## Chromosomal Abnormalities

■ **Chromosomal abnormalities** occur when there is no defect in a gene but rather, the individual has a different number, shape, etc. of chromosomes. Down Syndrome or Trisomy-21 is most common form of a chromosomal abnormality.

## Psychological Characteristics

■ While the role of genetics in determining physical characteristics is accepted, there is considerable debate as to the importance of genetics in causing, or even influencing, psychological characteristics.

■ However, most people accept the role of genetics to varying degrees.

■ A child's **temperament,** or characteristic way of behaving, has a strong genetic basis. At one end of the scale, some children are very easygoing while at the other end, some children react negatively to most changes and seem upset a lot of the time.

■ Some children have a genetic tendency to be shy.

■ Some of us have a genetic tendency to be **introverted** — our energy and interests are directed inward. Others tend to be **extraverted,** with their energy and interests directed to the external world.

■ Intelligence is known to have a strong genetic component.

■ Many gender characteristics originally thought to be socially conditioned now are known to be genetically determined. This issue is discussed in more detail in Chapter 18.

## Importance of Genetics

- Recent advances in genetics, including the mapping of the human genome, will lead to genetics becoming increasingly important in our understanding of physical and psychological issues.
- While the influence of genetics has been underestimated for the last 4 or 5 decades, it may be overestimated in the immediate future.

## Issues in Modern Genetics

Modern developments in genetics have led to the increased importance of this field in pregnancy and childbearing. These developments in turn have resulted in people being required to make ethical and emotional decisions that were not so common in the past.

- More and more prospective parents may want or be required to obtain genetic counselling in the desire or the requirement to avoid certain genetic defects or abnormalities.
- The role of substitute or surrogate parents will increase as the techniques of in-vitro fertilization improve.
- Genetic engineering raises the possibility of going beyond the avoidance of defects or abnormalities and introduces whole new issues of genetic selection and so-called genetic improvements.
- Each of the above three scenarios gives rise to a host of social, emotional, moral, and legal issues. These issues come to the centre of what it means to be human and must be treated with great sensitivity.

| Exercise 3–1 | Discussion of Issues in Modern Genetics |
| --- | --- |
| In groups of three or four discuss some of the concerns introduced by advancements in modern genetics. Perhaps groups could take separate issues and | report the results of their discussion to the whole class. It probably is not useful to say that everything should just be stopped; this will not occur. |

## EVOLUTIONARY PSYCHOLOGY

**Evolutionary psychology** attempts to explain human behaviour from the premise that the basic motivations behind all significant actions are controlled by either conscious or unconscious drives to increase the possibility of our genetic material surviving and increasing. The following issues are some of the more important ones for this approach to psychology.

## Territory

- Access to territory and resources is a prerequisite for reproductive success.
- This leads to a drive for MORE of all types of resources.

■ In the past MORE probably meant greater chances of our genes being spread because we could have more children and they would be more likely to survive. Birth control and the desire to limit population growth mean that this is no longer true in many situations, but the drive is still there.

## Kin

■ Kin relationships are strong because of similar genetic material.

■ Marriages are one method to increase kin relationships beyond the original families.

■ Kin of the wealthy tend to stay closer together than those of the poor, presumably because the wealthy have more resources to maintain the group.

## Reciprocal Altruism

■ In addition to kin relationships, we often enter into agreements with others to advance our interests.

■ These types of agreements are thought to be very susceptible to failure because of differences in genetic material between the individuals involved.

■ The breaking of an agreement results in moral outrage and guilt with claims of cheating.

## Choice of Mates

■ Evolutionary psychology predicts that males will chose female partners based on health, particularly as this relates to child bearing.

■ Females will chose males based on the male's resources and on his health.

■ In our society, where families tend not to know each other, information about health and wealth is gathered from appearance and employment.

## Conscious Control of Evolution

■ The premise behind the issue of a conscious control of the forces of evolution is that we need to understand the evolutionary forces that drive us, and attempt to control our responses to those forces. For example, the demand for MORE may be very destructive to us and to our environment if not understood and checked.

## ENVIRONMENT

Issues related to environment are very important in child and youth care, education, and social work courses. Discussions of environment need to have more depth than merely lamenting the limited environments that some people find themselves in, or debating what type of environment is optimal. Two concepts that must be understood initially are Goodness of Fit and Resiliency.

## Goodness of Fit

- **Goodness of fit** refers to the level that any given genetic mix is supported more by one environment than another.

- The type of genetic mix that may be supported varies with economic and social conditions. One set of conditions may support higher levels of physical activity than another, for instance. Under such conditions, hyperactivity could be seen as a positive characteristic.

## Resiliency (Hardiness)

- **Resiliency** or **hardiness** refers to the finding that some children raised in terrible environments do well later in life.

- The presence of some type of support system tends to be critical factor. This support system could be a neighbour, a teacher, a storeowner, etc.

- Perhaps some individuals are better prepared genetically to cope with difficult circumstances.

## Studies of the Role of Environment

- Much information about the role of environment arises from either accidental or deliberate deprivation studies. Examples of these studies include studies in which monkeys have been kept by themselves with only cloth mothers, as well as analysis of cases where children have been raised in very deprived conditions.

- Lost and found children also have been the infrequent source of information. These usually are children who were locked in rooms by parents with severe psychological difficulties.

- The role of environment also is determined from studying the damage done to a fetus by inter-uterine conditions that damage it. Examples of these conditions include the use of drugs or alcohol, various types of diseases, high levels of stress, smoking, and conditions that produce anoxia either during fetal development or at birth.

- Alcohol use by a pregnant mother with its resultant possibility of Fetal Alcohol Syndrome or Fetal Alcohol Effects has been a growing area of concern.

# HERITABILITY AND REACTION RANGE

## Heritability

- **Heritability** refers to the proportion of a particular biological or psychological characteristic that is inherited.

- This concept can become quite controversial when the issue becomes intelligence or any possible ethnic differences.

## Reaction Range

- **Genotype** is a person's genetic material or code.
- **Phenotype** is a person's observable characteristics.
- **Reaction Range** is the change in phenotype as determined by environmental conditions for any given genotype.
- Reaction range is much larger for some characteristics — such as temperament — than for others such as eye colour.
- There is a rapid rise in level of characteristic in the initial stages of moving from a limited to more normal environment. The change tends to be less for changes from normal to enriched.

Heritability and Reaction Range provide a means of conceptualizing and quantifying the role of environment.

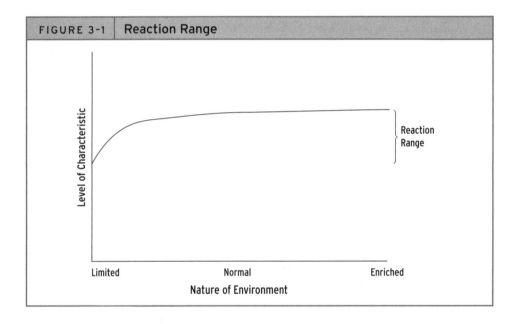

| FIGURE 3-1 | Reaction Range |

## INCORRECT INTERPRETATIONS

Discussions of the interaction between genetics and environment sometimes are simplistic. Assuming the relationship is 50-50 really gives the wrong impression. It is more a matter of the extent to which the environment supports or represses a genetic characteristic. The two incorrect poles of the genetic/environment interaction are genetic determinism and environmental determinism.

- **Genetic determinism** is the belief that genetics determines all of the major factors in our life.
- **Environmental determinism** is the belief that environment determines all of the major factors in our life.

## CASE 3-1: PERSONALITY AND TEACHING CAREER

Mrs. Liu hung up the phone and gazed at her daughter Pamela with a mixture of pride and concern. "She always has her nose stuck in a book," she had said during the phone conversation. "She went for a couple of walks and talked to two or three friends since coming home for Reading Break, but really hasn't gone out much. Not like Janet who seems to be always on the go."

Mrs. Liu marveled at the difference between her two daughters. "Like water and fire," she mused. She couldn't remember a time when the difference had not existed. As a child, Janet had been up shaking her crib, running around the house, talking to the cat, her parents, visitors, the letter carrier, anyone who happened to cross her path. Pamela on the other hand often would sit quietly in her crib and play with some toys. She was lively and determined but always seemed to be more interested in her own projects than Janet. When Pamela had her two or three friends over from school, it was not unusual to find them all sitting together in a big chair reading.

In university Pamela was attracted to a general arts program. Almost every field interested her. Concepts in Philosophy, History, and English all seemed to be connected. The excitement of learning new things and then seeing the connection to other ideas sometimes kept her reading for hours. Often she went off on a fascinating track that had little to do with her initial topic. She and a small group of friends meet over coffee to share their discoveries and to discuss current social and political issues.

The middle of third year brought a crisis in Pamela's academic life. The crisis had been percolating in the background but her mother's question during the holidays had brought it to a head. "What are you going to do when you graduate?" had been the dreaded question. Pamela had deflected the issue with comments about considering several possibilities and was relieved when her mother had not pursued the issue any further. Pamela came back to school in January and knew she would have to come to some type of decision. She heard a couple of students in History talking about registering in the Faculty of Education and thought she would check it out. When Pamela talked to the Advising Office in Education, she found there were a couple of courses she was lacking but she could pick them up in 4th year. Otherwise, with her grades and the courses she had taken, she would be accepted in the Post-Degree Secondary Program with Social Studies as a teaching area.

The program in Education was one of the most interesting she had taken in university. Everyone seemed so enthusiastic about the role of teachers and the importance of education. The fit seemed perfect for Pamela. She could use her role as a teacher to develop in her students the enthusiasm for learning that was so central to her own life. She really looked forward to her first Observation Period in a local high school. Perhaps she would get a chance to teach a couple of class although this depended on her sponsor teacher.

The Observation Period left Pamela very anxious about her future as a teacher. Most of the students did not seem to be very interested in their classes and took every opportunity to talk with their friends and goof off. Pamela taught one class on the changing concepts of ownership of creative work. She found it hard to keep the students' attention. It wasn't really that they were acting out and disrupting her class; rather, they seemed to be only mildly interested in her topic and only came to life when she mentioned the issue of sharing music on the Internet. A spontaneous debate broke out in class over whether the artists deserved to be paid or not.

Her sponsor teacher told Pamela that she had presented her topic well. When Pamela mentioned the students' lack of interest, the sponsor teacher had responded with, "Well they're teenagers; for most of them school is just an aspect of their social life. They don't get too excited about academics unless it relates directly to them."

Now Pamela was back in her classes and preparing for her practicum. She was wondering if she was cut out to be a teacher.

## Discussion Questions

1.  What are some of the reasons Pamela and Janet have differing personalities?
2.  Are some personalities better suited for teaching than others?
3.  If Pamela decides to continue with her teaching career, what types of activities might she have to build into her personal life?

## CASE 3-2: MORE IS BETTER

Alia started rescuing animals and birds when she was about two. Her room often looked like a convalescent ward for some strange zoo. Both her parents and even her younger brother were expected to contribute time and sometimes money to some project or other. As Alia got older, these projects moved from animal rescue to social issues. Her parents could only shake their heads when they saw a picture of her on the evening news leading a school demonstration against the genetically modified foods that apparently were being sold in the school cafeteria.

The apathy of people around her frustrated Alia and drove her to become more and more strident in her protests. Increasingly she found conspiracies and greed behind many developments in her community. Situations she had previously viewed as debates about concrete issues became ideological battlefields for her.

By her third year of university, Alia began to see the rhetoric that promoted one economic or social philosophy and denigrated others as being shallow. Most of these philosophies were unable to explain either the drive to accumulate more material goods by those who were already rich, or the spending of resources on weapons by groups of people who seemed to have such immediate needs for the basic necessities of life. She started to look for explanations of human behaviour that gave some insight to these behaviours. Unexpectedly she found a source of at least a possible explanation in the field she had campaigned against much earlier, the field of genetics.

## Discussion Questions:

1.  Are there more fundamental explanations for human behaviour than those offered by most economic or social theories?
2.  Can genetics be used to help explain concepts beyond the colour of someone's eyes?

## CASE 3-3: THE HOMECHILD

Her grandfather had always been Sheila's best friend. You could tell him anything and he never got upset. He always seemed to have lots of time to listen, go for a drive, or play ball. Chocolate was one of his favourite food groups followed closely by green jellybeans. The man was perfect in her eyes.

Sheila's close relationship with her grandfather declined somewhat after she graduated from high school and went on to college, career, and her own family. She always had a wonderful visit with him when she came home, however, and remembered how his eyes had sparkled when she brought her own son around to visit many years ago. The chocolate bar grandfather gave to her child was not so welcomed, however. He didn't have to ride in a car for three hours with a child that was bouncing from seat to seat!

On her last visit Sheila noticed that her grandfather was looking even more fragile and she realized, with a sense of deep sadness, that the phone would ring in the not-too-distant future to announce his death. She also realized that she knew very little about her grandfather and asked for a time to talk with him about his past.

"Well, there's not much to talk about," he said. "But if you want to listen to a boring story, how about coming down in a couple of weeks and we can go out for some dessert?"

Three weeks later they were seated in a window seat in a local restaurant that probably hadn't changed in 50 years. Grandfather ordered his usual apple pie with a big scoop of chocolate ice cream. Thoughts of diabetes, heart attacks and other terrible illnesses went through Sheila's mind and so she regretfully ordered herbal tea.

Grandfather started his tale with meeting his wife at a dance at a church social. He went on to describe their life together in glowing terms, emphasizing the joy that Sheila's mother and uncle had brought to their lives. The saddest moment of his life was the day his wife of so many years died.

"But were you born in Canada, Grandpa?" Sheila asked.

"No, I was born in England around 1902," he responded. He didn't volunteer anything further.

"Well, how did you get to Canada?" Sheila persisted.

Her grandfather was quiet for a long time and then asked her, "Have you ever heard of the homechildren?"

"No, never. Who were they?"

"Well, I was one of them. I was raised in an orphanage in London. I don't know for sure what happened to my parents. Around that time the British government was sending some of us kids in the orphanages to Canada. We were sort of adopted by families here, mostly rural families who needed a hand with the farm work. Some of us kids were treated pretty bad. Actually I had a pretty bad time myself and I was so lonely. I don't really want to think about those times. It doesn't do any good now."

"But you have been such a wonderful person," stated Sheila. "Ever kid in this town seems to know you and smile at you."

"Well I don't know about the wonderful part. I do know that a lot of the homechildren led quite unhappy lives. Maybe the schoolteacher and the pastor took a little more interest in me than in the others for some reason. Since then I have never wanted to see an unhappy child."

## Discussion Questions

1. What may be some of the reasons that Sheila's grandfather was able to have a rewarding life despite his difficult childhood?

2. What are some of the factors that may have made his outcome different from many other children with similar experiences?

*Note:* Homechildren were sent to Canada from 1870 to 1930. They sometimes were called Barnardo Children after an Irish social worker of the time.

# chapter four

# Brain and Biological Development

We cannot see, hear, or feel our brain, yet, at a fundamental level, it is us. Any understanding of psychology requires a basic understanding of the structure and function of our nervous system. The following is a summary of basic structures and concepts related to the operation of our brain and nerves.

## DIVISIONS OF THE NERVOUS SYSTEM

Our nervous system is a whole entity, but for the sake of understanding, it can be divided in a number of ways. One of these divisions is central and peripheral

- The **central** nervous system is composed of the brain, spinal cord, and cranial nerves.
- The **peripheral** nervous system is composed of all the rest of the nerves in the body.
- The peripheral nervous system in turn is often divided into somatic and autonomic.
  - The **somatic** nervous system carries information to and from sense organs and muscles.
  - The **autonomic** nervous system carries information to and from glands and internal organs.

■ The autonomic system in turn is divided into sympathetic and parasympathetic. These often function in antagonistic ways.

  ■ The **sympathetic** nervous system usually is involved in adjustments to the body to maintain temperature, heart rate etc. In times of danger, it causes a total body response called the 'fight or flight' response.

  ■ The **parasympathetic** nervous system is involved in maintenance of body, usually visceral organs. It acts to reduce heart rate and other effects of the 'fight or flight' response.

## Additional Ways of Dividing the Nervous System

■ Afferent/Efferent: **Afferent** nerves carry information to a structure, particularly the central nervous system. **Efferent** nerves carry information away from a structure, particularly the central nervous system.

■ Voluntary/Involuntary: **Voluntary** parts of the nervous system are under conscious control. **Involuntary** parts of the nervous system function without conscious control.

■ Voluntary and involuntary nerves are not completely separate. Some parts of the nervous system that usually are involuntary can be controlled voluntarily — breathing is an example. People also use techniques such as biofeedback to learn to control involuntary nerves.

## ORGANIZATION OF THE BRAIN

The brain functions as a unit but can be subdivided in terms of anatomy and function.

## Evolutionary Stages of Development

■ One way of subdividing the brain leads to three components based roughly on evolutionary stage of development: hindbrain, midbrain, and forebrain.

■ The **hindbrain** is the oldest part of the brain and is located at the back, lower portion of the skull.

■ The **midbrain** is located between the hindbrain and the forebrain, and is crucial in the relaying of information between the brain and the rest of the body.

■ The **forebrain** comprises approximately 80 percent of the brain's volume. Its most important component is the cerebral cortex, which is crucial in perception, cognition, and language. Other components of the forebrain control emotions, temperature, hunger, etc.

## Division By Function

■ Another way to divide the brain is in terms of its three principal functions: behaviour, emotions, and cognition. These three functions are not restricted to any particular area of the brain, nor are they separate from one another. The cerebral cortex in particular is involved in all three functions.

- Given this understanding, however, areas of the brain are more important for one function than another.
  - The cerebellum and brain stem are mainly involved in behaviour.
  - Lower levels of forebrain are important for emotions.
  - The cerebral cortex is crucial for cognition.
- Each of the three areas involved in these functions has the ability to sense, remember, and communicate.

## Left and Right Cerebral Hemispheres

- Sometimes approaches to education place considerable emphasis on the division between the left and right hemispheres of the cerebral cortex.
- The two hemispheres have somewhat specialized functions. For most people, the left hemisphere is more involved in logical thinking and language, and the right is more involved in emotions, spatial understanding and creativity.
- The hemispheres are connected by the broad band of neurons called the corpus callosum.
- While it is sometimes useful to consider the specialized functions of the two halves of the cortex, it is important to realize that they do not operate separately.

# BASIC COMPONENTS OF THE NERVOUS SYSTEM

## Nature of a Neuron

- The three principal components of a neuron are axon, cell body with nucleus, and branching fibres called dendrites.
- Human beings have approximately 100 billion neurons.

## Basic Nature of a Synapse

- Neurons are not fastened together or hardwired.
- The space between the axon of one neuron and the dendrite or cell body of another neuron is called a **synapse**.
- Humans have approximately 100 trillion synaptic connections.
  - The number of connections can easily go up or down by 25 percent based on our interactions with our environment.

## Neurotransmitters

- **Neurotransmitters** are specially shaped molecules that bridge synaptic gap.
- Neurotransmitters may excite or inhibit neural transmission.

- A large number of chemicals, each with a specialized role, are thought to be neuro-transmitters.
  - Those studied extensively include acetylcholine, norepinephrine, dopamine, and serotonin.
- Abnormal levels of particular neurotransmitters lead to various types of mental illnesses.
- Narcotics and other drugs duplicate or interfere with the functions of neurotransmitters.

## PROCESSES OF NEURAL DEVELOPMENT

Neurons undergo five processes of development from a person's conception to maturity.

1. **Proliferation**: The fetal brain produces about 25,000 neurons per minute.
   - This process is thought to be completed at birth.
2. **Migration** occurs as fetal brain neurons move from near the centre of brain to different parts of brain.
   - Migration of primitive cells may also be possible later in life.
3. **Cell Growth** is the result of use and growth in the body.
   - Larger cells are generally more efficient.
4. **Myelination** is the process by which neurons are covered with an insulating layer of fat cells.
   - These fatty cells provide electrical insulation for axons. This insulation speeds transmission.
   - Different areas of the brain are myelinated at different times.
   - Myelination begins before birth and continues until adolescence.
5. In the process of **differentiation**, primitive neurons become specialized.
   - There is a dramatic increase in connections with other neurons.
   - Differentiation occurs because of stimulation from the environment.
   - Even neurons that have established connections with other neurons may withdraw these connections if there is no stimulation.

## NEURAL PLASTICITY

- The brain uses stimulation from the outside world to shape itself.
- While genetics forms the basic framework of neuron structure and brain organization, demands from interaction with the environment determine the finished product at any given time.

## NEURAL NETS

- The concept of neural nets is similar to neural plasticity. Neurons build connections with one another to form neural nets based on demands from the environment.

■ The concepts of neural plasticity and neural nets have important implications for education because they indicate that our perception of the world and our approach to problem solving depend on the neural organization that has been built through our experience.

## INFORMATION PROCESSING, LEARNING STYLES, AND BRAIN-BASED LEARNING

These approaches to education attempt to deal with teaching and learning as if the brain mattered. They are discussed in more detail in later chapters.

## BIOLOGICAL DEVELOPMENT

Issues in biological development have important implications for psychology.

### Bonding

■ **Bonding** usually is thought of as attachment of parent to child.

■ There is a debate about whether bonding is biological or cultural.

■ Additional questions concern whether bonding occurs in all cases in all mothers and the role of bonding for fathers and extended family.

### Attachment

■ **Attachment** usually refers to the connection of child to parent.

■ Attachment exists on a continuum from secure through ambivalent to unattached. The degree of attachment is correlated with social difficulties.

■ Attachment theory raises the same debates and questions as bonding.

The issues of bonding and attachment are complex ones from both a biological and a social context. If it is mentioned at all, bonding now usually is covered as a part of attachment theory. Attachment theory usually is expanded to include relationships with others in the community including other caregivers, teachers, grandparents, etc.

### Progression of Motor Development

Progression of learning motor skills is one way of looking at motor development. Three components of this progression are:

■ Motor skills usually develop from **rhythmic** to **gross** to **fine**, which are considered the

■ Most people have more developed motor skills in their upper bodies than in their lower. As a result, motor skill development usually is cephalo/caudal or head to tail.

■ Motor skills are developed best when the centre of the body is trained before the extremities.

## Gender

- **Gender** refers to differences in physical and psychological characteristics between females and males.
- It is unclear how much of the difference in psychological characteristics between males and females is determined by genetics. Certainly it is much more than accepted in education. Environment may then serve to strengthen, weaken, or introduce new aspects.

## Growth Spurt

- Differences in ages of growth spurt for males and females is a critical factor for education.
  - The median age of growth spurt for females is 10.5 years while it is 12.5 years for males.

## Puberty

- The drop in age of menarche for females over the last hundred years is an issue of concern.
  - In North America the drop has been from about seventeen years to twelve years.
- Considerable debate exists as to the effects of early and late maturing for both females and males.

## Norms

- Detailed norms have been developed for many aspects of human biological and psychological growth.
- Often these norms are presented without any indication of variation. This can be very misleading for those who do not have an understanding of statistics.

## CASE 4-1: WHO AM I?

Tasha's thoughts whirled as she finished her first visit as a volunteer in an Intermediate Care Hospital. Her confusion continued while walking to meet her friends at the mall. Lia asked her if she was okay and Tasha responded with a nod of her head. The excitement of shopping in the mall and talking with her friends soon drew Tasha out of her reverie. A scolding from her mother for being late for supper and an hour's homework banished any thoughts about the hospital.

The next morning Tasha looked at herself in the mirror with the usual morning mixture of sleep and the jitters. She definitely was not a morning person. Brush teeth and hair she told herself, again amused by the idea of how easy it might be to confuse the two brushings. She went through the rest of her morning routine on automatic pilot. Some part of her brain seemed to know what had to be done.

Math was her first class of the day. Other students tended to dread math, but Tasha looked forward to it. She could see in her mind what was going on with the problems being discussed. She knew the right steps to take and felt a real pleasure in the logical way that the processes developed. Tasha really didn't have any problems with most of her classes, but Math was the only one where there was this kind of visceral feeling of pleasure.

Social studies, however, bored her. It wasn't that the work was hard, really; it was just that there never seemed to be any real point to it. When everyone stated different opinions during class discussions, Tasha got confused. She just wanted to know the facts about a situation. She was willing to accept in some measure that facts varied from person to person, but felt that there still must be some overall data about what happened and that it was important to know this data. Indeed, she had responded somewhat angrily to her teacher last Friday when he had suggested that students explore what racism meant for them. Tasha felt that the result was only a sort of pious listing of examples of racism that might or might not have occurred. There was no attempt to provide students with any information about what actually did happen in any specific situation.

At noon Lia stormed up to her shouting at her to stay away from Peter. Now there was no doubt that Tasha thought Peter was cute and that she felt a little buzz when he was around. Tasha knew that Lia was interested in Peter, however, and had never done anything beyond the usual social interactions she had with other students in the class. She was dumbstruck by Lia's accusations and her threat to break off their friendship if Tasha had anything more to do with Peter. "I didn't do anything," sputtered Tasha. Lia claimed that Tasha was 'making eyes' at Peter and that she had better stop if she wanted to keep their friendship. "Wow," thought Tasha. "What brought that on?"

She thought about her last interaction with Peter. He had told her about going to get his driver's licence and finding out that he was colour blind. He was still in a state of shock and Tasha didn't really know what to say. It did seem strange to her that Peter would not have realized earlier that he was colour blind. She found it quite interesting that he did not see colours the way they were. She also thought about other students who had more obvious sensory difficulties that kept them from experiencing her real world.

On Tasha's next visit to the hospital she went back to visit with Mrs. Henderson, an 89-year-old woman who had been in the hospital for a little over a year. A locked door that was opened by a simple code limited Mrs. Henderson's movements within the hospital. Mrs. Henderson couldn't remember the code and couldn't open the door. Tasha could take her for a walk outside, but usually Mrs. Henderson just wanted to talk. When Tasha came to visit, Mrs. Henderson couldn't remember who she was but was always very pleasant. Sometimes she confused Tasha with her own daughter and described things as if Tasha had been there. Tasha did not see the point of correcting her.

Mrs. Henderson told Tasha about her life on the prairies and about her family. She described events in great depth and seemed to remember the smallest details of her youth and childhood, details that Tasha didn't remember about her own, much more recent childhood! Tasha listened to these stories, often with interest. She liked Mrs. Henderson and respected the fact that Mrs. Henderson enjoyed her company without the emotional roller coaster of involvement with her other friends.

After four weeks of meeting with Mrs. Henderson Tasha arrived to find another woman visiting Mrs. Henderson. Tasha was about to leave, but the new woman smiled and invited her in. Initially, Mrs. Henderson seemed quite confused by both women being in the room, but she quickly went back to her pleasant manners and included Tasha in the conversation. Mrs. Henderson again was telling stories from years ago, this time about her daughter's childhood visit to Niagara Falls. Tasha quickly understood that the new woman was Elizabeth, one of Mrs. Henderson's three children. Elizabeth listened to Mrs. Henderson in much the same manner as Tasha had, responding with smiles and exclamations designed to keep the stories going.

At the end to the visit, Elizabeth invited Tasha to have tea with her. Tasha was a little apprehensive about talking with the woman, especially since she might have complaints or demands that Tasha wouldn't know how to handle. However, she agreed and soon they were in the dining room. Elizabeth expressed her thanks for Tasha's weekly visits. She lived in a nearby city, but the many demands of her life made it hard for her to visit her mother as often as she would like.

Eventually the conversation got around to some of the stories about her life that Mrs. Henderson was telling. Tasha commented on how Elizabeth and Mrs. Henderson must have had a great trip to Niagara Falls. Elizabeth smiled and replied, "That was my sister Jenny, and she remembers the trip very well. I was too young to go." Tasha was kind of shocked by this statement and asked why Elizabeth didn't correct her mother. Elizabeth replied, "At first I used to correct her, but it just seemed to confuse her and she often stopped talking. I know my mother enjoys her memories even if they are not quite what happened. Really her memories are all she has now."

That evening Tasha had her first serious introspection. She thought about how people seemed to have different aptitudes, interests, memories, perceptions, and sensory abilities. It was both disconcerting and fascinating. For the first time the question "Who am I?" took on more meaning than a simple statement of facts or a listing of likes and dislikes.

## Discussion Questions

1. What types of factors might influence our ability to see the world?
2. Is there some objective way to know what people mean by their actions?
3. Can I trust my memory of past events?
4. Other than the obvious physical differences, is everyone the same?
5. Who am I?

## CASE 4-2: LEARNING TO DRIVE

Saying that Jennifer Mendez wanted to drive was like saying a drowning person wanted air. She craved, desired, dreamed of, wished for, and prayed for the day to come when she could start her driving lessons. She had images of herself behind the wheel, radio playing, and the road ahead. Unlike some of her friends, the attraction was not simply convenience and an improved social life — it was the pure feeling of being on the road.

Jennifer's parents had promised her driving lessons for her sixteenth birthday. She had booked them already, for the very first Saturday after her Wednesday birthday. The first few classes took place in a room where the instructor taught a bunch of boring material about safe driving and road safety. She had read all of this stuff already and could hardly wait to get to the driving part.

The driving school even came by her house for her first actual driving experience so she did not have to deal with the rather strange situation of taking the bus to driving lessons. The instructor picked her up and they went to a parking lot at a nearby community college. The instructor spent some time explaining all the features of the car and showing her how the gearshift, brakes, and accelerator worked. Then it was her turn.

The car lurched forward and she headed toward a lamppost with what seemed like incredible speed. A panicked slamming on of the brakes brought a screech from the tires and stares from a couple on the sidewalk. The instructor merely smiled and responded with an annoying, "Good first try."

Slowly during the next hour Jennifer got so she could accelerate smoothly, although braking was still a bit of a challenge. She could even steer in a straight line without weaving back and forth. "Not ready for the highway," she thought at the end of the first lesson.

## Discussion Questions

1. Why could Jennifer not drive smoothly even though she had imagined herself driving for years?

2. What effects will practice have on her brain?

## CASE 4-3: THE STROKE

Ross was so tired — more tired than he had ever imagined was possible. There were people coming and going, but he was just too tired to talk to them, or to pay attention to what they were saying. He didn't know where he was, and he didn't care. He had a vague concern about getting some of his marking done, but wasn't sure what was left to do or when it was required. "I'll just go back to sleep for a while," he thought.

Later his room seemed brighter, although quite unfamiliar. There were two other men sleeping in the room and he soon realized that, for some reason, he was in a hospital. A nurse came by to check one of the other men and he called out to her. Amazingly there was no sound and the nurse left the room without coming over to him. He tried to move and found that he could lift his left arm and leg as well as move his right leg a bit. His right arm refused to move and he didn't have the energy to try and sit up. Feelings of panic overcame him but soon the tiredness forced him back to sleep.

The next thing Ross knew, a doctor was standing beside his bed. She was calling him by name. He opened his eyes and looked at her without moving his head. "Mr. Meier, you have had a stroke," she said. "You are now in St. Joseph's Hospital. Over the next two days we will be doing some tests. Please try to rest and not worry. You will improve a lot over the next few weeks."

The tests revealed that Mr. Meier had lost the ability to speak, although not the ability to understand language. He also had lost quite a bit of movement on the right side of his body. Fortunately, he had retained most of his memory except for events around the time of his stroke. He immediately recognized his wife and children, although couldn't recall the names of the two students who came to see him as representatives of his classes. The doctor told him that he could expect to recover a lot of his lost abilities, but that it would take time and a great deal of physical and mental work on his part.

## Discussion Questions

1. Why could Mr. Meier not perform actions even though he could think about doing them?
2. What changes would the physical and mental actions make in his brain?

## CASE 4-4: RATE OF DEVELOPMENT

George had worked very hard in his Methods courses and thought he was well prepared to teach his grade 5 class. He planned to intersperse his Math and Language Arts classes with Physical Education and Art classes. He felt the variety would relieve any potential boredom among the students. Besides, he was very interested in both Art and Physical Education and felt they were an important part of everyone's development.

George had taken a BA in English before going to a local community college for a year-long teacher-training program. He had worked as a supervisor in a teen program for two years, but had very little experience with 11- or 12-year-olds. While his college instructors talked about the importance of Art and Physical Education, the majority of class time was spent on Science, Math, and Language Arts Methods. George felt that he had plenty of ideas for Physical Education and Art activities though, and was not worried about these areas.

During the first three observation weeks of his practicum the class teacher spent very little time on anything other than 'academic' material. Class discussions were held, of course, and there was quite a bit of interaction among students. Art consisted mostly of drawing maps and diagrams, and there was no PE during the observation time.

The first part of George's practicum required his taking over specific classes. These classes usually were in Science or Math, and the sponsor teacher took the class back as soon as George was finished. George quickly noticed that there was quite a large variation in the ability of the students, so he often had to change some of his approaches to keep all of the students involved. He passed this difference off as mostly being due to differing experience. Some students apparently knew background material and others appear to have missed or not understood material that was supposed to have been covered in earlier grades.

By the fourth week of his practicum, George was supposed to be responsible for the programs in the morning. He and his sponsor teacher had gone over what he would be doing and George had asked the sponsor teacher about incorporating more Art. The whole issue had to be handled carefully as the sponsor teacher thought she was doing Art; George, however, wanted to include more personal expression in his assignment. The sponsor teacher was hesitant but agreed that George could spend 30 minutes each morning doing Art.

George's first Art class happened at 10:30 on Tuesday morning. He was to remember the time and day well. Because he wanted everyone to feel comfortable with the project, he had people work in self-chosen groups. The topic was a storyboard for an animation program they thought would be good for their age group for TV. He had explained the idea of a storyboard to them by sketching one for a popular comedy show. He emphasized that the concept of the show was more important than the actual drawings. The fact that George had not done much drawing since grade school and that his graphics were basically stick figures served to reinforce his emphasis on concept rather than drawing skills.

George was thrilled when the first group presented their idea for a panel where younger children could discuss things that interested them, interview their favourite musicians, and watch some music videos. Things were pretty rocky from then on, however. He will always remember the look on his sponsor teacher's face when one group of girls introduced the concept of quite a sexually explicit learning-to-date show. Actually the teacher was more concerned about a parent coming into the room than about the graphic nature of comments from students.

The real disaster came from a group of boys who had been excitedly involved in a project in the back. Their idea of a good show seemed to involve nothing more than a disconnected series of goofy stunts interspersed with a fair amount of maiming and killing. When George tried to save the day by asking them for the reasons that the characters were involved in all this different activities, the boys could only respond that it was fun to watch. They seemed to have no concept of character or motivation.

That night George decided he would have to rethink his whole idea of Art and Physical Education in the Grade 5 classroom. His experience with the storyboard project convinced him that he would have to be more careful in defining topics for his Art program. A mental review of the physical nature of the class alerted him to the need to alter his PE classes as well. His initial idea had been to run two soccer games across the playing field rather than lengthwise, with team members chosen on a random basis so that no one would be last chosen by a team captain. As he thought about the differing physical characteristics of his class members, he realized that alterations would have to be made if everyone was going to participate.

## Discussion Questions

1. Do all individuals develop at the same rate?
2. How does the rate of development in males and females relate to George's problem?
3. Do students in this age group share common social interests?
4. What could George do about his soccer game?

# chapter five

# Cognitive and
# Language Development

## COGNITIVE DEVELOPMENT

Cognitive development often is defined as the development of thinking. This is misleading if the concept of thinking is limited to include only the thoughts that might run through our mind. **Cognition** refers to our processes of knowing about, or perceiving, ourselves and our world. The underlying pattern is more about thinking patterns than individual thoughts.

## Issues in Cognitive Development

- Some important questions are the source of debate related to cognitive development and indeed, development in general.
- Do people develop at different rates? Almost everyone believes that the rate of development varies from person to person. Indeed, the rate of development varies among different factors in an individual. For instance, a child might understand the concept of *parent,* but not that of *brother* and *sister,* especially if the child had no siblings.
- Does development follow a relatively fixed path in the sense that an individual must be able to do one process before they are able to learn another? This principle is debated more than the concept of different rates. Exceptions to this process

are either demonstrated in experiments or pointed out in real life situations. The fact that a change in the order of development can be produced in a laboratory setting or that it occurs from time to time in the community does not mean that the general principle does not apply in most cases, however.

- Is development continuous or discontinuous? In other words, does development happen gradually, or are there sudden spurts? This question usually revolves around the word *sudden*. If *sudden* is taken to mean a few weeks or a couple of months, then there is little doubt that children can change dramatically in this time frame.

- Does development go through stages? This really is issue two and issue three combined. Piaget says there are stages while Vygotsky does not propose any general stages of cognitive development.

- How important are early events? Some theorists propose that early experiences in life are the most important factors in determining life-long development. Others emphasize the importance of experiences at every age.

  - Possibly at least some of this debate is due to not defining the nature of early experiences. Early physical or psychological traumas have life long effects; it may be the intensity of the experience rather than its timing that is the most important factor.

- What factors influence development? Again, writers tend to stress the importance of their own field of study. Someone with a neural development interest will stress the development of the brain and nerves, while someone with a more social-oriented field will place the emphasis on environment. The most obvious answer is that a variety of factors influence development.

## Jean Piaget

Jean Piaget usually is given prominence in any discussion of cognitive development. His ideas have influenced our concepts of how thinking develops and how education should be structured. Those interested in other cognitive theorists might want to look at writers such as Vygotsky, Donaldson, and Flavell.

## Basic Metaphor Underlying Piaget's Concept of the Development of Intelligence

- Intelligence develops through confrontation with environment.
- Development of intelligence involves the same processes as evolution.
- Intelligence moves from exclusively biological control to more abstract.

## Intelligence

- According to Piaget, intelligence is biological.
- Intelligence has two aspects: organization and adaptation.
- The organization of intelligence manifests itself in **schemata** or **schema** which are frameworks that develop in the mind to organize information.

- **Adaptation** occurs because forces require the establishment of a new state of equilibrium or equilibration. Adaptation occurs through the two processes of assimilation and accommodation.
    - **Assimilation** occurs when new information is incorporated into existing schemata.
    - **Accommodation** occurs when new information causes a change in schemata.

## Stages

- Piaget's theory states that cognitive development goes through a series of stages.
- These stages tend to occur at approximately the same age for individuals in a particular culture.
- Movement from one stage to another occurs because biological development leads to increased ability to deal with cognitive confrontations from the environment.
- The principal stages and the approximate ages for them are:

|                     |              |
|---------------------|--------------|
| Sensory-Motor       | 0-2 years.   |
| Pre-Operational     | 2-7 years.   |
| Concrete Operations | 7-12 years.  |
| Formal Operations   | 12+ years.   |

- **Operations** refers to a mental map for carrying out physical or cognitive tasks.
- Not everyone reaches the formal operations level. People must be confronted with problems that cannot be solved at the concrete operations level to reach formal operations.
- Each stage manifests typical abilities and difficulties.
    - At the Sensory Motor stage, typical problems involve coordination of sense organs and muscles, movement to goal directed activities, and developing concept of object permanence.
    - At the Pre-Operational stage, children are learning about language and symbols. They tend to centre on one aspect of a situation and have difficulty understand conservation of number and amount or reversing operations.
    - At the Concrete Operations stage, people are increasingly able to solve conservation problems. They are learning more and more about reversing operations and increasingly are able to classify an object based on more than one property of the object. They have problems with statements that are contrary to fact and with the concept of multiple solutions to a problem. People in concrete operations learn to understand humour and metaphor.
    - At the Formal Operations Stage, individuals can reason from hypothetical situations but have trouble dealing with particular types of adolescent egocentrism.

## Egocentrism

- The **ego** is an individual's personal construct — their map of the world. Individuals develop this map as a result of their interactions with their environment.

- **Egocentrism** refers to the degree to which individuals are centred in their constructs of the world.
    - Do they realize that their maps of the world are constructs or do they believe that their maps represent reality?
    - Do they understand that other people have different maps, or do they think that everyone perceives situations as they do?
- At birth, a child is almost completely egocentric. Experiences with the environment change the nature of egocentrism, although it continues to be an important aspect of interactions with other people and with events in our lives.
- Each stage of development involves struggles with particular forms of egocentrism.
    - Children at the Sensory Motor stage are gradually learning to separate the environment from themselves.
    - Children at the Pre-Operational level have to confront their magic thinking and animism.
    - Young people at the Concrete Operations stage learn to find multiple solutions to situations, and to distinguish between what actually exists in the world and what they believe to be true.
    - Individuals at the Formal Operations level deal with at least four types of egocentrism:
        1. the belief in an imaginary audience or that everyone is watching them;
        2. the concept of a personal fable in the sense that their lives are unique;
        3. idealism or the belief that there is some simple, ideal solution to situations and they know this solution, and
        4. difficulty in understanding that thoughts do not become concrete reality without effort.
- All people at all ages suffer from various forms of egocentrism.

## Piaget as Literature

Like Freud and Jung, Piaget perhaps is best viewed from a literary perspective rather than from a strictly scientific one. Debates about whether concrete operations starts at a particular age in all situations miss the power of Piaget's concepts. Rather, Piaget needs to be considered in terms of broader questions.

- How does Piaget's theory correspond to our lives?
- What are schemata, adaptation, and equilibration as seen in life?
- Why do we recognize humour in Calvin and Hobbes?

## Piaget and Education

- Piaget reminds us that children at various ages differ not only in the amount of material known, but, more importantly, in their basic thinking patterns.
- Teachers need to structure learning so that experiences confront the children's schemata in order to move them to higher levels of cognition.

## Concerns about Piaget

- Piaget lacks clarity about whether the cause of development is biological or cognitive.
- Piaget seems to assume that development is constant across all areas for a child.
- Some feel that Piaget did not consider cultural differences.
- Experimenters have found that children can do some operations beyond their stage if conditions are explained carefully.

## Approaches to Teaching Based on Piaget

- Several methods of teaching owe their foundation to Piaget's concepts. These include constructivist approaches, critical thinking, discovery learning, and problem solving.

## Lev Vygotsky

While Piaget placed great emphasis on children constructing their own patterns of thinking, Vygotsky placed emphasis on the role of people and tools in the environment. Vygotsky regarded language as the most important tool in the environment as it is not only used in communication but also in cognitive activities such as planning and thinking.

## Private Speech

- **Private speech** refers to talking to ourselves. Young children may do this out loud while adults usually do not — at least if they think anyone could hear!
- Piaget felt that private speech was a form of egocentric talking, while Vygotsky felt it had an important role in cognitive development.

## Zone of Proximal Development

- **Zone of Proximal Development** refers to the finding that children often can solve problems if adults structure experiences and conversations so that the children are led to the discovery of the answer.
  - The Zone of Proximal Development questions or modifies the concept of fixed stages.

## Scaffolding

- **Scaffolding** refers to the cues, examples, reminders and steps that can be used in problem solving.
- Scaffolding allows students to solve problems they couldn't do on their own and then gradually learn to solve these types of problems independently.

## Adult Mediated Learning

- **Adult Mediated Learning** postulates that development occurs through interaction with more capable members of the community who provide the right level of learning experiences.

## Vygotsky and Education

- Vygotsky's concepts provide a foundation for the concepts of scaffolding and mediated learning.
- Vygotsky encourages providing students with the support and the tools they need to consider issues near the upper limit of their zone of proximal development.

## Piaget and Vygotsky

While some texts make a great issue out of the differences between Piaget and Vygotsky, they both were constructivist in their approach, with Vygotsky placing more emphasis on the role of social interactions. Neither believed that decontextualized testing was an appropriate method to understand a child's present ability or potential. Rather, a dynamic interaction with the person doing the assessment is necessary to determine the true nature of the child's mental processes.

## Metacognition

**Metacognition** refers to thinking about the characteristics of our own or others' cognitive processes. Issues related to metacognition will be covered later under information processing in Chapter 11.

- Teachers work to produce strategic learners by providing them with appropriate information processing skills including attention, storage, and retrieval mechanisms, and by teaching effective problem solving strategies.
- Teachers help students learn cognitive monitoring skills such as self-checking to ensure that they are doing a process correctly.
  - Initial assistance and support with tools such as checklists often are steps in developing these skills.

## LANGUAGE DEVELOPMENT

## Nature of Speech and Hearing

- Speech and hearing probably developed for survival and communication.
- Sound includes all sounds — not just those made by humans.
- Sounds affect us cognitively, emotionally, and physically.

## Functions of Language

- Language includes spoken, written, and signed communications.
- Communication is one of the main functions of language. Interpersonal, instrumental, and regulatory are different types of communications.
- Language is also involved in imagination, perception and thinking.

## Characteristics of Language

- Language depends on words with conventional meanings.
- These words must be sequenced in a particular order for meaning to occur.
- Language allows for **displacement,** or the description of situations that are different from the one now occurring.
- In humans in particular, a relatively small number of words can be used to generate a virtual infinity of communication possibilities.
- All languages have rules related to grammar, pronunciation, and the process of holding conversations with others.

## Theories of Language

There are several theories that attempt to describe how humans learn language.

- The behaviourist approach claims that humans learn language through conditioning.
- The nativistic approach postulates that language is a built-in function of humans.
- The cognitive approach claims that learning a language involves cognitive processes.

## Language Development

- Preverbal communication is the first stage in language development. Babies are very efficient communicators even though they cannot speak.
- Children typically begin to speak using one or two word utterances. There is some debate about the level of language sophistication children are showing with these short words or phrases.
- Some type of language readiness test is used to measuring language abilities.

## Learning Two Languages

- There is considerable debate about whether learning a second language is easier for a child or an adult. Immersion seems to be the critical factor in both cases.
- Early second language learning often enables the learner to use the correct rhythm or accent with each language. This is much harder for older person to do.
- Debate also occurs over the issue of immersion. Some students have language difficulties in both the immersion language and their native language because of this process, while others seem to thrive with the combination.

## Approaches to Teaching Language

- One approach to teaching language involves having students learning to recognize whole words such as in the *See Dick and Jane* books.
- Phonics emphasizes learning speech sounds and the art of pronunciation.
- The whole language approach uses children's literature and children's own writing and speaking processes to build language skills.
- Most teachers use an eclectic mix of these and other approaches.

## CASE 5-1:  ADAPTATION

Julie Laroux was one of the most dynamic students in Mr. Tammaro's class. She was full of ideas and always greeted each new activity with a burst of enthusiasm. Exams were another matter for Julie, however. Saying that Julie suffered from exam anxiety would be an understatement. On the day of an exam Julie was very quiet, never smiled, and spent most of the day picking at her pens and looking around the class. She remarked several times through the term about how she hated exams. "I seem to know it in class," she stated, "but I just can't remember anything on the quiz."

Julie did well on her quizzes though, with most of her marks being in the B or B+ range. Unfortunately, she seemed to identify only with the questions she got wrong. Mr. Tammaro had remarked repeatedly about how well she did but Julie usually responded with, "Yeah but if I had just …." There was a section on report cards for parents to send comments to the teacher and Mr. Tammaro was somewhat upset to see that Julie's parents had mentioned they felt Julie needed to work harder.

Julie's situation actually mirrored that of a number of students in the class. Most of the students came from working class areas of the city with parents who had worked very hard to establish homes and small businesses. They wanted the best for their children and felt that education was an essential component of security for their children's futures.

Mr. Tammaro felt that he would like to reduce the level of exam anxiety in his class and also reduce the students' inclination to look to him for the what they thought was the right answer to problems or situations. Indeed, he often noticed that many of the students sat without saying anything during discussions and then wrote down his summary at the end. After the first report card he decided to modify his approach. He decided to use more group projects that did not involve having a right answer. Marking would still be rigorous but it would be based more on process than on having a specific content. He replaced his exams with weekly quizzes and sometimes even let the students discuss the questions before they had to write their answers.

Everything seemed to be going very well. Student participation picked up a great deal and even Julie was much more relaxed about the quizzes. Then on Thursday after school he received a call from Mrs. Leroux.

"Hello Mrs. Leroux," said Mr. Tammaro. "I have been looking forward to a chance to talk to you. The last parent teacher meeting was so busy I really didn't have time to talk to individual parents very much."

"Good to talk to you as well Mr. Tammaro, but my husband and I have a few concerns about Julie's reports from your class."

"Julie is doing very well in my class, Mrs. Leroux. As a matter of fact she has improved even more since I have changed my teaching style to include less direct instruction and exams."

"That's what I wanted to talk to you about, Mr. Tammaro. We feel that Julie needs to be taught rather than just the kind of playing she seems to be doing now."

Mr. Tammaro was taken aback but responded with, "Well the class is not playing Mrs. Leroux. They are working together to find possible answers to the problems I give them. I am finding they are learning a great deal — including how to work together to solve common problems."

"That may be, but Julie has plenty of group activities with Girl Guides and her church group. We sent her to school to learn. She also tells us that she doesn't have to study as much because you no longer have exams, and that the kids even talk about the answers to questions before they write your quizzes."

"It is true that I have reduced the emphasis on exams," explained Mr. Tammaro. "Too many of the students were getting very anxious before exams and I didn't think the exams were really telling me what the students knew. Julie is one of the students who was very anxious before exams but seems to be much more relaxed in class now. She is a real leader in her groups."

"Students have to learn to handle stress," countered Mrs. Leroux. "It is part of life. Also, if the students are doing group work how am I supposed to know if Julie is learning what she should be? She has to go on to other grades, you know, and then she will need to know what she was supposed to get in your class."

Mr. Tammaro tried hard to explain his motivation for his class and to assure her that Julie was learning what she was supposed to, but at the end of their phone conversation he felt that Mrs. Leroux was far from convinced. There were no further comments for almost two weeks however, and so he relaxed somewhat and thought that maybe Mr. and Mrs. Leroux had changed their minds.

That was until he saw the note in his box from the principal on Monday morning. The principal wanted to see him when Mr. Tammaro had a moment. Today at 4:15 would be good.

The meeting with the principal went just about as Mr. Tammaro had expected. It started with the usual pleasantries followed by an examination of the lesson outlines Mr. Tammaro had given the principal in September. The principal could not quite control her annoyance when she outlined her phone conversation with Mr. Leroux. She hadn't known about the details of the changes in Mr. Tammaro's class and had been forced to support her teacher without the details of what was going on in the class.

Mr. Tammaro apologized for his oversight and went on to explain what he was doing in the class and why. The principal sympathized and offered suggestions about how Mr. Tammaro might have better introduced the new approach into his classroom. She also explained that the parents in the area were very traditional in their views of education and that these views had to be taken into account. At the end of the conversation both agreed that Mr. Tammaro would introduce his changes more gradually over the next couple of years and with considerable explanation to parents about what he was doing. In the meantime, Mr. Tammaro would increase the value of exams again and go back to a more traditional format for them.

Mr. Tammaro couldn't think of a good explanation for the move back to the older approach when he explained the changes to his class the next morning. Most of the students were disappointed, although he was surprised to find that some of the students welcome the return to the older way. They stated that their parents were concerned with the new approach. Things reverted to the normal of previous weeks in the classroom. Students like Julie still got upset about exams and the class still waited for Mr. Tammaro to give the right answer.

In February Mr. Tammaro gave an exam that counted for almost 50 percent of that term's mark. He was disappointed to see that Julie only got 63 percent on the quiz. She seemed to have missed a fundamental concept and this led to her getting several questions wrong. When Julie got her quiz back, there was a look of shock on her face and Mr. Tammaro saw tears in her eyes. Later he tried to explain to her that she had just missed a concept and that the mark was not the end of the world.

Julie sort of smiled and said, "Ok." It didn't really look like she was listening.

Mr. Tammaro went home feeling sad that night and realized that he had to do something about changing the approach in his class. He was still thinking about the issue when the phone rang about 9:30 P.M. It was Mrs. Leroux and she was frantic. "Julie hasn't come home," she said. "Sometimes she goes to Andrea's house, but she always phones and comes home by 8:00 P.M. or so. We have phoned everybody we know and got your number from the newsletter you sent out at the beginning of the year. I'm sorry to be calling you but I don't know what to do."

"Have you phoned the police?" asked Mr. Tammaro.

"Yes we have, but they thought that probably there just was some problem at school and she had gone to a friend's house. Did something happen at school?"

"Julie had a bit of trouble with one of her exams," explained Mr. Tammaro. "She didn't do quite as well as she usually does. I tried to tell her that it wasn't the end of the world but she seemed quite upset."

"We always check on how the kids are doing with their exams," said Mrs. Leroux. "Our son John always seems to do well and our other daughter Alice doesn't seem to be the least worried. Julie works so hard and wants to be perfect all the time. Maybe we shouldn't push her so much."

"We all are trying to do what we think is best," said Mr. Tammaro. "Right now we have to find Julie. I know a couple of the girls she hangs around with in school. I will call their parents and see if Julie is there."

"Thank you. Please let us know what you find out, and we'll let you know if we hear from Julie.

Two phone calls later, Mr. Tammaro had located Julie at the Nadeau's. Mrs. Nadeau said that her daughter and Julie were talking in her daughter's room. Mrs. Nadeau had just arrived home from her shift at the local store. The two girls had told her that Julie was staying overnight and that it was all right with Julie's parents. However, Mrs. Nadeau had already come to the conclusion that something was wrong when she asked for Julie's parents' number so she could phone to check. The usual complaints about not trusting them did not disguise the fact that something was not right.

In about half an hour the situation was straightened out to the relief of everyone. Mr. Tammaro got a phone call after work the next day from Mrs. Leroux. He had expected the thank-you call and was not going to use the opportunity to push his concept of new directions in the classroom. As a result, he was surprised when Mrs. Leroux stated, "My husband and I think we were wrong when we criticized your new approach. We would like to help you talk about it with some of the other parents."

## Discussion Questions

1.  What roles did egocentrism play in this case?
2.  What often causes us to change our concepts of our world?
3.  According to Piaget, what are the two types of changes that can occur?
4.  What were the steps in the change process in this case?

## CASE 5-2: STAGES OF LEARNING

Ms. Silverstein has taught Grade Six for ten years. Her students usually have been involved in dynamic group activities using a variety of materials and formats to explore the topics of the different subjects being covered. Graphing, the use of images to convey ideas, and other forms of reporting data always have been a part of her classes. Students are taught how to obtain information from a variety of sources and how to integrate this information in various formats to summarize their findings. Sometimes a few students in the class have more difficulty than others, but she usually places them in groups where the others could help.

Even with these group activities, Ms. Silverstein gradually came to believe that she controlled her classes too much and did not allow enough discovery and experimentation by her students. Last January, she decided to implement some of the new approaches she had learned about from enthusiastic presentations at conferences. Rather than having the students explore issues she had assigned, she felt it was time to experiment with the idea of her students studying issues of interest to them.

Ms. Silverstein did not spring the changes on her class but introduced them gradually. Her first experiment occurred when the class was talking about gravity. She asked the class to explore what would happen if the gravity of earth were doubled. This seemed to her to be an interesting concept and she was looking forward to the student reports. One group did come to ask her if this doubling happened suddenly or whether it had always existed. This question led her to believe that the process was going well and that students were going to find the process interesting. She also was encouraged by the amount of discussion that seemed to be going on in the various groups.

However, final papers were less than she expected. Some of the groups seemed to get stuck on the issue of whether gravity on earth *could* double. Ms. Silverstein had assured them that it could not, but that it would still be interesting to explore what would happen if it did. This assurance apparently was not sufficient for some students to deal with the contradiction they saw in the assignment. Other groups responded with quite lurid accounts of people being squashed by their own weight, buildings falling down because their foundations could no longer support them, etc. She was more encouraged by these responses as at least they indicated a good understanding of the real world of gravity. Only one group looked at the issue from the point of view of how the world might adapt to this situation. This group even developed an experiment to test some of their assumptions such as adding weight to structures and animals to see how they would adapt.

The next time Ms. Silverstein got to try her new approach was during Social Studies. Previously the class had been looking at some of the causes of World War I. They had drawn maps of the various interactions of forces and discussed how one process related to another, eventually leading to the war. Ms. Silverstein thought it would be interesting for her class to explore the issue of the causes of war in general. She introduced the topic to her class by explaining that wars always seem to have occurred and showed on a map of the world where wars were occurring that month. She then asked the class what they thought might be the causes of wars in general. Several hands went up immediately and two or three students started to talk at the same time. "One at a time," said Ms. Silverstein. "Mary, what do you think?"

Mary responded, "Because people hate one another. They should just learn to like other people, even people who are different from them."

Christy then added, "They're just racist and don't like people who are different."

Tom claimed that wars occurred because people were trying to take things from other people and Dorothy added, "People just have to learn to live together and share."

These responses were a bit more simplistic that Ms. Silverstein was hoping for and she noticed that at least half the class was not paying attention. She tried again, "George, why do you think there are wars?"

George mumbled, "I think the same as the others. People fight wars because they want to beat other people."

Helen added, "Only men fight wars. There wouldn't be any wars if women ran things."

This started a general class argument that almost immediately spread from the issue of war to an argument about females and males. There was lots of participation but the class was out of control. Even as she tried to regain control of the class, Ms. Silverstein reflected that she had inadvertently started her own war.

In the lounge during lunch Ms. Silverstein discussed her experiences in the class with two other teachers. Ms. Philips claimed that she had tried these open discussions with her Grade 6 class but had found that a few students dominated the class with ideas that were usually just general statements lacking in specifics. "Besides," she said, "I have enough trouble just covering the material in the curriculum guide without introducing anything else."

Mr. Lin, on the other hand, explained that he had never tried such a general discussion with his grade 3 class, but that the class did love it when he read stories to them and often were able to understand quite complex situations and motivations when he questioned them in the right way.

"Right way," queried Ms. Silverstein?

"You have to kind of lead them along," explained Mr. Lin.

Ms. Silverstein spent the next few days mulling over her experience and the comments of her fellow teachers. Slowly she developed a strategy that seemed to provide more depth to class discussions and also involved more of the students.

## Discussion Questions

1. How does Piaget's concept of stages relate to this situation?

2. How does the concept of egocentrism relate to this situation?

3. How do the concepts of scaffolding and zone of proximal development relate to Ms. Silverstein's situation?

## CASE 5-3: THE MULTINATIONALS

"Look at them all," griped Perry Chan. "Heading off to the cafeteria for their name brand coffee. I can't understand why they are so apathetic."

Perry had been involved in social issues since Grade 10. His commitment had increased during his years in university. Taking part in protests of different kinds was almost a spiritual duty for him. People who didn't protest the system were supporting an obviously corrupt and abusive culture. People were being exploited, as was the environment. It was everyone's duty to do something.

It was obvious what had to be done. It had been obvious to Perry for many years. He remembered the flash of insight he had when doing a paper on logging in Canada. The paper had been another of those boring activities that teachers seemed to delight in assigning. What did he know or care about logging? Why not a paper on the music industry or something that interested him? All that changed when he saw some pictures of clear-cut logging. "Gross," he thought. "How can adults allow such a thing to happen?"

That was the beginning of his crusade. One issue led to another; then he started to see that they all had the same underlying factor — big business. The corporations, the multinationals were behind all of the problems in the world.

Perry had read enough about the issue to become convinced that the solution was small, cooperative, local enterprises where everyone was committed to a self-sustaining approach to life. Any thinking person should be confronting the big companies. Government funds should be available to support local industries. All rights to resources should be stripped from multinationals and made available to local groups that agreed to adhere to sustainable practices. Protests and media events had to be organized to convince the rest of the population to get involved.

### Discussion Questions

1. Which of Piaget's concepts apply to this case?
2. What type of additional information might cause Perry to re-examine some of his positions?

## CASE 5-4: DISCOVERING VYGOTSKY

Mrs. Singh felt that Grade 6 students should be able to do at least 30 minutes of homework each evening. While she usually assigned some activities to be done at home, often the results that were handed in the next day made her wonder if the whole process was worth the bother. Many of the students obviously had tried to do what was asked of them; a few succeeded, but most complained that they couldn't understand what they were supposed to do. Other students produced colourful masterpieces that could only have been the work of a parent with several university degrees. A few had the usual run of excuses that could be combined under the mythical heading 'the dog ate it'.

At the next parent-teacher night Mrs. Singh stressed the importance of homework and asked all the parents to cooperate with her in having their children do 30 minutes of work each evening. This increased the number of students who had done something as well as the number who submitted masterpieces. There was not much improvement in the quality of work, however. Over the next couple of days she spoke to a few parents about the homework issue and was surprised to find that the parents did not know what to do other than complete the work for their children or threaten to punish them if the work was not completed.

A short workshop on helping children with homework seemed to be in order, and she sent a notice home advertising one in two week's time. Meanwhile, Mrs. Singh thought about a way of structuring the workshop so parents could understand the concept behind working with their children. Looking through some old textbooks from university she came across Vygotsky again and realized that his concepts might provide her with the foundation for the workshop.

## Discussion Questions

1.  Which of Vygotsky's principles apply to the homework situation?
2.  What points might Mrs. Singh want to make in her workshop?
3.  What type of activity might Mrs. Singh do to demonstrate her approach?

## CASE 5-5: ABRACADABRA

By some mysterious grapevine that allows information to spread through the school without particular direction, all of the students knew by noon on that December day that Ms. Cochrane would not be back for classes in January. Her place was to be taken by a Teacher-on-Call (TOC) who had been to the school from time to time. No one knew much about the TOC, other than his name, Mr. Wilson, but the general consensus was that he was a bit weird. One of the students apparently recalled seeing him actually reading a dictionary.

Grade 10 Language Arts were the first students to have Mr. Wilson after the winter break, and there was a fair amount of anticipation as to what he would be like. There was a general feeling of 'same old, same old' when he immediately started talking about how words from other times stay in our vocabulary and influence our thinking even if we not longer know exactly what they mean.

"Could at least have told us about himself," lamented one.

"Boring, boring," whispered another.

Mr. Wilson then broke the class into groups and gave each group five words or phrases that they were to find the original meaning of before the next class. At first, there was the kind of lethargic response that often accompanies assignments but this changed as students got into the detective work involved in searching out what the words and phrases meant. One group's words and phrases were:

dog in a manger

sincere

abracadabra

distaff

let the cat out of the bag

## Discussion Questions

1. What function(s) of language does this case illustrate?
2. Why is it helpful to know the precise meaning of words?
3. What are the meanings of the words and phrases in the above list?

# Social, Emotional, and Moral Development

## SOCIAL DEVELOPMENT

### Bronfenbrenner's Ecological Theory

Bronfenbrenner's Ecological Theory states that development occurs in a number of social contexts or systems.

- **Microsystem** refers to the context in which individuals spend most of their time and includes school, family, peers, and church.
- **Mesosystem** refers to the interactions between microsystems.
- **Exosystem** refers to individuals, groups, organizations with which individuals do not have direct connection, but that influence their microsystem. Examples include courts, government, media, and neighbours.
- **Macrosystem** refers to the broad culture in which individuals live.
- **Chronosystem** refers to the social and cultural history of individuals.

Bronfenbrenner's theory orients us to the importance of social context in social development, but leaves out biological and cognitive factors related to social development. It also fails to consider the step-by-step development theories of Freud, Piaget, and Erikson.

## Freud's Psychoanalytical Model

It is hard to know where to place Freud's psychoanalytical theories in the present divisions of psychology. They cannot be ignored, however, as in many ways they are the foundation of psychology, are good predictors of many aspects of personal and social behaviour, and provide a foundation for other theorists such as Piaget and Erikson. Twenty-three volumes are needed to house Freud's collected works, so any short summary is misleading.

## Freud as Metaphor

- The truth of Freud's theories should be judged in terms of how they relate to our lives rather than whether they are factually true in every instance.
- Freud thought that a person's mind was a battleground between unconscious forces and the individual's concept of external reality or ego.
- People are healthy to the extent that their resolution of this war allows them to work and love.
- This is a real and great battle, however, and we all have suffered wounds as a result of it.

## Energy

- Freud's model was influenced by the mechanical, steam engine concepts of his time.
- He proposed that people had positive and negative psychic or mental energies that built up and needed to be released or at least controlled.
  - Freud called the positive energies **libido**.
  - He called the negative energies **thanatos**.
- The negative or death instinct energies often are allowed into consciousness only as dreams or in some symbolic form.

## Stages

- According to Freud, stages occur in development based on areas of the body that are sensitized for the release of energy at that time.
- Freud's stages and their time frame are oral (early infancy), anal (late infancy), phallic (early childhood), latent (middle and late childhood), and genital (adolescence).

## Personality Structure

- Freud's concept of self or personality involves the interplay of three components.
  1. **Id** represents an individual's unconscious instincts and desires.
  2. **Ego** is an individual's conscious construct of world.
  3. **Superego** represents an individual's conscious and unconscious moral model or ideal.

## Defense Mechanisms

- The ego must maintain itself in the face of mental energy attacks from within and challenges from the environment.
- A variety of defense mechanisms are used to maintain equilibrium.
- Types of defense mechanisms include projection, rationalization, regression, and sublimation.

## Evaluation of Freud's Psychoanalytic Model

- Freud's psychoanalytical model has had many positive aspects.
  - His theory made the concept of the unconscious more accessible to psychology.
  - He introduced the concept of stages.
  - Freud provided a new approach to the issue of mental conflict in children and adults.
  - Freud's writings stimulated the fields of both psychiatry and psychology.
- Freud's psychoanalytical model also has encountered a number of criticisms.
  - Researchers claim that Freud's approach has not been open to experimental study.
  - Most post- Freudians believe that Freud placed too much emphasis on sexuality.
  - Freud concentrated on negative experiences.
  - Freud probably placed too much emphasis on early experiences.

## Eric Erikson's Psychosocial Theory

- Erikson's theory explains that all individuals have the same basic psychological needs, and experience them in somewhat the same order.
- How these needs might express themselves or how they might be resolved depend on the social context in which the individual lives. As a result, Erikson's theory is called **psychosocial.**
- According to Erikson, each individual goes through a series of crises that occur in stages based on age and social environment. The relative success or failure in resolving each of these crises influences later stages.

## Psychosocial Stages

- Erikson's stages and their age time frame are trust/mistrust (0-1), autonomy/shame (1-2), initiative/guilt (3-5), industry/inferiority (6-10), identity/role confusion (11-20), intimacy/isolation (20s, 30s), generativity/stagnation (40s, 50s), and ego integrity/despair (60s+).
- James Marcia expands Erikson's 5th Stage — identity versus role confusion — by developing four ways that young people resolve their identity crisis. The four ways are achievement, foreclosure, diffusion, and moratorium.

## SELF-PERCEPTION

### Definitions

■ Self-perception is a combination of self-concept and self-esteem.

    ■ **Self-concept** refers to what individuals know or believe about themselves.

    ■ **Self-esteem** refers to the overall value individuals place on themselves based on what they know or believe about themselves.

■ Both self-concept and self-esteem can be considered in a general sense or applied to specific contexts.

### Determinants of Self-Perception

■ Genetics exercises a strong influence on emotional and thought patterns.

■ Early childhood experiences may provide a general cognitive and affective foundation.

■ Present emotional states strongly influence self-perception.

■ The issue of gender's influence on self-perception is a complex one. Most texts point out an apparent drop in self-esteem for females versus males in the adolescent period. Most of these studies depend on self-ratings, however. Other measures such as drops in school performance, higher suicide rates, and increased criminal behaviour might indicate that males may be the ones that are suffering the greatest decline in self-esteem as they enter their adolescent years.

■ In addition to personal self-perception issues, there are also group or collective issues involving culture and ethnicity. Individuals can be influenced by the way the groups they identify with are perceived by the larger population.

■ Self-perception probably is determined by a dynamic interaction of the above factors.

### Improving Self-Perception

■ Methods of improving self-esteem are the principal concerns of many programs in education and counselling.

■ Competency-based education, teaching for success, and mastery learning all are thought to improve self-perception.

■ Social skills training and social support lead to higher levels of self-perception.

■ Cognitive therapies such as assertiveness training, positive self-talk, and visualization have been shown to be effective.

■ Changes in approach to spirituality influence self-perception.

■ Teachers must realize that they have the power to influence a student's self-concept and self-esteem in positive or negative ways.

## Concerns About Self-Perception

- The concept of improving self-perception, particularly as it relates to self-esteem, has been given considerable emphasis and resources in counselling and education.
- It is a heresy to question the supposedly tremendous importance of self-esteem approaches to personal or social difficulties.
- Questioning whether people's mental health has been improved as a result of these approaches is answered by a demand for more of the same type of programs.
- Three fundamental questions arise, however:
    1. Will an improvement in self-esteem result in an improvement in performance, or is the reverse actually the case?
    2. Will an improvement in self-esteem result in increased feelings of meaning or fulfillment in life?
    3. Will an improvement in self-esteem result in an improvement in society?

## CONCEPTS RELATED TO SELF-PERCEPTION

Several concepts border on issues in self-perception. These concepts are very powerful in their own right, however, and an understanding of them can be very beneficial.

### Shame

- Shame refers not to guilt but to being exposed in a negative way.
- Shame challenges our need for power and status.
- An initial shaming incident gives rise to internalized governing scenes.
    - Any similar situation gives rise to feelings of expected shame and avoidance.
- Shame has both good and bad aspects.
- Desensitization and cognitive strategies are used to counter inappropriate levels of shame.

### Attribution Theory

- Attribution theory deals with the reasons people give for the success or failure of their actions.
- Individuals might attribute the outcomes of their actions to the internal, stable factor of ability or the internal, unstable factor of effort.
- Individuals might attribute the outcomes of their actions to the external, stable factor of task difficulty or the external, unstable factor of luck.
- Generally, self-perception is improved by attributing success to internal factors, since internal factors usually underlie any success.
    - Failure needs to be analyzed and attributed accurately.

## Locus of Control

- Locus of control deals with whether individuals feel the control of particular incidents — or their lives in general — is internal or external.
- Sometimes authors emphasize internal locus of control, but this may not be realistic when referring especially to an external reality.
- The concept of locus of control is often combined with attribution.

## Self-Efficacy

- Self-efficacy refers to expectations about ability to perform in specific situations or in life in general.

## Internal Critic

- Our internal critic is the voice in us that judges our own and other's performance.
- The internal critic can be useful for our safety.
- The internal critic also can become a block to emotional health and performance when not controlled.

## VICTOR FRANKL

- Frankl found that there was little or no relationship between success (as defined by either society or individuals themselves) and feelings of happiness or contentment.
- Contentment arose from a sense of meaning.
- Three of the ways Frankl proposed for creating meaning were delivering our best work to the past, experiencing things and people in their uniqueness, and developing our own way of dealing with different forms of suffering.

## MORAL DEVELOPMENT

## Relative vs. Absolute Morality

- Is there a fixed moral code or does appropriate moral behaviour depend on the situation?

## Concept of Stages

- Most theorists postulate that moral development occurs in a series of stages.
- The concept of stages is similar to that used by Erikson, Freud and Piaget.
- Kohlberg's Stages of Moral Reasoning has been a seminal approach to the issue of moral development.

■ Selman's Perspective Taking Scale also has components similar to those used for moral development levels.

## Kohlberg's Stages

■ Preconventional Reasoning is the first level of Kohlberg's approach.

    ■ Preconventional reasoning has Stage 1, Avoid Punishment, and Stage 2, Individualism and Purpose where the purpose is to obtain positive feelings and rewards.

■ Conventional Reasoning is the second level.

    ■ Conventional Reasoning has Stage 3, Interpersonal Expectations and Conformity, and Stage 4, Social Systems Morality.

■ Postconventional Reasoning is the third level of Kohlberg's theory.

    ■ Postconventional Reasoning has Stage 5, Social Contract, and Stage 6, Universal Ethical Principles.

## Criticisms of Kohlberg's Stages of Moral Reasoning

■ Kohlberg's stages may be culturally specific.

■ The stories that Kohlberg used to generate stages may be too complex for children and unrelated to their personal experiences.

■ Gilligan claims that caring would be a more appropriate perspective for moral reasoning than Kohlberg's concept of justice.

■ Gilligan states that Kohlberg's stages are only appropriate for males, since they were developed using only males in the study.

## Selman's Perspective Taking Scale

■ Selman's Perspective Taking Scale looks at the ability of an individual to take the perspective of others. This ability is related to both Kohlberg's and Gilligan's approaches to morality.

■ Selman postulates that the ability to take the perspective of others goes through five stages ranging from Stage O, the Egocentric Viewpoint of the young child, to Stage 4, the Social and Conventional Perspective Taking of the adolescent.

## Moral Education

■ The role of schools in moral education is controversial.

    ■ Teachers have little training in this area and no certification.

    ■ The involvement of schools in direct moral education is very offensive to some religious groups.

- Values clarification programs have been important components of many education programs.
  - Critics claim that these programs support the concept that morality is decided by discussion.
- Other schools use a cognitive moral education approach.
  - Typically, these approaches teach moral positions from a heavily western and humanist point of view.

## Indirect Moral Education

- Schools, teachers, books, etc all carry moral messages.
- Even attempts to use materials without moral messages carry moral messages.

## CASE 6-1: OUTBURSTS

"That's nonsense," stated Miriam. "The real reason that the decision to cut funding was made was because they just don't give a damn about the situation."

There was complete silence in the meeting. Up to this point Miriam had been quiet and had only supplied a bit of information about experiences in her class. Everyone was completely unprepared for her outburst. Miriam could feel the tension in her body. The tight jaw muscles, the slight burning sensation in her face, and the increased awareness of her arms all were familiar to her. "I've done it again," she thought. "Another stupid outburst."

Outbursts were infrequent but disconcerting because Miriam never knew when they might occur. She knew that often her points were missed because people were alarmed or amused by her outbursts. She also knew that she felt anxious and scattered after the outbursts; she had difficulty settling down to her work. These outbursts had damaged her personal life as well. A relationship of several years finally collapsed over one outburst too many. Now she really missed her partner and often rehearsed the way in which she could have handled the situation differently. Miriam actually spent a great deal of time reviewing situations that had triggered her outbursts and developing more effective strategies. She visualized upcoming meetings and her responses. In spite of all this effort, she really could detect little or no decline in the number of outbursts.

Miriam had often thought about getting counselling or signing up for a course that would help her understand this troublesome part of herself. She was thinking about this as she headed into the staff room. Someone was always sticking up posters near the coffee machine about courses, things for sale, and cartoons. Stuck among the others was one advertising a workshop called *Learn to Analyse Your Dreams*. The advertisement claimed that participants would, "Find out more about the forces in your life." The course started two weeks from Wednesday. "I think I'll sign up," mused Miriam. "Wednesday night would be a good night to take a bit of a break and do something different."

The workshop instructor described different views of dreams including communications from the gods, messages to our conscious mind from our unconscious, and random firings or housecleaning by the brain. While she could offer no proof of which of these approaches was correct or indeed if any of them were, she stated that she believed our dreams often have important messages for us. The instructor taught the class how to record their dreams and gave two accounts of her own dreams. Miriam thought the dream analyses discussed in class were a bit on the flaky side, but she had committed her time and decided to try for at least the six weeks of the workshop.

Next morning the dog's whining woke her up and she hurried to let him out of the house. She was half way through her morning routine before she remembered about the dream recording. She couldn't recall even dreaming. Friday morning she could recall little fragments when she lay back after shutting off the alarm but these fragments seemed distant and unreal. On Saturday morning she didn't need the alarm and was able to stay in that state between sleeping and waking. She felt herself coming out of a dream and panicked for a moment because the dream seemed so real. There were no angels or flowers in her dream, however — no peaceful, floating moments. Rather, she was in a rage at some figure that was almost completely turned away from her. She couldn't hit the figure and the figure seemed to be unaware of the words coming from the dreaming Miriam.

Miriam was shaken by the dream. "What does it mean?" she wondered. "Who is the other person in the dream? Why can't she hear me? What can't I hit her?"

Miriam decided this was definitely not a dream she was going to share with the group next Wednesday evening. It felt far too personal.

## Discussion Questions

1. What is the relationship between dreams and Freud's theory?
2. What is your interpretation of Miriam's dream?
3. How do you feel her dream relates to her outbursts?

## CASE 6-2: SOMETHING WILL COME UP

Joshua spent his whole school life surrounding by friends. He didn't find any of his classes particularly difficult and so was always able to maintain the relatively good grades that pleased his parents. Indeed, he often only thought of a course in terms of his final mark and otherwise paid little attention to any content.

Sports were the big thing for Joshua. He seemed to excel in all of them and was able to make several school and community teams. Practices, games, and discussions related to these sports occupied his whole life. They were the source of his social relations, including his relatively infrequent dates. Professional sports were not really a part of his thoughts about the future, however. He realized that he was not pro-career material early in his teens, and never felt motivated to look at other ways he might be involved in sports later in life. Next week's or yesterday's games were the limit of his focus.

His father and mother had asked him several times about what he wanted to do with his life. "I don't know yet," was the way he usually responded. "I'll probably go to university."

This response alleviated his parents' concern as they felt those vague statements about going to university actually showed at least some sense of direction. "At least he isn't out all hours of the night hanging around on the street," his father stated.

A minor crisis occurred when he had to choose some of his subjects for Grades 10 to 12. The school counsellor held a brief interview with him. When Joshua said he didn't know for sure which subjects he wanted to take, the counsellor asked him what he planned to do after high school. Joshua fell back on his old response of, "Well I guess I will go to university." The counsellor asked Joshua what he planned to take at university and Joshua claimed, "I don't know yet. Probably just start with some general courses."

The counsellor explained how to determine the courses that were acceptable to universities from their calendars and closed the interview. As well as thinking about the different courses, Joshua talked to his friends. They did not seem to be willing to discuss their future in any detail and many of them considered courses only in terms of how much homework they thought there would be, and how the homework would interfere with their sports and their part-time work. Joshua took these ideas into account, ruled out any art courses because none of his friends were taking them, and avoided algebra and physics because he often found them difficult. There were lots of courses left that would qualify him for a general university program and he chose some of these.

Choosing a university also involved a bit of a crisis. He really hadn't gathered any information on a career, although he enjoyed the conversations of a couple of engineers that often visited with his parents. The lack of algebra and physics ruled out getting into engineering, however, and his other marks were borderline for acceptance anyway. Three of his friends were going to a university about 150 kilometers from their hometown. They were going to take general courses for the first year or so and then make up their minds. Joshua decided to follow their lead.

Joshua made one of the university's B level sport teams and was involved in a number of house leagues. His social life expanded and occupied most of his weekends. Courses and concentrations were selected largely on the basis of having the prerequisites and time tabling concerns. Without any real decision, he found himself in fourth year with an area of concentration that did not have a clear career path.

Joshua noticed that many of his friends had made decisions and were becoming involved in their future careers through co-op experiences. His casual dates also were becoming less interested in talking about the sport or music scene and were more interested in what was happening after university. Joshua increasingly was finding that his standard, "I don't know for sure" was being countered by, "But you must have some idea" rather than the more familiar, "Yeah, me too".

Finally it was October of his fourth year; graduation was looming and then what would Joshua do? There was a range of occupations that were open to him, but none that seemed to have a specific title or career direction. Joshua decided that he had to get serious about his future. A poster in his building advertised a talk about jobs of the future and Joshua decided to attend. The presenter claimed, "The names of many of the jobs of the future are not even known yet. It is a wonderful time for those with self-direction to define their own careers. Become *Me Inc.*"

This idea appealed enormously to Joshua but he could see no path to implementing the concept. He liked the idea of being responsible for his future outside of the more common career paths, but also felt he needed something that would give him direction. His experiences with the university athletics lead him to think about sport. Unfortunately he hadn't taken any courses in physical education or sport while in university. This fact alone struck him as amazing. How could something that was so much a part of his life not be reflected in the courses he had chosen to take?

His parents had suggested teaching to him during the summer and now he heard a couple of students in his class talking about enrolling in the education faculty for the next year. Joshua had spent two summers working in a summer camp and so had some experience working with young people. He had really enjoyed this time and felt that teaching would be a good thing to try.

Registration in education was a little more difficult than he expected. His marks were okay but the education advisor indicated they were marginal and that his situation would be reviewed after the next year's Fall term. In addition Joshua would have to take another English course before the start of his Education program.

Education turned out to be quite a shock to Joshua. The courses were difficult and very time-consuming. Most of his spare time was spent in class preparation. He had to abandon many of his sport activities and reduce the number of hours in his part-time job. He also was amazed to find that most of his fellow students had wanted to be teachers for years and were not very accepting of his 'good enough' attitude. They put a great deal of effort into all of their work even if they felt some of it was unnecessary, and became angry if Joshua suggested that they had done enough when he was part of a group activity.

During the fall he had a two-week observation period in a local school. Some parts of this were interesting, although sitting in the classroom sometimes had been a bit boring. His sponsor suggested that he help a couple of the students and that he might like to visit a few other teachers while his was there. His practicum supervisor at the university also had given him a number of questions he had to answer related to practices in the school.

A couple of times during noon hour he asked if he could join a pick up game of basketball on the parking lot. The students had said, "Yeah, sure", but had seemed somewhat hesitant. He noticed that after they had played for a while many of the students wandered off without saying anything to him.

After the observation period, Joshua went back to his education classes to prepare for his practicum starting in January. Joshua found he had to spend hours preparing his units. He was surprised at the amount of emphasis instructors placed on teaching methods and classroom management as opposed to content, and found he had to spend hours on his own preparing his units.

Two weeks before his practicum was to begin he started to worry about whether he was doing the right thing. Other students in the class were talking about jobs and even looking forward to the possibilities of being Teachers-on-Call (TOCs) when they had completed their practicum experience. A few were planning on teaching in other countries, but most had districts they were checking out. Joshua really didn't know where he would like to go to work. Perhaps a job would come up in the school where he was doing his practicum.

## Discussion Questions

1. What is the definition of Joshua's crisis?
2. What should Joshua's parents and teachers have done to help him?
3. What are your suggestions for him now?

## CASE 6-3: THE FRAUD

Knowing that he was a fraud had been an underlying current in Jason Osolit's life since Grade 8 or 9. His parents and teachers never detected his pretense; indeed, they usually complimented him on his schoolwork and his involvement in many art and drama activities. Even most of his friends would responded with the dreaded, "Oh, he's really nice" if asked. He had all the right moves to make everyone believe he was this capable person who could do all these different things.

In private, though, he knew there was another Jason Osolit, a person who didn't feel at all confident. This other person felt empty, even unreal. Doing one activity after another kept both others and himself from clearly detecting his true nature. From time to time though, Jason realized that he was just acting. At his core he was this kind of useless presence going through the motions. Thoughts of running away came from time to time; he even contemplated suicide on a couple of occasions. He knew that these actions would disappoint his family and friends, however. Thoughts of their disappointment were too painful to contemplate.

In his second year of university he discovered the self-help section of the library. Jacket blurbs on books about self-esteem immediately captured his interest. They promised positive feelings about himself and a life of happiness and achievement. He devoured them one after another. Each advocated a different and sometimes incompatible set of mental and physical behaviours. He learned about the value of affirmations and visualizations for generating positive feelings and outcomes. Over the next three or four years, monitoring his self talk became almost a natural occurrence and gradually he learned to make his self comments more positive and supportive.

Over time he did begin to feel more positive about himself and experienced more of a sense of real confidence when he interacted with others. He finished university and started his career as a counsellor in a social service agency. He was able to use all the concepts he had obtained from his extensive reading and from the workshops he had attended. He even offered a few workshops on his own and was very pleased with the comments from participants about the way he had changed their lives. He began to think of self-esteem as being the answer to most people's problems and words like affirmation, attribution, and visualization became a regular part of his professional vocabulary. Public endorsement led to professional success. Within five years he was able to set up his own counselling practice. Seminars and workshops lead to a continuous stream of clients, not to mention a sizeable amount of income. A new book and web site promised even greater returns.

Strangely, it was at this time of great external success and even internal confidence that the old feelings of emptiness started to come back. He fought them with all the techniques he promoted to others, and was largely successful in maintaining positive feelings about himself and his work. Finally though, he had to admit that even with the tremendous benefits of the techniques he had learned, something was missing. He would have to go on another search.

## Discussion Questions

1.  What were some of the factors that contributed to Jason's early feelings about himself in high school?

2.  What steps did he take to improve these feelings?

3.  What do you feel might be the issue for him now?

4.  How might he go about dealing with this new challenge to his self-perception?

## CASE 6-4: DEFINING MORALITY

Ted was raised in a home where the values of helping others and working in the community were very important. His parents gave money to many charitable groups and attended at least one fundraising activity a month. As long as Ted could remember, his parents had encouraged him to volunteer. They supported him enthusiastically when he joined different types of advocacy groups.

Ted's parents both were well-paid professionals who had worked hard to get through university and who now went to their offices many hours per week to support the lifestyle they valued. On the one hand, they had a lot of empathy for others in less fortunate circumstances and often commented about how tough it was for some. On the other hand, they also thought that people needed to take responsibility for their lives. For them, a rough childhood for instance was no excuse for violence and drug use.

When Ted finished his Education program, he looked for a school in one of the areas in the city where social problems were most pronounced. He felt that he could really make a difference there. "I think that many of these young people just have to learn to take responsibility for their lives," he claimed. "I know I can show them how to succeed by giving them success experiences in my class."

Ted had worked in an inner city recreation program for a couple evenings per week for two years. He was familiar with the types of interactions that went on between students and was prepared for the rough language and pushing and shoving that often characterized their social interaction. He also was prepared for the difficulties he would have in getting the students interested in his classes. The first few months were a real struggle. Students often were away. They frequently didn't have their homework done. Students had difficulties with concepts that they should have known a couple of years previously. It was hard to keep the attention of some of the students. Stories of problems are home were disheartening, especially since there usually was nothing that Ted could do.

A few students seemed to be making changes however. Sybil in particular was showing real progress. She was very intelligent and often brought a depth of understanding to her work that the other students never showed. Ted sometimes saw Sybil working on her homework in the library during noon hour when most of the students were out on the sidewalk or in the local mall.

In the last couple of years a small group of refugees had settled in the area. One of these young refugee women was having trouble in Ted's class and so he thought he would ask Sybil to work as her mentor for a while. He was sure that Sybil would feel the need to help; indeed she probably also was concerned about integrating the new people into the community.

Ted was surprised and disappointed by Sybil's response to his request. "I don't think I can help her, Mr. Andrews," said Sybil. "I have a lot of work to do at home in addition to my school work. I really want to get into university."

"I just thought you could work with her in class," said Ted. "It wouldn't take too much of your time. I really think we need to help others."

"I'd just as soon not," said Sybil. "I don't hate her or anything. I just have to make sure I get the best marks I can, that's all."

Disappointment and anger overwhelmed Ted. "That's pretty selfish," he stated.

## Discussion Questions

1. Do you think Sybil is being selfish?
2. What level of moral development would you give Ted?
3. What level of moral development would you give Sybil?
4. Does the criteria for moral development vary from one situation to another?

# chapter seven

# Peers and Social Relations

## COMPLEXITY OF SOCIAL INTERACTIONS

### Ambiguous Meaning of Actions

Human social interaction is an amazingly complex process. One of the main difficulties revolves around ambiguity about the meaning of a social action. This ambiguity arises because the meanings of social behaviours are not fixed or instinctive in humans and other higher mammals. Consider the following examples.

- A push is not necessarily a push; it could be a joke or an invitation to come and play.
- Someone calling, "Hey, stupid" might be a verbal attack, but it also might be a shout of affection across a parking lot.
- A wink could mean almost anything.

Similarly, objects do not have a fixed meaning. A broom could be a horse, a guitar, or just a broom. Further confusion is added when people from different cultures interact because the various meanings of actions may not be consistent across cultures.

## Frames

- Because the meaning of social behaviour cannot be understood instinctively, interactions require a higher order of signals to indicate the specific meaning of a behaviour in a specific situation.
- These signals define the social context or frame in which the behaviour is to be viewed. For instance, a smile accompanying a push probably would indicate the desire to play. Other signals such as words like, "Come on, let's go" would strengthen the interpretation of the push as an invitation to further friendly social interaction.

## Ambiguous Intentions

- Most people's motivations for action in social situations are mixed.
  - I may want you as a friend and enjoy your presence. I also may want to be leader of a group, ride in your car, meet some sexual need, or get you to help me with some activity.
- It is not easy to separate the intentions of others when they interact with us; indeed, it is not easy to discern our own intentions.

## Fundamental Issue

- Learning to understand the ambiguous meaning of actions and the levels of intentions in our social interaction are very complex processes.
  - Often attempts to teach social skills on an individual or group basis fail to consider the issues of ambiguity and intentions and, as a result, fail to help people understand the fundamental difficulties of social interaction.
- Those individuals with social skills deficits need to be helped to understand the concept of interpreting actions in frames and of the appropriateness of people having mixed intentions in social interactions if positive results are expected.

## DOUBLE BIND AND SOCIAL INTERACTION

- During social interactions we often have to reduce our emphasis on our own needs and concentrate on the intentions of others in order to have the possibility of meeting our own needs.
- The bind of reducing the emphasis on our needs in order to get them met is a very difficult concept for people to learn and accept.

## SOCIAL INTERACTION AND CONTEXT

- People's contexts have to be known before decisions can be made about the level of their social abilities.

- Interpretations of appropriate social behaviour will vary from one culture or situation to another.
- People's ability to engage in social events may be influenced by home environment, poverty, substance abuse, etc.

## VALUE OF FRIENDS

- Humans have a strong drive to belong to a group because belonging meets both physical and psychological needs.
- Research shows that people who are deprived of social relations because of tragedies or social difficulties encounter a variety of health challenges in much greater numbers than for those who report the presence of social support.

## PEER PRESSURE

- Peer pressure often is mentioned when social relations are discussed.
- The assumption usually is made that peer pressure is always negative.
- Peer pressure can be positive in the sense that it helps us learn to behave in ways that are socially acceptable.
- Some children who are resistant to peer pressure eventually encounter psychological and social difficulties.
  - This is particularly true for individuals who don't seem to care, or who deliberately act to make themselves unacceptable to their peers.
- Young people encounter a conflict between the need to develop a sense of personal identity and the need to belong.

## EGOCENTRISM

- The concept of egocentrism was discussed in Chapter Five.
- High levels of egocentrism reduce a person's ability to engage in social interactions.

## LEVELS OF POPULARITY

- Typical popularity ratings are popular, unpopular, and controversial.
- Popular people tend to be liked by most and disliked by few.
- Unpopular people are comprised of two groups: the neglected, and the rejected.
  - Neglected people usually are not chosen often by others but are not disliked or rejected.
  - Rejected people are not chosen by others, are not liked, and tend to be avoided as much as possible.
- Controversial people are liked by some and disliked by others.

## SEX DIFFERENCES

- While there is a lot of overlap between females and males, there are some general sex differences in nature and underlying function of social groups.
  - Females tend to be membership- and relationship-oriented in their social groups.
  - Males tend to view social groups as opportunities to engage in activities.
- The differences may be decreasing as the importance of sport and recreation activities increases for females.

## AGE DIFFERENCES

- At elementary school age groups tend to be single sex.
- By middle school more young people engage in coed activities.
- Cliques become more important in the middle school years.
  - Cliques can give a strong feel of belonging and social support.
  - Cliques also can lead to the drive for exclusion of others and to higher levels of anti-social behaviours.

## RATING OF SOCIAL COMPETENCY

- It is very hard to rule out personal and cultural biases in any rating of social competency.
- A tool such as Selman's Perspective Taking Scale, discussed in Chapter Six, could be used.

## IMPROVING SOCIAL SKILLS

- The most important factor in improving social skills involves helping people understand the issues of ambiguity and frames discussed above.
  - Direct instruction, role playing, and the use of movies and plays to demonstrate intricacies of social interaction all assist in learning about these issues.
- Social skills training also should include direct teaching of skills such as in how to address someone, talk on the phone, etc.
- Many people benefit from programs that include concepts of detecting and expressing emotions.
- Programs that teach tolerance and respect as well as programs that help build self-esteem have also been proven effective.

## SPECIAL CASES

### The Shy Person

- Social anxiety or shyness is at least partially genetic.

- Since shy people reduce social anxiety by avoidance of social situation, they tend to become more and more isolated.
- Sometimes shyness is rewarded by parents and teachers.
- Techniques discussed above for dealing with social skills deficits can be used to help those who suffer from high levels of social anxiety.
- Other helpful strategies include training in visualization and relaxation skills and teaching shy persons to concentrate on other aspects of social environment rather than their own feelings.
  - Examples include clothes others are wearing, number of people with glasses, etc.

## The Bully

- Teachers and others working with young people need to try and distinguish bullying from assertiveness and leadership.
- Both females and males can be bullies.
- Bullying can be physical or emotional.
  - Concentrating on physical bullying reduces respect for anti-bullying programs.
- Bullying may be an individual or group behaviour.
- Teachers and parents must understand that bullies are trying to meet their needs in the best and most successful way they know.
  - If bullying is not controlled, bullies can be quite successful at meeting many of their needs.
- Schools and the rest of the community have to demonstrate clearly to bullies that their behaviour is not going to be an effective way to meet their needs, and that their behaviour is not acceptable.
  - They also need to help bullies meet their needs in other ways.
- On the other hand, adults need to accept that some children may be more aggressive or irritable than others are.

## The Bullied

- Anyone can be the victim of bullying, but victims are most likely to be those who are vulnerable for either physical or emotional reasons.
- Teachers and parents need to help all young people realize that telling appropriate adults about incidents of bullying either experienced or viewed is a desirable behaviour.
- Adults also need to help the bullied directly.
- One approach to helping the bullied involves reducing their vulnerabilities through social skills training and building social support among both peers and adults.
- Important social skills include assertiveness training and learning to use humour to diffuse awkward situations.
- The bullied also can be taught to avoid bullying situations.

- Bullying situations are difficult to avoid when attendance is mandatory, such as in schools.

- Sometimes the bullied are encouraged to fight back. This usually is a dangerous and inappropriate action.

- While it is almost a platitude to talk about reducing bullying, teachers and parents may not be able to do so in some situations.

  - Alternatives such as moving the child to another school or social situation need to be considered.

## CASE 7-1: JAKE IS HERE

The preschool was located in a lower middle class area. Children of all shapes, sizes, and colours played, fought, laughed and cried together. Parents volunteered on a regular basis to help the teacher and sometimes even parents who were not on duty that day stayed around to chat and watch the children. The large church basement was divided into a number of play areas and areas for quiet activities. The playground outside was covered with grass and contained the usual assortment of swings, slides, and various other articles that could be 'morphed' into almost anything that the kids desired.

Anyone watching the children in the preschool would see a mass of play activities with children running, laughing, talking, hollering. Any brief squabbles immediately were broken up with a homily about sharing. Indeed 'share' had to be the most common word uttered in the whole place. The kids even used it in a manipulative way by saying the 'share' word to mean that another child should give them a toy they wanted.

Careful watching of individual children, however, would lead to a quite different understanding of the types of social interactions that were taking place. A surface mass of activity would break down into an enormous web of social interactions. Each child would be seen to be trying to accomplish a personal goal through some type of social strategy. Some of these strategies would be quite basic and involved nothing more than trying to order others around or take toys. Other strategies would be very subtle and show either an instinctive or a quickly learned understanding of Machiavelli and other advanced strategy texts.

Jake was a member of the 3- to 4-year-old group. There was nothing to distinguish him physically or socially from the other students. He was just one of the group. He didn't get into fights with the others kids, nor did he seem to be by himself very much. Indeed, he appeared to be an out-going child; he was constantly running from one group to another and always seemed to have a big smile on his face. Closer examination of his interactions raised some concerns, however. When he approached another group, he ran up to them, stopped just outside their playgroup, smiled and loudly announced, "Jake's here." He didn't pay any attention to what was going on in the group before he approached it and never varied his strategy for trying to join the others

The children being approached usually ignored Jake, although sometimes they would look at him. They never said anything to him or indicated in any way that he could join their playgroup. Jake would watch them for a few minutes, turn away with a frown, and run to another group. Sometimes he stopped in his efforts at joining other children to talk to an adult or to sit in the swing by himself.

Jake's situation went completely unnoticed by the adults. Indeed, his situation only came to the attention of the teacher when Jake started to complain to his parents about none of the kids in the preschool wanting to play with him. At first the preschool teacher doubted this until she spent a few days watching his social interactions carefully. Even then she wasn't sure why he was having difficulties playing with others.

## Discussion Questions

1. Why do you think Jake was not able to join the others?
2. What mistake was he making when he approached a group?
3. What kinds of training might help Jake?

## CASE 7-2: NOBODY PHONES

Mr. McAvoy looked at his daughter Tara with a hollow feeling of pain in his chest combined with a desire to just hold her and tell her everything was fine. It was obvious that Tara had been crying before he entered the room, and was now trying to keep him from asking any questions by putting the 'big pout' on her face and rushing from the room. There just didn't seem to be much he could say or do for his 12-year-old daughter. Even telling her about the sense of shame, anger, and longing he had experienced under similar conditions when he was in school would not have helped. He knew that 12-year-olds do not respond well to old stories about difficulties in an adult's past.

He knew the story though; indeed, it was always a part of him. He didn't even know how it got started. It seemed that everything had been all right in the early grades. But by Grade 4 or Grade 5, he noticed there were bunches of boys playing together while he was by himself. It didn't seem to be anything in particular that led to his isolation. He just wasn't part of the group.

Mr. McAvoy liked school otherwise. He enjoyed learning stuff and his teachers always praised his work. His parents never said much about his report cards, although there were no complaints. Indeed, the absence of complaints was what he interpreted as approval. If the teacher put him as part of a group with other students, they seemed to accept him without any problem. Perhaps the only difficulty was that he so wanted to be with the others that when he got a chance, he tried too hard to win their approval. When he noticed this happening, he would keep quiet for a while, hoping that the others still liked him. Every social interaction seemed to have this watcher analysing and commenting on his behaviour and what he should and shouldn't be doing to win membership in the group. He listened to these inner voices with their suggestions and criticisms. He could never just relax in a group.

Mr. McAvoy still remembered the pain of not being invited to birthday parties or not being part of the group that pushed each other around, shouting insults, and then swooping off to a store or to some unknown part of the field by the tracks. Again, it wasn't that the others drove him away; they just seemed to never consider him, never ask if he wanted to go. Couldn't they see him standing there fiddling with his stupid books and waiting for any slight hint that he could join the group?

He knew the same thing was happening to his daughter now. She had been waiting by the phone for two or three hours for a phone call inviting her to a classmate's party. She was so like him: conscientious in doing her homework, quiet, nice, and pleasant looking. And the phone never rang.

## Discussion Questions

1. How would you classify Tara's level of popularity?
2. What are some ways she could change her situation?
3. What types of training activities would you recommend for Tara?

## CASE 7-3: MY HOME AT THE MALL

Jeremy hung out at the mall every day after school and seemed to spend the whole weekend at the food fair or in the video games area. He did his homework at the tables in the food fair, seemingly ate all his meals there, talked on his cellphone, joked with the regulars, and often joined other students who had come down for a break from parents and school.

Jeremy was popular in a way; he certainly had no trouble interacting with other kids. He was funny and outgoing, friends with both males and females. He listened to comments about what other people were doing or thinking, but tended to laugh off any questions about his own life and started some silly joking around if pressed for information. When asked, he gladly went to informal parties at people's homes, but never invited anyone to his place. Indeed, no one seemed to know where he lived. When someone suggested that the group go to a movie for instance, Jeremy always wanted to meet at the mall or at the theatre.

A couple of the boys decided to follow him after the mall closed. Firstly he hung out at a nearby convenience store for about an hour but then the older kids told him to get lost. After a couple of blocks of shuffling along, he entered a home with no lights in the front windows. After a few seconds the two boys heard hollering from inside the home and a crash. They assumed that Jeremy must have gotten into trouble for coming home late.

When Jeremy's peers entered Grades 11 and 12, they spent less time hanging out at the mall. When they did come though, Jeremy was still there and came right over to be with them. His goofing around was less and less accepted, however. People wanted to talk about some of the issues in their lives including girlfriends or boyfriends, what was going on at home, and their plans for the future. Jeremy offered no comments of his own and soon would suggest some game they could do. Most found his suggestions quite immature.

During a group project in Biology, Aviva asked Jeremy if they could work at his house. Jeremy responded, "My grandma is visiting. She is quite old and doesn't like noise."

Later Aviva heard Jeremy tell another student that his grandmother was dead. She discussed Jeremy's lie with a couple of other students. The agreed that Jeremy's behaviour was very strange. "What's the big secret about his home," they wondered? One student commented that Jeremy's behaviour disturbed her and several others agreed.

"I don't think I would feel safe being alone with him," stated Aviva.

## Discussion Questions

1. What are some of the reasons that Jeremy might not want the others to know about his home?

2.  Why does his refusal to discuss his home have more impact on his peers as they get older?

3.  If you found out about the situation, what could you do to help Jeremy's situation with his peers?

## CASE 7-4: THE JUGS

Brenda could remember when she had felt the first tightening in the pit of her stomach but then dismissed it because it couldn't possibly be true. She had always been part of the group, even in elementary school. The group even had a name — 'THE JUGS'. It stood for "Just Us Girls" and had started in Grade 4 in her bedroom. They were looking for a name for their group. Kai had suggested Just Girls, but the initials didn't mean anything. A bit of brainstorming lead to JUGS and the name stuck. Even teachers learned of the name and sometimes referred to the group as the Juggies. When the girls found out later that the name had another less socially acceptable meaning, it only made the label that much more delicious. They were one of the hip in-groups at the school, although they had no specific label like the cheerleaders, the school council group, or the troublemakers. They were just a group of laughing, rambunctious teenagers who seemed always to be chatting to one another and planning small social events such as trips to the mall or birthday parties.

Brenda saw herself as a central member of the group, if member was the right term for a loose knit group of young people. Other people had come into the group or left over the years. This was due mostly to girls leaving or moving into the area. There did not seem to be any fixed routine for joining; you just sort of slid in sideways. Over the last five years until now in Grade 9, the group had been the centre of her social life. They were just there, her friends. Some were better friends than others, but they all were friends. Boys were only fodder for gossip rather than any serious challenge to the group. None of the group would think of going out with a boy on a night that some group event was planned.

The incident that started everything occurred right after Grade 9 Social Studies. Lucy, a member of the group since Grade 8 but not someone with whom Brenda shared her deepest thoughts, called to Brenda in the hall, "Nice shoes, Brenda." Brenda wasn't sure but she thought the comment had a bit of a bite to it. This feeling was reinforced by another JUG frowning at Lucy and pulling her along the hall.

Despite Brenda's unease, everything seemed the same as usual in the group and Brenda began to think that she was mistaken. Everyone was laughing and joking and they all made plans to meet at 11:00 a.m. on Saturday at the mall. Later than week, though, Lucy made another comment about Brenda's clothes and a couple of the members of the group laughed a bit. Two or three others spoke and said, "That's not nice."

A week later Brenda was answering a question in class and said that Toronto was the capital of Canada. Several of the boys laughed but Brenda ignored them. They didn't know anything anyway. A few of the girls who were not part of the JUGS also laughed but again their opinions were not important. The fact that two members of THE JUGS had a smirk on their faces hurt a great deal; members of the group had an implicit agreement never to embarrass each other.

A couple of days later Brenda overheard a couple of JUGS discussing what had apparently been a car ride with one of the members who had just got her licence. Brenda hadn't heard anything about the car ride; the others sort of downplayed the whole issue when she asked them about it. "No big deal. We just went for a little ride. You weren't around."

On Friday, one of the boys sang out to her, "How's Carl?" Brenda didn't know what he was talking about. She didn't know any Carls except for a couple of boys in other classes. Then she remembered that the rather strange man who stocked shelves in the pharmacy was called Carl. He was always trying to talk to the girls and they used to joke about it. They even talked to him a couple of times to distract him so that a friend could stick some lipstick in her pocket. Her fears were later confirmed when one of the new girls in the class said, "You're not going out with Carl are you?"

"No way," exclaimed Brenda. "How did you ever get such a goofy idea?"

"Just that a couple of the other girls said you were and didn't want anyone to know."

The first phone call came that night. "Slut" was all that was said before the phone was slammed down. Over the next couple of weeks the phone calls became more frequent and more horrible to hear. She was called names, listened to stories about what she and Carl had done, and was threatened. She even heard that someone had pasted her face on a pornographic picture and posted it on some web site. Apparently a lot of the kids had seen it.

The Jugs didn't involve her any more. Some of her long time friends would still say "Hi" but they didn't invite her to join them and made excuses when she tried to talk to them. Other students made rude comments to her in the hall and someone poured glue into her lock. Brenda felt too embarrassed to discuss what was happening to her with parents or teachers. Somehow she felt that it would be just too much if any adult found out about her difficulties. The adults would have pity for her and she didn't want anyone's pity. They might even try to intervene and that would only make matters worse.

School became a place of torture that had to be faced every morning. Headaches and nausea were a part of every morning. She didn't want to tell her parents that she wasn't feeling well because they would ask all kinds of questions. They noticed the change in her though, and with obviously growing concern asked her if she was all right. She tried to laugh it off with, "Yeah, fine – well, maybe just a bit of the flu. You know that all schools are just germ pits."

Everything came to a head on Sunday night when her parents asked her to sit down and talk to them. They talked about the changes they had seen in her and the fact that she didn't seem to go out with her friends anymore, or have them over. Her parents wanted to know what was going on. In a flood of tears she told them the whole story.

## Discussion Questions

1. What type of group were The Jugs?
2. What was the purpose of the group?
3. Can you think of any reason why Brenda might be excluded from the group?
4. What types of behaviour were at least some members of the group doing to Brenda now?
5. What suggestions do you have for helping Brenda?

chapter eight

# Variations in Learning

A single chapter on variations in learning presents a misleading impression of the importance of the topic in education and child and youth care. People who are working with others are always dealing with individual differences. Each client or student comes with a variety of strengths and areas of potential concern. Those working with young people constantly are making decisions about how to maximize strengths and how to improve areas of concern, or at least reduce their impact. The following then are a series of topics that are being dealt with in a single chapter for convenience sake, but that need to be seen as spread through any discussion of education psychology.

## INTELLIGENCE

### Nature of Intelligence

- There is a tremendous amount of debate about the definition of intelligence.
  - Some of this debate results from concerns about labeling.
  - Political and social beliefs underlie other issues in the debate.
- Regardless of any debate about definitions, there are clear differences in mental abilities among individuals.

- Some of these differences have very important consequences in school and in other aspects of life.
- A working definition of intelligence usually includes verbal and problem-solving skills.
- Any useful definition also needs to include the ability to adapt to, and learn from, events in life.

## Intelligence Quotient

- The concept of Intelligence Quotient or IQ arose from an early concept of **Mental Age** or cognitive level.
- In the historical formula IQ = Mental Age/Chronological Age × 100.
- IQ tests not involve comparing an individual's performance with others of the same age group. A normal distribution is assumed.

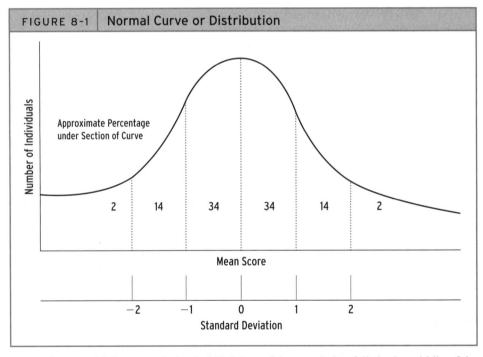

| FIGURE 8-1 | Normal Curve or Distribution |

- The mean IQ for a population is 100. Most of the population falls in the middle of the range, with approximately 68 percent having IQs between approximately 84 and 116.

## Norms

- IQ scores are not absolute measures. Rather, they are a comparison of an individual's performance with a group's performance.

■ While the group or population used to obtain the norms is very large, they do not represent all individuals or situations.

## Factor vs. General IQ Scores

■ Some IQ tests given a general IQ score while others give a series of factor scores that can be combined to produce an overall IQ score.

■ Usually tests that give factor scores are more valuable for education than those that only produce a general score.

■ Care needs to be taken in interpreting IQ scores derived from factor scores.

    ■ For instance, a person might have an IQ of 100 with all the factor scores being in the mid range, or might have an IQ score of 100 with most of the factors being very high while one or two are much lower than the mean.

## Group vs. Individual Tests

■ IQ tests are most valid when they are administered on an individual basis by a trained psychometrican.

■ IQ type tests administered in a classroom on a group basis by an educator have almost no validity for individual students.

■ Computer-based tests sold commercially to parents or others have no validity for any individuals who might have any type of individual need related to the test.

## Nature vs. Nurture

■ Intelligence probably is about 50 percent genetic.

■ Early fetal environment is crucial, especially in terms of any damage to brain development.

■ A child's environment is also extremely important because the brain is not some fixed structure. The brain is molded by interaction with environment as discussed in Chapter Four.

■ The concept of reaction range discussed in Chapter Three shows that limited environments result in a large deficit in performance. In other words, sufficient stimulation results in increased neural networks; the value of increased stimulation beyond that point is debated.

## IQ and Culture or Ethnicity

■ Because the population used to calculate IQ norms may not represent all cultures or situations, individual performances on IQ tests by persons different from the norm group have to be approached with great care.

    ■ Some of the issues may have to do with the inappropriateness of the test materials.

    ■ Other concerns revolve around the perception of testing in general among a particular group of people.

■ Simple presentations of IQ differences based on race are completely inappropriate. In addition to issues of environment, culture, etc., modern genetics shows that the whole concept of races is meaningless.

## Intelligence and Problem Solving

■ Intelligence is not the only issue in ability to solve problems.

■ Emotional factors strongly influence our ability to make appropriate decisions about our lives.

## Multiple Intelligences

■ The concept of multiple intelligences has become very prominent.

■ Sternberg proposes three types of intelligences: analytical, creative, and practical.

■ Gardner proposes seven domains in which intelligence demonstrates itself: linguistic, logical-mathematical, musical, spatial, bodily-kinesthetic, interpersonal, intrapersonal.

■ Sternberg and Gardner have worked together to develop an approach to education called Practical Intelligence for Schools.

■ The strength of the multiple intelligences approach is that it reminds us to view the concept of intelligence as being beyond just IQ.

■ The weaknesses of the multiple intelligences approach are that any number of intelligences could be proposed, and that a simplistic approach to multiple intelligences may cause educators to give too little weight to issues of low intelligence in the traditional sense.

## Information Processing Model

■ The Information Processing Model states that intelligence is the result of three interacting factors: brain and neural development, sophistication of information processing strategies, and understanding of specific concepts and situations related to the test or to the more general social environment.

## Intelligence and Disabilities

■ Great care must be taken in interpretation of any intelligence score when disabilities are present.

■ In particular, there is no relationship between learning disabilities and intelligence.

## Special Cases

■ Marginal intelligence is defined as having an IQ in range of 70-85.
  ■ Individuals with marginal intelligence may have difficulty performing beyond Grade Nine level in school.

- Mild retardation is defined as having an IQ in range of 55-69.
  - Mild retardation represents 80% of individuals diagnosed as retarded.
  - Individuals with mild retardation usually have difficulty working beyond the Grade Four level in school.
- Moderate retardation is defined as having an IQ in range of 35-54.
  - Individuals with moderate retardation usually are not in schools.
  - They may be involved in community training programs.
- Severe retardation is defined as having an IQ below 35.
  - Individuals with severe retardation usually need extensive care.
- Gifted sometimes is defined as having an IQ above a certain level such as 120.

## Improving IQ

- A variety of techniques have been proposed for improving IQ.
  - Examples include: improving diet and other health factors; lowering stress; providing more stimulation in environment; training in test-taking and in the type of concepts on tests, and several relaxation and meditation techniques.

## Four Questions To Ask A Psychometrician

- When a teacher or youth worker is told by a psychometrician that a young person has a low IQ, four questions should be asked:
  1. What are the factor scores?
  2. Was there any cultural or other bias for this individual with this test?
  3. Were there any learning difficulties that might affect the test score?
  4. Do you have any suggestions about what I might do to help?

# CREATIVITY

## Definition

- **Creativity** has numerous definitions. Some of the more common ones are: access to feelings, control of internal censor, convergent thinking, divergent thinking, intuition, and self-confidence.
- The only definitions that seem to have any predictive value are self-confidence and control of internal censor.
  - **Internal censor** is that small voice in our heads that criticizes our actions including our creative actions.

## Vehicle

- Some believe that a skill or talent is required to demonstrate true creativity.
- Others hold that solutions to any type of problem show the same type of creativity as that demonstrated by the skilled or talented.

## Tests of Creativity

- Tests of creativity include the ability to develop possibilities in terms of endings of stories, establish connections between seemingly unrelated concepts, and find solutions to specific demands or problems.

## Stimulation of Creativity

- Strategies for stimulating creativity include brainstorming, discussions about blocks to creativity, permission to experiment, practice playing with ideas, and teaching relaxation.

# LEARNING STYLES

## General Nature

- The concept of learning styles refers to a preference for perceiving or processing information in a particular way. The style is a preference rather than being an essential condition.
- Learning styles may be biological, or learned, or a combination.
- There are several approaches to the concept of learning styles.
  - One approach divides people into visual, auditory, or kinesthetic learners.
  - Another approach divides people into impulsive or reflective learners.
  - A third approach distinguishes between deep and surface learners. Deep learners look for the meaning of material. Surface learners tend to concentrate only on the content to be learned.
- Schools may favour one style over another.
- The main strength of the learning styles approach is that it alerts us to the need to present information in a variety of formats.
- The main weakness of the approach comes when people are designated or labeled as particular types of learners, with the underlying assumption that they cannot learn in other ways.
  - This labeling becomes particularly inappropriate when cultural groups are designated as a particular type of learners.
  - The labeling is often then used as a justification for lower performance in classroom settings.

## TEMPERAMENT AND PERSONALITY

- **Temperament** is a person's characteristic way of responding.
  - One way of defining temperament is along a continuum from easy or relaxed to difficult or irritable.
- **Personality** involves the qualities of the individual that makes one person act differently from another.
  - Examples of personality variables include introversion and extraversion.
- Both temperament and personality have genetic as well as environmental determinants.

## CHILDREN WITH DISABILITIES

### Disability vs. Handicap

- A disability refers to some limitation of an individual's ability to function.
- Disabilities become handicaps only in particular situations.
- In other situations, a disability may confer a benefit.
  - Difficulty in hearing may be an advantage in some work situations.

### Labeling

- People with disabilities should be described as having a disability rather than being a disability.
  - Rather than using the term 'deaf student,' use the phrase 'student who has difficulty hearing'.
  - This change reminds others and us that a disability is only one characteristic of the student, and perhaps an unimportant one.
- Labels can lead to reduced expectations about performance.
- On the other hand, generic terms such as 'deaf' when not applied to a particular individual aid in communication, advocacy, fund raising, etc.

### Mainstreaming and Inclusion

- Every child has a right to be educated in the least restrictive environment possible.
  - In most cases the least restrictive environment is the regular classroom.
- Traditional approaches use a **mainstreaming** philosophy that emphasizes dual categories of regular and special students.
- **Inclusion** philosophies advocate the abandonment of categories and the development of a unified approach for all students.

■ Supporters of mainstreaming and inclusion believe that the only exception to these approaches is when the needs of the child or some other special circumstance indicate another approach would be most beneficial.

■ Any program for students with special needs that involves other than the regular classroom must be justified with documentation from the appropriate experts.

## Individual Education Plan (IEP)

■ All students who are receiving special education require some type of document with a name similar to an Individual Education Plan or IEP.

■ This is particularly true where additional funding and any deviation from the regular classroom program are involved.

■ The development of an IEP is usually a team effort.

■ The IEP must have a series of measurable objectives that are monitored on a regular basis.

## Expected Outcomes

■ All school districts have designations that indicate whether the student is expected to meet the outcomes for a particular grade, or individual expected outcomes.

■ Those who are meeting the outcomes for different grades, even though some special arrangements are made, will graduate with a regular diploma.

■ Those who are meeting individual outcomes different from those in regular grades will not be eligible for regular graduation diploma.

■ It is very important that parents and the student understand the difference.

■ Sometimes counsellors and teachers hesitate to explain the issue clearly.

## Total Numbers

■ Approximately 10 percent of the Canadian population are disabled.

■ At any time, approximately 7.5 percent of Canadian students are receiving special services.

■ During their school life approximately 15 percent of students will require special services.

## Types of Disabilities

■ As discussed above, disabilities often are divided into different categories for ease of communication. Most students with disabilities do not fit neatly into one category.

■ Physical and sensory challenges include vision and hearing difficulties, cerebral palsy, etc.

■ Communication problems include various types of language and speech impairments.

- Emotional and behavioural disorders involve anti-social and conduct disorders, chronic depression, attention deficit/hyperactive disorder, etc.
- Learning disability refers to a group of disabilities that manifest as difficulty in learning that cannot be explained by other types of disabilities including physical or sensory, mental retardation, social or emotional conditions, or environment.
  - Learning difficulties include problems in reading, mathematics, speaking, listening, and remembering.

## Low/High Incidence

- Some disabilities are much more common than others.
  - Those with various types of learning difficulties represent about 50 percent of special needs students and are the most common designated disability.
- The more severe disabilities always are less frequent or low incidence.

## TECHNOLOGY IN SPECIAL EDUCATION

Covering specific technologies is not useful because of their rapid change and the varying availability of specific equipment in different areas of the country. Some trends are important however, as all classrooms will contain students with special needs, and specialized equipment increasingly will be a part of these students' lives. The technology behind this equipment has broad general applications in education.

## Present Trends

- Mechanical or powered equipment is being replaced by computer-assisted equipment.
- Modern equipment not only can perform more functions but it can make decisions based on input from the disabled person or from the environment.
- More and more equipment is being designed for a particular person or is capable of external or self-modification to meet individual needs.
- Computer-based equipment goes beyond the old concepts of just coping with a disability to reaching normal functioning or beyond.
- Electronic learning technologies have broad implications for all areas of education as discussed in Chapter 20.

## Future Trends

- In the future, more and more computer technologies will be implanted within the person with little or no external evidence.
- Computer programs increasingly can be expected to learn and modify their behaviour.
- Many future 'computers' will be either completely biological or will have biological components.

■ Virtual reality programs will become so sophisticated that the brain will be unable to distinguish virtual from concrete.

## CASE 8-1: AN IQ OF 85

Antonio was one of the 'slower' students in Mr. Shapiro's Grade 8 class. He struggled with almost all his subjects but managed to get enough Ds and Cs to pass each year. Sometimes the marks were not really deserved, but teachers could not bring themselves to say that Antonio could not pass to the next grade.

All of the teachers knew that Antonio had a relatively low IQ. Indeed, when Mr. Shapiro checked Antonio's Permanent Record File, he found that an IQ test done in Grade 2 indicated Antonio had an IQ of 85. It was not clear where or by whom the intelligence test had been done, but someone had noted that he had marginal intelligence. Mr. Shapiro thought that Antonio had done well to get this far in school and reminded himself to keep Antonio's ability in mind when giving him assignments.

About a week later Mr. Shapiro decided to visit a small grocery store on his way home. When he entered the store, he was surprised to see Antonio stocking shelves. In response to his questions, Antonio explained that he worked in the store most evenings and on the weekends. His parents owned the store.

Antonio's father noticed him talking to a stranger and came over to see what was happening. Mr. Shapiro explained that he was Antonio's teacher and was surprised to see him working in the store. "Yeah, I don't know what we would do without Antonio," stated the owner. "He does our books and keeps track of the inventory. His English is better than mine so I get him to phone in any orders and write any letters we need."

Mr. Shapiro was amazed at this information. He almost asked how someone with Antonio's ability could do all these things. Luckily he caught himself in time.

### Discussion Questions

1. What is your perception of Antonio's intelligence?
2. Is the intelligence Antonio demonstrates in the store specific to the store or does it indicate something about his general intelligence?
3. Why might his earlier intelligence test be suspect?
4. Why has he been doing poorly in school?

## CASE 8-2: NOT A CREATIVE BONE IN MY BODY

"It looks like a mess," thought Kassandra. "Who was this young teacher trying to kid? I couldn't draw something if my life depended on it." Kassandra Jack had been a teacher for 15 years. Two kids and a husband in that time as well. "The whole catastrophe," she remembered Anthony Quinn saying in Zorba the Greek.

This autumn she promised that she was going to do something just for herself. She had looked over the courses being offered at the local community college. Some sounded too boring or technical; others just reminded her of the types of problems she dealt with every day. "Who on earth wants to hear more about the problems of stress? Then I'll be stressed about being stressed."

There was a class on drawing for absolute beginners that seemed interesting. Kassandra couldn't remember the last time she had drawn anything for fun. It must have been back in Grade 3 or Grade 4 — and seemed like several lifetimes ago. Once in a while she tried to draw something on the board, but the hoots of laughter from her students discouraged most such attempts.

The first few drawing classes consisted of learning about the materials and making lines of different shapes and sizes on the paper. This was no challenge since there was no 'right' way to do them. During the fourth class the instructor placed a basket on a table and suggested that the class draw the basket as they saw it. The whole idea immediately made Kassandra nervous and her finished drawing showed her clearly that she had lots to be nervous about. The drawing looked like an elementary school student had done it. It didn't help much that the drawings by the others weren't much better when Kassandra peaked at their work.

The teacher, who looked to Kassandra like he was about 15 years old, went around the class praising everyone's work and encouraging them to continue. Kassandra thought he sounded a lot like her when she was trying to get one of her students to work on a project that needed a lot of improvement. "Got to encourage them no matter how bad it is," she thought. "He probably goes out for coffee afterwards with his friends and they laugh about our drawing."

Kassandra couldn't understand why she couldn't draw better. "I just don't seem to have a creative bone in my body," she thought. "Every time I try to make something artistic, it looks terrible. Good thing I have a job where I don't have to be creative."

## Discussion Questions

1. What is Kassandra's definition of creativity?
2. What are some of the things blocking her creativity?
3. Do you think she is creative at work?

## CASE 8-3: ANNETTE IS DIFFERENT

Susan Carstairs had been raised to have a very strict view regarding proper behaviour; indeed, misbehaviours of any kind were seen as indications of a weak moral character and poor parenting. She could remember the strong feelings of disapproval expressed by both her parents and grandparents when there was any mention of someone doing something that was not acceptable to the community. One of her uncles had been accused of stealing a small amount of money from his parents' home when he was a teenager. The incident was remembered 50 years later and there still was some underlying concern about whether the man could be trusted.

Her brothers and sisters had done all the right things. Sure there were outbursts of anger when they were growing up, but these were met with such disapproval that everyone learned to keep 'unhappy' feelings to themselves. One of her sisters had got a speeding ticket and had been denied access to the family car for a year. It wasn't so much that no one had difficulties in their lives; it was more a matter of trying to keep all these difficulties hidden from family members and certainly from the rest of the community.

When Susan had children of her own, she continued the parenting practices of her childhood. Rambunctious childhood behaviour was expected and everyone smiled at the energy of the young children. Even the odd broken dish or spilt milk was laughed away with the comments about the young age of the children. She was even amazed when her father didn't get angry when one of her children accidentally spilt juice on a book her father was reading. She had been bracing for a comment about "being more careful."

The situation went far beyond concern about the approval of her family with one of her children, however. Annette had been different from the other children since birth. She had cried more than the others and had been more difficulty to calm. She always seemed to be anxious or upset. Even her sleep was not peaceful. She reacted with anger when any of her siblings came near where she was playing, and actually seemed to enjoy kicking or hitting the family's beagle. Visits to any of her family were nightmares of apprehension and embarrassment. By the time Annette had reached her second birthday Susan's parents were becoming increasingly critical of Annette's behaviour and had become more forceful in their statements about how Susan should discipline Annette. Susan tried using increasing levels of punishment when Annette misbehaved, but this didn't seem to help and seemed only to make Annette more frustrated and angry.

Susan noticed that visits to her sisters also were becoming strained; usually one of her siblings followed Annette around whenever they visited to make sure that nothing got broken or that no one got hurt. Smiles of greeting became increasingly brittle and there were no requests to stay when Susan and her husband said it was time to go home. One of her sisters had stopped inviting her over at all and had suggested they go to a restaurant for a meal any time Susan mentioned getting together. This behaviour from her parents and sisters was not unexpected, although it was very difficult to accept.

The behaviour of her brother was a total surprise to her however. He had been living with his girlfriend for the past year, although everyone pretended not to notice. Neither he nor his girlfriend seemed to mind Annette's visit. Susan noticed that one room was firmly locked when they visited and that the apartment was cleared of most breakable objects. Her brother seemed to understand Annette's outbursts and the pressure Susan and her husband were experiencing. Sometimes her brother even offered to take all of the kids on a little outing. This small break was such a source of joy for Susan.

Susan felt that Annette might just be a little 'young for her age' and so decided to delay placing her in a preschool. By the time Annette was four though, Susan felt she would benefit from playing with the other children and chose a parent cooperative preschool in the neighbourhood. That way Susan could be involved in Annette's preschool and perhaps learn some strategies from the teacher or from other parents about what she could do to help Annette control her aggressive and emotional behaviour.

The first few days at the preschool were a disaster. Annette screamed and hollered that she wanted to go home on the first day. Susan had to be with her constantly and point out the new toys to get Annette to stay. She didn't seem to be very interested in the other children, and even hit a child with a spoon when the child came over to the play area where Annette was.

"Don't worry. She'll be alright," said the preschool teacher. "Sometimes it just takes them a few days to fit in."

However, the situation only got worse. Annette did move around the preschool more as time went on, and she did interact with some of the other children. Indeed, she seemed to really want to play with the other children and would often approach them to play. Often though, the play activity would quickly disintegrate when Annette got too bossy or when she became very angry when one of the other children did something that Annette did not like. About two months later, the teacher asked Susan to meet her after the school closed. Susan was very apprehensive, as she knew the meeting would be about Annette and her behaviour.

"Susan, we have to talk about Annette," said the preschool teacher in the voice she used for discussing problems with the children. "I know that you are very much hoping that Annette would benefit from being in the school and playing with the other children. Actually I think that Annette has improved in the last two months and really needs a program like this. Unfortunately some of the other parents are complaining about their children being hit or toys being taken from them, and are hinting that they will take their kids out of the school unless something is done. I don't want that to happen and I don't have time to be watching Annette all the time. I think the only way she can continue her is if you agree to come every day with her and stay with her on a one-to-one basis. I know this would be a big commitment from you but I don't have any other resources to help Annette."

Susan thought about the situation that night and discussed it with her husband. They had two other children besides Annette. Susan had stayed home with the children rather than using a daycare service partially because Annette had been so demanding. Now the youngest would be three in a couple of months and could go to a preschool as well. Susan was looking forward to having a few hours to herself when all of the children were in school and eventually getting a part-time job. In a couple of years all of the children would be in school and she could resume her career.

This was really the first time that Susan and her husband had discussed their feelings about Annette and her future. When the issue was opened they were surprised to feel the depth of their concern and apprehension. There also were feelings of sadness, fear, and embarrassment. Their child often was such a wonderful person; she learned quickly and wanted so much to be liked by others. But then there were those outbursts of anger, hitting, and taking things that did not belong to her and breaking things. Susan knew that she would have to accompany Annette to preschool every day. She hoped that the situation would change for the better, but had a deep feeling that the future held many years of crises.

## Discussion Questions

1. How would you define Annette's personality and temperament?
2. What assumptions were Susan's family making about personality and temperament?
3. What strategies do you think Susan and her husband could use to help Annette's situation?

## CASE 8-4: THE MILITARY BRAT

Families came and went on a frequent basis in the area around Marine Park High School. Part of the reason for this was the nearby airforce base, but the main reason was the relatively low cost of the housing near the base. Families often bought their first home in the area and then moved on when they had accumulated enough money. Tom Jackson had taught at Marine Park for three years but still had not got used to the uncertainty about the make-up of his classes. In August he could not be sure what grade he was going to teach, never mind what students would be in his class.

By the end of September Tom was getting to know his new students a bit better. One student in particular was causing him a lot of concern. Mary Bradshaw's parents had moved into the area when her mother was posted there after a three-year stint in Germany. Her father was a carpenter and was able to find a new job whenever his wife had to transfer. Mary's record file gave very few details about her performance other than to show that she had not done well in many of her classes although she had passed each year. This was her first year in a high school as well as being the first time she had been in Canada since she was ten.

Mary had not made any friends in the class and a couple of the students had laughed when she could not read a section of the text in class. Usually the military 'brats' were quick to meet other students who had been on the same bases as themselves and formed cliques based on these previous relationships. Sometimes these cliques were quite disruptive and picked on other students. Tom was concerned that they might start picking on Mary; when this started it was very hard to get it stopped.

Mary seemed to understand what was going on in class. She could answer questions about topics he had covered as well as any of the other students, although she sometimes used the wrong word when she was speaking. Tom couldn't help but smile when he remembered her using the word astrology instead of astronomy. The other students did not realize how close the two words were historically. The results on her first quiz, a multiple-choice exam, were very poor, however, and her first lab report had been very brief and contained several spelling mistakes. Yesterday the issue had become very pronounced. Tom had asked the class to read a relatively easy science article and to answer a few questions. To be honest about the whole thing, he had substituted the activity for his regular class because his throat was a bit sore and he wanted to give it a rest.

Mary appeared to be working very hard but looked very unhappy when she handed in her sheet. When Tom looked at her sheet he was very concerned although not totally surprised to see that Mary had answered only one of the five questions and that her answer was a direct copy of a couple of sentences from the text. Even then she had made a spelling mistake.

## Discussion Questions

1. What initial steps should Tom take?
2. If Mary has a disability, what type do you think it is likely to be?
3. What might be some of the components of Mary's IEP if one were done?
4. What kinds of things could Tom do to help?

# chapter nine

# Cultural and Ethnic Issues

Issues of culture, ethnicity, race, and religion are flash points for very emotional confrontations. Some of these confrontations are based on real ignorance, injury, and misunderstandings; others are the result of professional agitators looking for new areas to express their mock outrage as they try to control public comment and opinion. Regardless of the source of these confrontations, the potential for them adds considerable stress to the life of the teacher and reduces the discussion of any issues related to these topics to vague generalizations and meaningless platitudes. Because of this concern, any discussion of these topics probably should start with a series of definitions, recognizing that even attempts to define almost certainly will result in some type of argument.

## DEFINITIONS

- **Culture:** the civilization of a given people or nation at a given time.
- **Ethnic:** of, or having to do with, various cultural groups of people, and the characteristics, language, and customs of each.
- **Ethnocentric:** regarding one's race or culture as the most important.
- **Memes:** self-replicating unit of culture.

- **Memetics:** study of the replication, spread, and evolution of memes.
- **Race:** one of the major divisions of humankind having certain physical characteristics in common.
- **Racism:** a prejudice in favour of particular races.

## RACE VS. ETHNICITY

- While there might be some biological or medical reasons to use the concept of race in some contexts, use of the term in a chapter such as this usually is misleading.
    - Indeed, when most people speak of race, they usually mean a cultural or ethnic group.
- In any but very prescribed situations, ethnicity is a much more valid concept than race.

## MEMES

- At the end of his book *The Selfish Gene*, Richard Dawkins introduced the concept of memes; the concept itself has been obeying the rules that were used to define it.
- The concept of memes has spread throughout the world and produced thousands of papers, books, and web sites. Fashions in dress, slang, and media are examples of memes.
    - A public figure adopts a particular way of behaving and soon the behaviour has spread throughout the country, or perhaps throughout the world.
- Memes travel both vertically and horizontally in that they go between generations and also across different individuals and cultures.
- While memes can be thought of as evolving in a sense, the process of evolution is not the same as the process of natural selection: natural selection tends to rely on a relatively random process of selection, while people deliberately try to 'infect' others with their memes.

## MULTICULTURALISM

### The Basic Concept of Multiculturalism

- Canada employs a mosaic model when dealing with multiculturalism.
    - Cultures maintain their separate identity to some extent, and each contributes to an overall masterpiece.
- The United States tends to employ a melting point model.
    - All cultural groups are expected to identify mainly with a relatively uniform American culture.
- There are proponents and opponents of both concepts in both countries.
- For a dominant group, multiculturalism might be an interesting concept; for groups with significantly less power, it may be a matter of survival.

■ Even with support for multiculturalism, some cultures may not survive because of the loss of opportunity to use a language or engage in activities that are related to a particular location, time, or way of life.

## Difficulties with the Mosaic Concept

■ There tends to be one mainstream with others viewed as exotic fringe groups.

■ Smaller groups are seen as having unusual clothes, foods, and customs.

■ One week of the year we all celebrate different cultures and eat unfamiliar foods.

■ The mosaic model fails to identify the varied day-to-day experiences of individuals with perhaps different backgrounds.

## INTER-CULTURALISM

■ Inter-culturalism involves an examination of the inter-relationships among people with different cultural backgrounds.

■ The previously designated mainstream culture now is seen as one of the components of a fluid, dynamic interaction.

■ Memes 'infect' from dominant to minority cultures, but also from minority to dominant.

## OUTSIDE VIEWS OF CANADA

■ People in other countries get their views of Canada from a variety of sources including information sent back by immigrants who have moved to Canada, material from the Canadian government, non-governmental organizations, and the media.

■ All of the above sources of information may be quite misleading.

## IMMIGRANTS IN CANADA

## Adjustment Process

■ When people immigrate to Canada, they go through an adjustment process made up of the following 5 stages:

1. Honeymoon period
2. Cultural shock
3. Initial adjustment
4. Mental isolation
5. Acceptance and integration

■ The process is not a continuous one, and the lengths of the stages vary from individual to individual.

■ Dates of festivals, family events, etc., can cause a person to experience again a stage that had not been felt for some time.

## Adjustment Problems

- Immigrants experience a staggering list of adjustment problems. Adjustment problems increase as the amount of change from the home country increases.
- The number of suicides among immigrant students is an area of growing concern for schools.

## Conflicts in Schools and Community

- Students who are new to Canada experience a number of conflicts between their views of institutions and social interactions and what is expected of them in Canada. Some of these conflicts are:
  - The roles of teachers and other authority figures may be quite different.
  - Behaviours that are considered appropriate in one country may not be considered appropriate in the other.
  - Gender roles and the role of older people may vary.
  - Concepts of moral behaviour and the relationship between religion and other areas of life such as medicine may have to change.
  - Language differences may reflect not only the actual meaning of words, but also the existence of different realities.
  - More or less emphasis may be placed on the importance of achievement versus social interaction, and the value of material goods.
  - Collectivism may be more valued than individualism in the home culture.
  - There may be more of a stigma attached to counselling and special education than is the case in Canada.

## Conflict Between Community and Home

- Many students from other cultures experience conflict between behaviours expected from their parents and their cultural group and behaviours expected from their peers in school or in the community.

## Racism

- Racism is experienced and expressed by all groups and individuals.
- Racism has much more serious consequences for individuals who are a minority in a particular context than for those who are part of the dominant group in that context.
- Usually government ministries related to education and social services have web sites with material related to antiracism and cultural equity
- Many institutions are involved in structural and content changes related to racial ethnic equity.

# ENGLISH AS A SECOND LANGUAGE (ESL)

- ESL students may be acquiring English as a second language or as a third or fourth. As a result, ESL might more appropriately be called EAL, or English as an Additional Language. In schools where French is used, ESL would become French as a Second Language (FSL).

- There is no typical ESL student. Some are born in other countries while others immigrate with their families. Some have excellent educational backgrounds while others may have deficits in particular areas. Some speak a dialect of English that may allow them to communicate more easily on the playground, but limits their ability to function in the academic environment of the classroom.

- Approximately the same percentage of ESL students have additional special education needs as in the English-speaking groups.

## Basic Difficulty

- Students' abilities and education may be advanced in terms of the course content, but they cannot communicate this because of difficulty with English.

- This can lead to high levels of frustration and various additional behavioural and social problems.

## Definition

- For students to qualify for ESL programs and for any additional funds to be designated for ESL, generally two conditions must be met:
  1. Annual assessment to demonstrate difficulty must be done. This difficulty refers to cognitive academic language proficiency, not playground language.
  2. They must be in an approved program.
- In addition, the student must qualify to be in the public school system.

## Numbers

- Average numbers of students involved in ESL programs generally are quite meaningless.
  - While the percentage of students involved in the provinces of British Columbia and Ontario may be low, over half of the students in the Vancouver School District have English as a second language, and Toronto has been called the most culturally diverse city in the world.
- In addition to areas with concentrations of ESL students, every class in every district can expect to have at least one or two students who do not speak English as their first language.

## Teaching Techniques

- While having students who do not understand English introduces special difficulties, teachers need to approach these difficulties using the same general principles as they would use for the rest of their students. These principles are given below.
  - Provide a supportive environment.
  - Involve all students in the class.
  - Value the experience of ESL students.
  - Use groups and mentors.
  - Employ multiple methods of coding information including colour, music, graphics, and non-verbal expressions.
  - Build by approximation.
  - Be sensitive to the possibility of cultural differences including the role of questions, touching, and moral issues.

## Assessment Techniques

- Teachers have to decide how much a student's proficiency in English is influencing their evaluations.
- It is important to develop ways to assess comprehension that do not rely as much on language.
- Provincial Ministries of Education usually have guidelines for assessment of ESL students.

## Communicating with Parents

- Some type of translation may be important for teacher/parent interviews and for sending reports home to parents.
  - The translation may be provided by volunteers from the community, from local cultural associations, and from translation agencies.
- Teachers have to be sensitive to confidentiality. Siblings and other relatives may not be suitable as translators.
- Sometimes schools or parents have to pay for translation services.

## Advocacy

- Teachers with ESL students often find they have to be advocates.
  - This sometimes involves looking for funding for translation, computer programs, etc.

## Support

- Most Ministries of Education have information related to ESL on their web sites. The British Columbia Ministry of Education has particularly useful information at its site.
  - Most provincial teachers' organizations also have information related to ESL.
- School boards and individual schools may have specialists related to ESL.
- In addition, there are numerous sources of information and teaching resource materials among community groups, on university campuses, and on the Internet.

# FIRST NATIONS EDUCATION

## Terminology

- **Aboriginal** refers to Inuit, First Nations and Métis peoples. The issues of terminology are confusing however.
  - Federally there is Indian and Northern Affairs Canada, while often provincial organizations are called something like Aboriginal Affairs.
  - The central legislation is called the Indian Act while many government communications refer to First Nations.
  - Ministries of Education often use a general category of Aboriginal Education but then use First Nations throughout publications.
- When referring to a particular group, use the name they call themselves.

## Numbers of First Nations Students

- First Nations people represent approximately 3 percent of the Canadian population.
- While there are First Nations students in almost all of the schools in the country, some communities have a much higher percentage than others.
- First Nations populations tend to be younger than the general population. For instance, in British Columbia, status Indians make up 3.3 percent of the general population, but seven percent of the school population.

## Problems

- The media regularly carries distressing stories about the much higher levels of difficulties experienced by First Nations and other Aboriginal peoples as compared to the rest of the Canadian population.
  - There is very little emphasis placed on the strengths of these cultures.

## Goals of Education and Social Programs

- Most education and social programs share the same goals in their First Nations programs.
  1. Increase the success level of First Nations people.

2. Recognize and honour First Nations' approaches to education and social services.

3. Recognize and honour First Nations' ways of learning and learning strengths.

4. Provide a voice for First Nations.

5. Increase levels of satisfaction about government services in the First Nations.

6. Help teachers and others working with First Nations peoples to understand the importance of building a support network among chiefs, elders, and other authorities in the local First Nation's population.

## Resources

■ There are an enormous number of articles and books related to First Nations education.

■ The most up-to-date sources of information tend to be web sites maintained by government departments, First Nations groups, teachers' organizations, etc.

 ■ The British Columbia Ministry of Education's web site is particularly useful.

## CASE 9-1: OUR OWN CHARTER SCHOOL

At one time, the neighbourhood had a very mixed population. People used to joke about taking a world cruise just by walking down their street. The local school had been the centre of the community, with many taking part in school events — including Christmas plays and a St. Patrick's Day parade that somehow had started 25 or 30 years earlier. Many of the parents had no idea who St. Patrick was; they were only interested in the parade.

In the last decade school officials had made a conscious effort to become more inclusive. Christmas festivals became winter celebrations, and the St. Patrick's Day parade was replaced by a multicultural fair. These events still attracted good parent support but they suffered from a curious lack of energy, almost as if everyone knew they were play-acting.

Another more wrenching change had occurred in only the last five years. The composition of the community was changing rapidly. In the past, the relatively lower prices of homes had attracted a large variety of new immigrants to the city. Now the majority of new homeowners came from one particular group. In a very short length of time, this group established their own stores and rented a small hall as a community centre. Both religious services and social activities were held there, although attempts were being made to raise enough money to build a separate space for worship.

Because they were more concentrated in parts of the neighbourhood, the new group tended to interact with one another. Slowly this started to build feelings of animosity among the long-term population. People didn't go of their way to be unpleasant; indeed the opposite was true — members of the new group invited others in the community to their activities, and many of the long-term residents appreciated the services of the new businesses. Despite these interactions, gradually there developed a feeling of *them* and *us*.

This feeling was perhaps most noticeable in the local school. Parents from the new group asked that their children not participate in family life education classes. These parents also did not participate at a very high level in school activities, mainly because there always seemed to be activities going on at the same time at their community centre.

Last year a group of the new immigrants started to talk about wanting their own school. They didn't have any particular objections to the existing school, but wanted the opportunity to teach their religious beliefs to their children and to control some of the types of information related to social behaviours that seemed to be more and more common at the local school.

At first the discussion centred on building a small private school. This was viewed with alarm by other parents in the area as it would reduce drastically the number of students in the local public school and maybe lead to its closure. It also was felt it would split the community even further, and perhaps lead to even greater social disruption. Leaders of the new group listened to these concerns and then raised the issue of perhaps changing how the local public school operated and replacing it with a charter school.

Most of the parents in the area had never heard of a charter school but were apprehensive about any change, especially a change that seemed to have such strong support from one group. They learned that the charter school would have a strong code of conduct and would teach in a relatively traditional format. Family life education and any discussions that dealt with religious views would not be part of the curriculum.

Some of the members of the long standing community thought this would be a good idea as they felt the school was now placing too little emphasis on traditional academic subjects. Many others, though, felt that their children needed to learn about many social issues given the rapid changes in the city around them. They also felt that their children benefited from the non-traditional subjects. Underlying it all was a concern that a particular group was driving this change and that they might push their agenda even further.

## Discussion Questions

1. Who should control school structure and curriculum?
2. Does conflict necessarily involve ill will toward another individual or group?
3. What are some of the underlying issues related to multiculturalism in this case?

## CASE 9-2: THE IMMIGRANT TEACHER

Sanjai Desai's life had taken so many twists and turns before it had reached this Grade Six classroom in a Canadian School. India was her first home, the home of her family and everything she knew. University, and then a career and family of her own, were the visions she had of her life. She had met Rajan at one of the numerous family parties when he had come as the guest of a cousin. Rajan was an engineer working for a subsidiary of a Canadian firm. Their marriage had the support of both families, and parents immediately started making comments about grandchildren. Sangai wanted a family but also a career; Rajan supported her in this. Indeed, it was one of the things they discussed before their marriage.

After about two years, Sanjai and Rajan had their first child, a baby girl who became the centre of their lives and a source of great emotional satisfaction to the child's grandparents. Both sets of grandparents expressed a depth of love for the grandchild that neither Sanjai or Rajan could ever remember being given to them. The grandparents were ever so happy to look after the child when Sangai went back to work a year later.

The first real twist in the road came when Rajan came home one night and said he had been offered a much better job in the company's home office in Burlington, Ontario. Sangai's emotions were in such turmoil that all she could do was try to say the unusual word

'Burlington'. She did not have her husband's ability to speak English and had not traveled within Canada as he had. The whole idea of leaving everything she knew was terrifying.

Grandparents and the rest of the extended family responded with disbelief and grief when the move was explained to them. Her mother choked on tears every time she tried to discuss the move and her father seemed to age in a manner of a few days. There were questions about what Sangai would do with the baby if she had to work and how they would cope without family. Mostly though, these were just words to try to deal with the huge sense of loss.

Gradually over the next few months, the grandparents came to understand that Burlington was near Toronto and that they had family in Toronto. These people would be some source of support and some connection to family. There was still a sense of loss, even of death, but an image could be held of Sanjai and Rajan at least being with people the family knew rather than all alone.

As the day of the move approach, Sanjai's sense of excitement grew, although there always was that deep well of loss. There was so much packing to do, family to visit, phone calls to make, that every minute seemed to be filled. The situation was even more hectic when they reached Burlington. The company helped them find a new house, but getting the home arranged took every minute.

Sanjai lack of ability to speak English meant she could not even go and buy something at the corner store; she had to have her husband there to talk to the storeowners. The family members who lived in Toronto were very helpful, but they had very busy lives and few seemed to keep the old family ways. Indeed, often the only people she could phone during the day were some of the grandmothers who also couldn't speak English and were more than happy to chat on the phone.

Sanjai's lack of English skills meant that she could not get a job even if they could find someone to look after their daughter. In any case, childcare costs would eat up most of any salary she could make. Gradually a sense of loss and longing overwhelmed Sanjai and she sank further and further into depression. The situation was much better for Rajan as he went to work every day and became more and more involved in the community while Sanjai withdrew more and more.

Another child a year after they came to Canada was a source of joy of course, but also a further weight on Sanjai. Now she had little contact in the community and two small children to look after. Depression was her constant companion.

One of the pediatricians in the area had a large number of East Indian patients and it was there that Sanjai saw a poster for an English class for mothers with children. The organization putting on the course would provide babysitting while the mothers spent two hours on Monday and Wednesday mornings learning English. Sanjai grabbed the lifeline and the next stage of her life started with that course.

Six years later, and following an enormous effort to juggle children, home, and university courses, Sanjai had completed all the courses the university required her to take for a Canadian degree. Then she applied to the Faculty of Education and was accepted. Her practicum was a little rough but the sponsor teacher intervened when the students started to get out of hand, and everyone seemed very anxious to make sure she completed her program and got her teacher's certificate.

Luckily Ontario was hiring new teachers and she got a job teaching a Grade Six class the first year after graduation. She spent the whole summer preparing lessons, handouts and activities for the class. Being a teacher was an important position and she took her responsibilities very seriously.

Everything seemed to go wrong right from the first day. She waited, smiling, for the students to take their seats and listen to her plans for them. A few students did quit talking and turn to her but many kept right on with their conversations. She finally had to raise her voice to quite a rude level to get their attention. Even then their attitude did not seem to be attentiveness so much as a momentary pause before flight in another direction.

This pattern of indifference continued for the next few weeks. Sanjai felt that the students were not paying attention to her and were not willing to work as they should. Homework seemed to them to be a choice; if there was something more interesting going on, then homework did not have to be done. Students even used 'important' TV programs or not getting back from the mall in time as excuses for not having homework done. Many students complained about the amount of homework Sanjai expected them to do.

Sanjai phoned many of the parents to talk with them about homework. She was amazed to find that some of the parents also viewed homework as only one of the options that might be done on a particular evening. She was dismayed to find that some parents were antagonistic to the concept of homework and thought that it was Sanjai's job to do any schoolwork during school time. They also complained that Sanjai was expecting their children to do too much and pointed out all the other activities their children were involved in. School was merely one of the activities in which their children participated.

Students also confronted Sanjai about the content of their classes. They complained that the topics were boring. Sanjai pointed out that she had spent a lot of time preparing the classes and that they were required to cover certain topics. They were not impressed by this argument and kept asking to do other activities, to go outside, to use the computers, etc. They always seemed to want to do something rather than pay attention to their classes. They didn't seem to place any value on getting an education.

## Discussion Questions

1.  How do culture and views of the role of education interact?
2.  Whose view of education should dominate?

## CASE 9-3: WHAT'S OUR CULTURE, DADDY?

Tim Brennan grew up in an extended Irish Canadian family in a small city in southern Ontario. Along with his family he attended the local church and went to school at the Catholic elementary and secondary schools. University was his first experience with being away from his family and with attending a secular educational institution. Gradually, his attendance at church declined while he was at the university, but he accompanied his family without protest when he was home for holidays. He never actually considered doing otherwise.

After graduation Tim went to Sarnia to work. He married a woman with no religious background and started a family. Church became far from a central focus of his life; indeed it really had very little meaning for him except for festivals such as Christmas and Easter. Neither he nor his wife attended any of the social events at the church, preferring to socialize with people from work and members of his wife's curling group. The opportunity to use a friend's cottage meant that he often was not even in town during about half of the year.

When his first child reached school age, it just was assumed that she would go to the local public school down the street. Tim didn't really decide not to enroll his child in a religious education program at the church; it just never occurred to him.

One evening his daughter brought home a flier from the school advertising an upcoming multicultural night and asking parents to volunteer to demonstrate their culture. Tim read the flier and formed an image in his mind of people in colourful dress maybe doing some dances and selling unusual desserts. He noted the date in his diary and told his daughter that he and his wife would love to go. Then he dropped the matter from his mind.

About a week later his daughter mentioned the multicultural night again, and again asked her father if he was going to go. He thought this repeat request was a bit odd, but assured her that both her parents would be there. He was totally unprepared for the comments from his daughter that followed.

"What are you going to wear?" she asked with that feeling of anticipation of some whole new aspect of life opening up that only young children seem to be able to project.

"Why, I'll just wear my clothes," he responded.

"But Dad, it's multicultural night," she said with that tone of exasperation that only young children seem also to be able to manage.

By this time Tim was totally confused and could only respond with, "What do you mean, dear?"

"Well, what culture are you going to be?" she asked.

Tim started to respond that they didn't have a culture but then realized that he really needed a better answer for his daughter.

## Discussion Questions

1. What is meant by culture?
2. Does everyone live in a culture?
3. What types of conditions cause organized cultures to disintegrate?

## CASE 9-4: THE BAND SCHOOL

Ken Williams knew that his situation had reached a crisis point. There were only 13 of the 21 students in the class present and the whole class was far behind his instruction plan for the year. He had heard that three of the students had dropped out and were not coming to school again. Many of the others might as well have dropped out; they were using the school only as one of a several possible places to go on any particular morning. The fact that it was now winter merely meant that some of the other places they could have gone were less desirable than they had been a couple of months ago.

Ken had seen the position at the First Nation's band school advertised in the *Globe and Mail*. He had already taught for four years in a school in a middle-sized city and was looking for an opportunity to try something else. The rural nature of the band school fitted into a vague dream of living outside urban areas. He knew that the idea of 'communing with nature' was a throw back to his parents' generation but he still wanted a change.

He had applied for the position and was interviewed by the principal and a band elder in May of the previous year. The interview had not gone well from his point of view. Neither of the people interviewing him seemed to be all that impressed with his teaching plans and seemed to be much more interested in his philosophical and religious views. He hadn't thought very much about these things, and felt they were private in any case and really should not be part of a job interview.

Despite his concern about the interview, Ken was offered the job and moved halfway across the country in late August to the small community. The principal and the band had made him feel welcome, inviting him to several of their events, and welcoming him into their homes. Band elders had repeatedly told him to come to them if he needed any help.

September had been a bit of a rude awaking. On the first day only about 75 percent of the students who were supposed to be in class showed up. Some were supposedly away with their parents while nobody seemed to know where four or five of them were. After lunch, three more were missing but one new student appeared.

Ken liked to involve his students in a discussion about the topics they were covering. In the past his students were very involved but now he got little response to his requests for questions or comments. The situation improved somewhat if there was any discussion about events in the community but deteriorated dramatically when he attempted to have the students discuss motivation and behaviour in some of the Language Arts texts he was using. He has chosen the texts because they were supposedly of interest to the majority of young people. Discussion worked better than seat work though, and he kept at it. The fluctuating attendance made his attempts at continuity in content from one day to the next very difficult.

Even more disconcerting than the changing attendance and the low levels of student participation was the tremendous variation in student performance. Some of the students were up to grade level or above, but many were functioning well below what would be expected for their age. While he could understand the pressure on previous teachers that would cause them to pass the children to the next grade almost without meeting any criteria, he also realized that this practice would mean that some of the students would leave school without even basic literary skills.

From time to time one of the elders would come and sit in the back of the class. After class he or she would congratulate Ken on his class and offer a little suggestion. He remembered one saying that she found it easier to work with the kids in the community centre when she had them involved in some group activity and let them talk to each other quite a bit. She, like the others, let Ken know that he could come for help if he needed any. She also invited him to come and watch one of her dance classes the next night but Ken had a lot of marking and class preparation to do and declined the invitation.

## Discussion Questions

1. What are some of the assumptions Ken is making?
2. What mistake(s) is he making in dealing with the elders?

## CASE 9-5: THE HOCKEY COACH

Nathan lived in a rural area about 35 kilometers from the nearest town of any size. The local community had an adult baseball team that many of the boys played on when they got to be about 16 or so, but there was no other organized sport. Of course the kids played all kinds of pickup games; indeed they had more opportunities for sport than many urban children. Hockey games on local ponds were a constant feature of every weekend during the winter.

When Nathan's oldest son was six, he started to talk about wanting to play hockey in one of the leagues in town. The boy seemed to have all the attributes of a future good athlete and so Nathan looked into the possibility of his son playing in the urban leagues. The cost and time demands seemed prohibitive, especially when you added the 45-minute winter drive but the boy kept asking to be able to play and laying on guilt trips about not getting to do anything because they lived out in the sticks. That was how it all started — first one son, then a second son, and then a daughter who wanted to play soccer. Nathan seemed to be constantly on the road going from one game or practice to another.

One year the coach asked for some help from the parents and Nathan volunteered because he felt that he was the best one. Indeed he wasn't too happy with the attitude of some of the parents and definitely did not want his children involved with them. Two years later the coach had to withdraw at the last moment and the job of coaching fell to Nathan. He already had taken a couple of coaching clinics that started him on the path to coaching certification. This was the beginning of his volunteer coaching career.

He really liked coaching the kids and most of them responded well to his relatively relaxed style. Sometimes parents would complain about the team's lack of a 'killer' drive, or that their child was not playing enough. Even more difficult to deal with were the negative comments directed to some of the players. Some kids did not play as well as others, but that was no reason for demands that they stay on the bench or personal comments against them. Nathan spoke to the parents as a group several times about this and took a couple of the most vocal parents aside to tell them about the damage they were doing. One of these parents became quite angry and told Nathan that, "They have to learn to deal with it and get out there and win. Winning was what life was all about."

The comments became more and more personal as his boys got older. It seemed that the parents identified with the older players as hometown favourites especially when they played teams from nearby communities. One of the most distasteful aspects of the job of coach for Nathan was listening to parents hollering insults from stands about players from these communities. Nathan often knew these players and their parents and he felt both embarrassed and angry.

Nathan's oldest son quit when he was 15; his youngest son held on until he turned 16. Both left for a variety of reasons but certainly one of them was the behaviour of parents and some of the players. They couldn't seem to realize that none of the players in the league were going on to pro careers and that the pro career model was not suitable for just a bunch of young people who wanted to play hockey.

When his youngest son said that he didn't want to play next winter, Nathan also told the local hockey association that he wouldn't be available to coach in the fall. There were several phone calls from parents trying to get him to come back, but Nathan really felt that he needed a break. He had been involved now for more than 12 years and hockey had taken up so much of his time. He was looking forward to a bit of free time.

In January he received a call from the band office of a nearby First Nation. The Band had built a recreation centre of their own and had been running recreation programs. About ten to fifteen boys and four or five girls wanted to play hockey on a more organized basis and learn more of the skills involved. The band official wanted to know if Nathan, "…would be willing to help them a bit. Nothing major. Just a few pointers. Maybe a clinic or something." Nathan agreed to come around and look at the recreation centre and talk to some of the band officials. He was very impressed with the centre and with the attitude of the officials and so agreed to run a series of three Saturday morning workshops for any young person interested starting in two weeks.

At the first workshop there were nineteen boys and eight girls on the ice. They all had the required safety equipment and some of them could skate quite well. Others needed some skills training. He was amazed to see that there were at least fifty people in the stands as well. The whole thing seemed to be a kind of a party. Over that winter, the three work-shops expanded to include weekly pickup games among the people who showed up. There was a core group of about fifteen boys and three or four girls. It was fun having teams of mixed ages and sex playing together. At the end of the season they put on an exhibition game and had a big meal afterwards.

The next year there were enough players to form teams for the younger boys, younger girls, and older boys. Unfortunately, there was only one girl for an older group; she played with the boys. Near the end of the season one of the band officials who had been very supportive came to Nathan and said that another band was interested in an exhibition game for the older players.

Nathan was quite hesitant at first. "I really don't want to be involved where parents are cheering for one side or the other and I especially don't want negative comments to any of the players," he stated.

The band official went away and came back in about half an hour with another idea. "How about a clinic for all the players and then a pickup game."

"Sounds like a great idea," said Nathan.

"We'll organize it," said the official. "All you have to do is show up."

Over the next two years these clinics and pickup demonstration games expanded to include other nearby bands. By the end of the three years there now were about fifteen older boys who were quite good hockey players. These boys started to talk about playing in the local amateur league as a team. Nathan was uncomfortable with this idea as well but he could not see any other opportunities to give his players the game experience they desired. He approached the local amateur association and after some discussions having to do with payment of fees, etc., the association allowed the First Nations team to play.

The First Nation boys loved their first year but won only one game and that was a bit of a fluke. The players did get experience though, and most of the younger players came to watch. Gradually their game improved as well. In the second year the First Nations team won three games and put on a good show in most of the other games. Nathan had been concerned about the reaction of community parents when his team went to their arenas but there did not seem to be any of the name-calling he expected. There was a lot of cheering for the local team but mostly silence for his team and once in a while there even was applause when his team executed a good play.

Things started to change in the third year. The First Nations team won more than half their games and actually made the playoffs, although they were eliminated in the first round. Nathan noticed an increase in negative comments directed to his players, however. Most of these comments were the usual ones that he remembered from the past, 'jerk, goon, etc'. Once in a while, however, there was a war whoop and he saw one of the parents making a chopping motion toward one of his players.

The situation got worse the next year. Nathan's team now was beating other teams on a regular basis and spectators were trying to discourage his team or put them off their game. The war whoops and chopping motions increased. Someone came dressed up in a feather costume and starting doing a movie version of a First Nations dance. Other comments were derogatory ones about Indians and savages. These comments upset his team, but Nathan explained about the spectators trying to discourage their team and emphasized that the players maintain their concentration.

At the end of the season Nathan felt tired and dispirited for the first time in the last four or five years. He had enjoyed working with the First Nations teams but didn't like having to deal with the comments from the spectators. On one side he realized that the comments were much the same as he had heard years before when his sons played. The spectators used any little hook to get something to rattle the opposing team. On the other side, he worried about the racist nature of some of the comments. Did these comments represent an underlying racism, or were they just another example of the terrible way that some parents behave?

## Discussion Questions

1.  What is the difference between racism and negative comments or behaviours that might be directed to anyone?
2.  Does the fact than an action is just part of a game or fun activity mean that it should be subjected to less scrutiny?
3.  Do you think the parents of the others teams were being racist?

## REFERENCES

Dawkins, R. (1989). *The selfish gene*. Oxford: Oxford University Press.

The British Columbia Ministry of Education Web Site: http://www.gov.bc.ca/bced

# chapter ten

# Behavioural Learning Theories

## DEFINITION

- Learning is a relatively permanent change in behaviour or thought caused by experiences that cannot be explained by reflexes, instincts, maturation, fatigue, injury, disease, or drugs.

## CLASSICAL (PAVLOVIAN) CONDITIONING

- Classical and Pavlovian conditioning mean the same thing.
- Classical conditioning involves pairing a neutral or conditioned stimulus with an automatic or instinctive unconditioned stimulus, unconditioned response situation.
- The result of this pairing is a conditioned response that is similar to the unconditioned response, although weaker.
  - This pairing can be totally unconscious.
- Examples of automatic or instinctive unconditioned stimulus and responses include salivation at the sight of food or attempts to avoid pain.
- **Generalization** is the extent to which a pairing generalizes to other stimuli that are similar to the conditioned stimulus.

- Being bitten by a large black dog might cause me to react with fear whenever I see a large black dog. I might also generalize my experience to include all dogs or even other animals.

- **Discrimination,** on the other hand, refers to how much I am able to select between similar stimuli.

- **Extinction** involves decreasing the likelihood of a response by non-pairing.

- Advertising uses the concepts of classical conditioning when a product is associated with some desirable situation or person. An example would be associating a particular beverage with exciting social gatherings.

- One of the ways to prevent or cure undesirable classical conditioning learning is through extinction.

- Another approach to prevention or curing involves counter-conditioning, where the same conditioned stimulus is paired with a pleasant, instinctive reaction.

| Exercise 10–1 | Conditioning and Advertising |
|---|---|

Gather a wide variety of ads from magazines and papers. Analyze the ads to see with what automatic/instinctive relationship the product is being associated. In more sophisticated ads it may be more difficult to detect the pairing. Sometimes products are paired to socially desirable, or at least approved, conditions. Examples include linking a particular industry to wilderness settings.

## OPERANT CONDITIONING

### Prominent Researchers

- Prominent researchers include Thorndike, Watson, and Skinner

## Thorndike

- Thorndike showed that repetition and rewards strengthen learning.
- Thorndike defined learning in terms of observable behaviour.

## Watson

- Watson stated that behaviour was a combination of responses.
- Every response was caused by the environment and had an effect on the environment.

## Skinner

- Skinner used pigeons and rats doing observable acts to record and evaluate the behavioural effects of positive and negative reinforcement.

■ Reinforcement schedules were shown to be important.

■ Skinner's theory provided the foundation for the use of programmed learning materials in education.

## Operant Conditioning Theory

■ Behaviour leads to consequences.

■ Consequences can be perceived as reinforcement or punishment.

   ■ **Reinforcement** leads to an increase in the number of responses.

   ■ **Punishment** leads to a decrease in the number or responses.

■ Both reinforcement and punishment can involve the presentation of some condition, or the withdrawal of some condition.

■ Operant research involves starting with some baseline level of behaviour and recording changes.

■ Researchers often have to **shape** the desired behaviour by first reinforcing approximations to the desired behaviour.

■ Sometimes researchers have to provide cues as to which behaviours will be reinforced.

■ For learning to occur, reinforcement must be delivered on some type of **schedule**.

   ■ The schedule could be fixed or variable.

   ■ The schedule could be dependent upon the number of responses, the time interval, or a combination.

■ Operant approaches to learning are the foundation of behaviour modification programs.

■ **Premack's Principle** is another way that operant conditioning is used in schools. More desirable activities are linked to the completion of less desirable activities.

■ **Extinction** for operant conditioning occurs when behaviours are no longer reinforced.

   ■ Usually there is a temporary increase in behaviour called an **extinction burst** before behaviour declines.

## Punishment vs. Reward

■ Rewards are more effective than punishment in changing behaviour.

■ Punishment — especially if severe — doesn't teach new behaviour. It may cause emotional damage, it provides poor modeling, and sometimes doesn't stop the behaviour anyway.

## BEHAVIOUR MODIFICATION

■ Teachers and others working with young people always are involved in a process of behaviour modification.

■ Usually this process is not as effective as it could be because it is not part of a pre-established plan.

- A behaviour modification plan would involve the following steps.
  - Define the specific behaviour change desired.
  - Establish the baseline levels.
  - Establish the appropriate reinforcement or punishment.
  - Apply the reinforcement or punishment as close to the time of behaviour as possible.
- Appropriate reinforcers are best chosen based on the known preferences of the person or persons involved.
- Possible punishments in a school or other youth program include time out, logical or natural consequences, and satiation.
  - The length of the time out can be decided by the teacher or by the student meeting some condition.
  - **Logical consequences** are determined by some prearranged set of conditions.
  - **Natural consequences** occur when the natural or social environment is allowed to act.
  - **Satiation** involves forcing the repetition of original problem behaviour such as requiring someone to smoke several cigarettes when caught smoking.
- Behaviour modification does have difficulties.
  - Intrinsic motivation is not developed.
  - The reinforcement may come to be valued more than the behaviour.
  - Peers may pressure a young person to not change behaviour.

## AVOIDANCE AS A REWARD

- As the time to do an unpleasant activity approaches, anxiety increases.
- If the activity is avoided, anxiety level decreases and the avoidance is rewarded.
- This rewarding of avoidance is the basis of procrastination.
- As a result, we may never do the activity, even though we cognitively may desire to do it.

## LEARNED HELPLESSNESS

- Learned helplessness can result when punishment is perceived to be severe and uncontrollable.
- The process of becoming learned helpless can be divided into four stages.
  1. Punishment from the environment occurs that is not seen as related to a person's behaviour.
  2. No behaviour seems to reduce the incidence of punishment.
  3. The individual decides that they are somehow responsible for the punishment; they make a misattribution.
  4. The individual comes to believe that they somehow are defective and thus are doomed to perform in a way that others find suitable.

■ Dealing with learned helplessness involves steps to help individuals learned they are worthwhile, effective people.

## SOCIAL LEARNING

■ The concept of social learning expands operant conditioning to include issues of expectations and models.

   ■ Alfred Bandura is the best known presenter of this position.

■ The basic concept is that we may be able to do behaviours we have never performed before, either because we have observed others doing them, or we have otherwise learned how they are to be done.

■ Models are chosen for high status, like interests, and perception of rewards.

■ Important factors in observational learning are:

   ■ Observer must be focused on the model.

   ■ Observer must remember what the model did.

   ■ Observer must be able to perform the observed action.

   ■ Observer must expect reinforcement in the same manner as that received by model, or be vicariously reinforced through the model.

## COGNITIVE BEHAVIOUR APPROACHES

■ Cognitive behaviour approaches involve helping students learn to monitor and control their own behaviour.

■ These approaches enable students to generalize behaviour management skills to other areas of their lives.

■ They also relieve the teacher of having to monitor a student's progress on a constant basis.

■ Typical steps in a cognitive behaviour approach include the following:

   ■ Help students set goals.

   ■ Record baseline behaviours and progress.

   ■ Teach students to talk themselves through an activity.

   ■ Help students learn to monitor and control thoughts, feelings, and behaviours to reach a goal.

   ■ Teach students to self-reward.

## CASE 10-1: GRADE 3 DROPOUT

"I don't like school anymore; we just do stupid stuff. It's no fun," Kai whined.

    Kai's mother was amazed at the change in her daughter's attitude to school in the last couple of months. In Grades 1 and 2, Kai had loved school and always was excited about going. Somehow things had changed in the first couple of months of Grade 3.

    Even before Kai had started to school she talked about going. She told everyone that she would be in Grade 1 in September. She even learned the name of the first grade teacher and recited the name to herself during the summer so she would not forget it in September. When she did start, there was a continuous stream of enthusiastic stories about what she had done in class, or what the teacher had said. Sometimes Kai's sister complained that she couldn't get a word in at supper because of Kai's stories.

Grade 2 was much the same. Kai seemed to be having a little difficulty with her printing and was not very interested in books. Her teacher assured Kai's parents that there was no reason for concern as Kai was so enthusiastic about all the activities in the classroom and had a lot of friends in the class.

The first sign of any change occurred around the third week of September in Grade 3. Kai seemed less excited about school and responded to questions about what she was learning with brief comments. Her mother thought it might be just an indication of Kai getting a bit older and recognizing that it was not cool to be telling stories about school.

"Ms. Zimmerman doesn't like me," Kai announced at supper. This comment was so out of character for Kai that everyone stopped eating and talking.

"What do you mean she doesn't like you?" asked Kai's father. "I'm sure your teacher likes you. What has happened to you? You used to like school so much."

"School was a lot better when I was younger," responded Kai. "Now we have to do all that stupid stuff." With that comment she got up and left the table. During the next two weeks there were more comments about not liking school. Her father decided he had better find out what was going on and phoned Ms. Zimmerman to request a meeting.

"I'm so glad you phoned," said Ms. Zimmerman. "I have been worried about Kai but was hoping the situation would improve. I understand from her Grade 1 and 2 teachers that she used to love school, but her Grade 2 teacher did notice that Kai was having some difficulty with academic material, especially reading and printing."

At the meeting Kai's parents were surprised to find that Kai was not keeping pace with the other students. "I don't understand. She always was so interested in school. She seems bright," her mother said.

"Kai is an intelligent and wonderful child," responded Ms. Zimmerman. "There probably is just some specific difficulty that Kai is having. Unfortunately, she realizes she is behind the other students and I have heard students call her 'stupid' a couple of times. I don't allow anything like that in my class but can't be sure what is going on in the playground or outside the school."

## Discussion Questions

1. How might classical conditioning explain Kai's change in attitude toward school?
2. What kinds of steps might help deal with Kai's situation?

## CASE 10-2: ENDORSEMENTS

The real change came in high school. Pearl had always been very active, playing almost every sport going. Often she played with the boys because there didn't seem to be enough girls who were interested. When she was 10 or 11 the boys sometimes objected, but a show of her ability soon had them accepting her as a member of the team. Indeed, they sometimes tried to get her on their side, especially if it looked like the other team was stronger.

Mr. Sisson, a local high school coach, first noticed Pearl when she was in Grade 6. He had been walking into the recreation centre and had stopped to watch a pickup game of basketball. Pearl caught his eye firstly because she was the only female playing. As he watched, he saw that Pearl played with a smoothness and fluidity that the boys lacked. They relied on a lot of pushing and shoving to move the ball around while she seemed to be able to slip through openings, dribbling easily with her head up looking around. Pearl was always in a stable position when she shot. There were no 'I hope' shots, no shots while falling or when there was little chance of the ball going in. Her outside shots arced into the basket while her drives to the basket did not involve the desperate charge that he usually saw in his students. Pearl seemed to understand that the purpose was to get the ball in the basket, not the drive itself.

Mr. Sisson didn't know the girl's name but recognized immediately that she was one to keep his eye on for the females' basketball team. The next day in the lounge he mentioned her to Ms. Voyer who coached the females' team. Ms. Voyer was very interested and asked the girl's name.

"Didn't ask anyone," responded Mr. Sisson.

"Why not?" asked Ms. Voyer. "How can I keep my eye out for someone I don't even know? Maybe she'll go to another high school, and even if she comes here she may not come out for the basketball team."

"Let me get this right," said Mr. Sisson. "You wanted me to ask a girl's name in the parking lot of the recreation centre. Not likely. Somebody would phone the police before I could turn around."

"Well, the next time you see her try to find out who she is," replied Ms. Voyer. "I think you are being a bit paranoid."

Mr. Sisson next saw Pearl in a local mall. She was there with some of her friends from school and Mr. Sisson overheard them mention something about their teacher Ms. Frogier, someone Mr. Sisson knew, being at a movie with the some man. While the chatter about who he was and what he looked like was interesting, Mr. Sisson moved on so as not to be noticed by the girls. He had the information he needed to identify Pearl.

After a phone call to Ms. Frogier the next day after school with a brief explanation, Mr. Sisson knew Pearl Leung's name. Mr. Sisson asked Ms. Frogier not to say anything to Pearl right now, but that he would send her information about a summer sport camp that was being run in the local recreation centre; he hoped Pearl could participate in it.

The camp had many sports. He and Ms. Voyer looked after the basketball component. They participated in the camp because of their commitment to youth sport in the city. The cheque for specialist coach didn't hurt, either. Pearl registered for the camp the next summer and her involvement with Ms. Voyer started from there. Pearl far surpassed all of the other girls of her age group at the camp. Indeed, she played better than most of the older girls although her smaller size meant that she really could not compete at the higher level. Ms. Voyer saw the potential, however, and encouraged Pearl and her parents to take every opportunity to develop her skills.

In high school Pearl was the player to watch. Newspapers and radio and TV sport announcers commented on her play. By Grade 11 even a few people from the community were coming to the basketball games. One night a stranger could be seen taking notes while the team played. Rumour had it that she was a coach for a university team. The university coach did not have a scholarship to offer Pearl but she did have a reputation as a great coach and the university's team usually was in the national finals. She also was the coach of the Canadian National Team and offered the possibility of Pearl playing for Canada. While there were scholarships in the U.S., Pearl liked the idea of staying in Canada and possibly playing for the National Team. She had never thought much about Canada before but now felt an attraction to the idea of playing for her country's team.

Pearl's career took off after her first year on the university team. Her picture started appearing in the university paper and then in local papers. A shot of her playing in the national finals even appeared in the *Globe and Mail*. A local charity asked her to be part of a fund raising campaign. All she had to do was appear in a couple of pictures and make a few brief comments at a couple of local events. This was followed by requests from other agencies. In one of these Pearl was somewhat upset to find her picture prominently shown as part of a local business' advertisement where they had tied the ad to the charity event.

Pearl was not completely surprised to get a phone call from someone who claimed to be a sports agent. She didn't know the person; he said he was just getting started. Pearl politely declined to become involved but this put the idea in her head. At a YWCA reception for local women in sport she met a tennis player who had done well on the international scene. Pearl asked her about an agent and the tennis player offered to introduce Pearl to her agent. The meeting went well and the agent promised to keep in touch. He asked Pearl to contact him before making any public appearances or endorsements and warned her about the dangers of taking any form of payment or signing any contracts, as this would affect her amateur status. Pearl continued her charitable work, however.

Pearl had a fantastic university career. She also played on the National Team. Her ability, as well as her dynamic personality and ready smile, made her a constant feature of reports about the team. In her third year she became team captain. Pearl tried out for and made the Olympic team. It was a glorious time in her life. The team did not do particularly well in the Olympic trials and were eliminated from the final competitions, but Pearl's face was splashed over all the national media. *Sports Illustrated* even interviewed her about the rising importance of women's basketball and the role of sports for young women in general.

With the end of university, however, and the next Olympics four years away, Pearl had to make a decision about what she would do next. There really was no place for her to play in Canada and so she turned pro and went to Europe. Turning pro also meant that she could be paid for endorsements of products. At this point her agent helped her select three non-competing products that had good solid reputations. The money was not fantastic, but combined with her salary as a player, she was doing well. Her family was excited about seeing her face in the media and she enjoyed the touch of glamour herself. Europe was lonely, however. She actually missed the routine of classes, practices, camps, etc.

Sometimes the players were invited to parties after games. Usually Pearl did not go; she heard from some of the other players about what went on and she didn't want any part of it. One Saturday night all the other women went to a party and Pearl went back to her apartment. The weight of her loneliness was just too much, however, and she decided to go down to the local pub for a drink and to just sit and watch the people.

This was how she met Noel. He actually recognized her as one of the basketball players and asked her if she would like a drink. A couple of drinks later she said she had to get back as the team had a practice in the morning. Noel had no objections and said he should be going as well. He asked if they could meet again and Pearl agreed. As Pearl was leaving the parking lot she noticed Noel looking for a taxi. She pulled up beside him and asked him if he would like a ride home. He said he lived over three kilometers away and Pearl responded with, "No problem." Pearl always was amazed about how people in Europe looked at distance. Three kilometers in Canada would be considered next door. In the dark Pearl didn't notice that Noel hadn't fastened his seat belt. She certainly would have said something if she had. They resumed their animated conversation from the bar. While she was concentrating on her driving, she was a couple of seconds too late seeing the dark car backing out of the driveway.

The accident really was quite minor considering what could have happened. There was some damage to both cars and Noel had quite a nasty cut on his forehead but otherwise everyone was fine. A police car was going the opposite way on the street and immediately swung in behind Pearl's car. The police radioed for an ambulance for Noel although he claimed that he was fine and that the bleeding had already stopped. The police officer came up to Pearl and asked her for her driver's licence and vehicle registration. At this point the officer became a little bit more stern and asked Pearl to come over to the police car. Pearl was required to blow into a breath analyzer.

Pearl's blood alcohol was slightly over the limit allowed for driving. Pearl was going to be charged with driving while intoxicated, although the police indicated that she would only get a fine since the level was low and this was her first offense. Pearl got Noel's phone number and promised to call him in the morning before the ambulance took him away. The whole thing was very embarrassing and she didn't look forward to all the hassles of the court case or dealing with the insurance company. Life went back to normal, however, and she and Noel had even gone out a couple of times.

Two weekends later she received her regular call from her mother. This time her mother seemed worried and asked several times if Pearl was all right. Finally Pearl asked her mother if there was some problem. Her mother told her about the story in the national newspaper of Pearl's drinking and driving and how a young man who she had picked up in a bar had been hurt in the accident. Pearl was horrified for her family. The story had been factually true but had turned a minor incident into a big scandal. She assured her mother that she was fine and that the whole issue had been blown completely out of proportion. Indeed, Noel planned to accompany her to Canada during her next visit and Pearl was going to bring him to the house.

After the phone call Pearl had a feeling of anxiety that she couldn't shake. She knew that the story had done her reputation a lot of damage. After several hours of fretting she phoned her agent in Toronto. He also had seen the story and was starting a program of damage control. He indicated, though, that the whole issue was difficult; any explanation seemed only to make the problem worse. They decided to issue a press release stating that Pearl had been involved in a minor accident where no one was seriously hurt and that no charges had been laid.

Pearl was due to be in Toronto in two weeks and was to be the feature speakers at a campaign to open a new research centre for women in sport. The centre phoned Pearl and said they had changed the format of their opening somewhat; Pearl's speech was no longer required. Pearl was still welcome to come to the opening however and her fee would be paid because of the late notice.

A month later one of Pearl's sponsors called her agent to talk about next year's contract. They were thinking of moving from endorsement by athletes to including other forms of advertising. As a result they wanted to reduce their involvement with Pearl. No one said anything about the article in the paper but Pearl was sure these changes were not coincidences. She really started to understand the underlying principles of endorsements.

## Discussion Questions

1. What qualities must a person have if they are going to be paid to endorse products or agencies?
2. Why might agencies and businesses be hesitant about using Pearl?
3. What kinds of things could she do?
4. How does a particular learning theory explain the power of endorsements?

## CASE 10-3:  WILL PUNISHMENT HELP?

Nina was just getting to know her Grade 4 class. September was such an exciting time of the year. "It seems I get to start life all over again each September," she had remarked in the lounge just yesterday. A couple of other teachers smiled and nodded their heads in agreement. Nina's class seemed to be the usual mixture of sizes and colours. She remembered her professional year in Education and how she had though of a Grade 4 class as a unit. "Boy, was I off the mark," she mused.

Three students in the class had been designated special needs. There might be others who had moved into the area, but she knew that she had three to start. Actually, the designation was sort of an arbitrary point on a continuum for many of her students. When it came to learning difficulties in particular it seemed that there usually were a lot of similarities between those who were designated and others in the class who perhaps could be.

Bernice was one of the names that jumped out at her. She remembered Bernice from the comments of the Grade 3 teacher last year. The teacher often sank into the old couch in the lounge and lamented, "You just wouldn't believe what she did today." This was followed by another escapade from Bernice's saga of hyperactive and inappropriate behaviour. In addition, Bernice still read at the Grade 1 level and was having increasing difficulties with math.

After class that day a well-dressed woman knocked on Nina's door and walked into the classroom. "Can I talk to you for a minute about Bernice? I'm her mother," the woman said. Nina would have preferred an appointment but always tried to get to know the parents and this seemed like a good opportunity. In addition, she hoped that the parent would have some ideas about how Nina could help Bernice in her class.

Bernice's mother turned out to be quite negative, however, and began to recite a list of problems that she and her husband had with Bernice. "We pushed to get her designated as special needs in Grade 1," she stated. "It was so obvious that she had all kinds of difficulties."

When Nina asked if Bernice's mother had found any strategies that helped Bernice, she got a list of increasingly severe punishments that the parents had used. These punishments always involved the removal of some privilege. While Nina found Bernice to be a handful, she felt this listing of behaviours and punishments was quite troublesome.

Bernice was constantly out of her seat, knocking stuff over, running into other students' seats in her rush to get some place and constantly looking around to get someone's attention. In addition, Bernice's academic problems had not been exaggerated. She really was operating some place in the Grade 1 and 2 level. Nina found herself liking Bernice, however. She was hardly ever deliberately mean to other students. In addition, she often came up with odd facts or approaches to stories that amused and interested Nina. Yesterday for instance she had explained to the class what 'dog in a manger' meant and had turned the assignment of drawing a map of Canada into an exercise in cartooning. One picture Nina remembered in particular showed a mosquito attacking a snowball. "That could be the true symbol for Canada," though Nina.

Nina decided to concentrate on Bernice's strengths and try to ignore her off-task behaviour. When she praised Bernice for her symbol of Canada, Bernice seemed to be kind of stunned. Then Bernice was out of her seat again. Rather than saying anything about it, Nina waited until Bernice had settled down in a chair at the back. She then asked her, "Bernice, could you summarize for us the main points of the video we watched yesterday before we move on?" Bernice did a great job and went into details that even Nina had forgotten. Nina decided to continue on with her approach of ignoring Bernice's inappropriate behavior unless it was disrupting the class. She even began to suspect that her efforts to keep Bernice on task were more disruptive than Bernice's behaviour.

As the month of September moved into October Nina noticed that Bernice's behaviour had lost its frantic nature. She still was off-task a lot but there was something less demanding in her behaviour. She even was starting to use some of the reading and work strategies Nina had introduced. On Bernice's first term report card Nina was able to point with enthusiasm to the improvements that Bernice had made, although she had to note that Bernice was well behind the other students in some areas. Nina felt she could be very positive about the future for Bernice.

The next parent-teacher meeting was not very positive. Bernice's mother came and Nina was looking forward to sharing her progress. Bernice's mother swept Nina's comments aside however and stated that, "We're having a lot of problems with her at home. Sending her to her room or taking away her allowance doesn't seem to help. I just don't know what's going to happen to her when she grows up."

## Discussion Questions

1. What are some of the differences between punishments and reinforcements for influencing behaviour?

2. Why might concentrating on problems cause them to increase?

3. What are some reasons that Bernice's parents might be using punishment as opposed to reinforcement to influence her behaviour?

## CASE 10-4: ART OR POPCORN?

All his teachers agreed that he was a gifted artist. Some commented that they expected to see his name mentioned in the arts media within a decade. Others were doubtful that he would ever amount to anything. "Michael never finishes anything," one teacher was heard to comment. Another complained that Michael always managed to sabotage any goodwill he had built up by some cruel or thoughtless act.

"Yesterday he dribbled paint on another student's work," stated his present teacher. "The student was so upset that she started to cry. Michael had that smirk on his face even when I asked him to leave the room. It is such a tragedy that all his talent seems to be going to waste."

Michael was one of the few boys from the neighbourhood to actually make it to Grade 12. The majority dropped out in Grades 10 and 11 or took just a few courses each year to maintain the illusion they were still in school. Mostly they just hung out and made nuisances of themselves. Storeowners constantly were phoning the police about some relatively minor incident, although sometimes the boys were suspected in more serious crimes.

A core group of these boys called themselves The Popcorns. No one knew where the name came from but some thought it was appropriate. "A bunch of airheads," sneered a teacher. Michael was a member of this group and often could be seen hanging around with them and taunting other students. Michael seemed to pick on what he called the 'suckers'. They usually were students who did well in school and seem to be very serious about their academic work. The Popcorn members laughed at his comments and clapped him on the back when he made what they called 'a good one'.

Michael also was suspected in some of the graffiti that was painted on the outside wall of the gym. These often were demeaning pictures of the principal or some of the teachers. The art teacher often was the subject of one of these satirical masterpieces. "It must be Michael," commented the principal. "I don't think any of the other kids can draw like that."

Despite Michael's behaviour in class and his graffiti, his art teacher wanted him to go on to Art College. She constantly praised his work and told him he would have great success in the art world. She pointed out a couple of established artists who had graduated from the school and had gone on to exciting careers. "It's your ticket out of here doing something you love," she reasoned. "Can't you see what a tremendous gift you have and how much it could do for you?" She just couldn't understand why Michael refused to grab the chance that clearly had been so rewarding for others.

## Discussion Questions

1.  What might be some of the tensions leading to the conflicts in Michael's behaviour?
2.  Why might he reject the chance to continue his art career?

## CASE 10-5: I'LL DO IT IN THE MORNING

Saying that Bjorn found Physics difficult was definitely an understatement. He really didn't seem to have a clue about how to approach some of the problems. He always left Physics until the end when he was doing his homework, and then usually found some excuse to take a break before he started. He could solve the problems where the correct formula to use was obvious — just plug the numbers in and write out the answer. The teacher liked to give mostly tough problems, however. There were a lot of words and Bjorn found the whole thing confusing. He didn't know where to start. Bjorn didn't know how many times he had left them until morning. "Perhaps I'll think of something during the night," he always reasoned. The fact that sleep did not bring solutions never stopped him from hoping.

Bjorn's Physics teacher thought there was a good chance Bjorn might fail the class. She was a bit surprised to find that Bjorn was not having problems in other classes and indeed, was doing very well in his Language Arts classes. "So much for a reading difficulty," thought the teacher.

After the next class she asked Bjorn to come in to talk about his problems in the class. The meeting was a bit strained at first as Bjorn thought he was going to be criticized for not doing better. It took a little while for him to accept that the teacher really thought there might be some way he could improve his work in the class. This was a surprise to Bjorn as he always thought of Physics as being a better measure of intelligence than Language Arts. "Anybody can do English," he thought. "Only the bright kids can do Physics."

Bjorn didn't know what to say when the teacher asked him how he approached his Physics problems; surely the answer was obvious. "Well I just look at them and sometimes I see the answer," he stated.

"What do you do if the answer isn't obvious?" asked the teacher.

"Then I know I can't do it," explained Bjorn. "Usually I just leave it until morning."

## Discussion Questions

1. Why does Bjorn leave his Physics until the last?

2. Why does he leave the questions he finds difficult until the morning?

3. What type of behaviours could the teacher explain to Bjorn to help with his approach to Physics?

# chapter eleven

# Cognitive Learning Theories

## COMPARISON OF BEHAVIOURAL AND COGNITIVE APPROACHES

- Behavioural approaches state that behaviours change as a result of reinforcement or punishment.
  - You only need to know the nature of feedback from the environment to understand behaviour.
- Cognitive approaches state that changes in knowledge lead to changes in behaviour.
  - Individuals are active in developing knowledge.
- Perhaps it is more productive to consider behavioural and cognitive approaches to learning as being on a continuum.

## COGNITIVE APPROACHES TO LEARNING

- **Information processing** theories, where the emphasis is placed on how an individual learns, stores, and retrieves information, represent one cognitive approach to learning.

- **Constructivist** approaches, where the emphasis is placed on how an individual transforms and gives personal meaning to knowledge, represent the other principal cognitive approach to learning.
- These two approaches are not mutually exclusive but rather could be seen as being on a continuum.

# INFORMATION PROCESSING

## General Nature of Approach

- Information processing models are based largely on the concept of the brain as a type of computer.
  - The brain is not seen as a computer in a mechanical sense but rather as an organ involved in the sensing, storing, and retrieving of information.
- This brain 'computer' has both processing speed and capacity.
  - **Speed** refers to how quickly a mental process can be completed.
  - **Capacity** refers to the amount of information that can be held in conscious awareness at one time.
- **Memory span** is closely related to processing speed and capacity, and refers to the amount of new material that can be absorbed at one time.
  - Memory ability increases as the child ages.
- Greater depth and organization of previous knowledge in a field increases the ease of learning new material in that field.
- Over time, some processes become automatic and do not need conscious awareness, while new activities may have to be controlled consciously.
  - University students usually can write and listen at the same time; Grade 2 students usually cannot do the two activities at the same time.

## Attention

- Computers are designed to pay attention to even the most boring of information; human beings are not.
- The ability to pay attention changes with age.
  - Young children tend to be attracted to the most pronounced stimulus in the environment; older students usually become better able to focus on a task.
- Difficulty in paying attention sometimes leads to a diagnosis of Attention Deficit Disorder (ADD).
  - There is considerable controversy about this diagnosis and its broader label of Attention Deficit Hyperactive Disorder (ADHD). Some believe that sometimes this diagnosis is more of a reflection of an anti-child bias in our society than it is of any problem the child might have.

## Gaining the Attention of Students

- Obviously students won't learn if they are not paying attention.
- On the other hand, some attempts to get students' attention may be counter-productive. For example, gaining their attention with an unrelated bit of trivia might be successful initially, but also might be all the students remember about the class.
- Use of cues is helpful.
- Emphasizing the personal value of information helps if it is true. Some material must be learned even if it is a big stretch to find any immediate value.
- Signaling that the information to follow is important helps students pay attention.
  - Teachers can write critical information on the board.
  - Saying "this is on the test" usually gets a response.
  - Hesitating before speaking can be used to indicate that important information is to follow.

## SENSATION AND PERCEPTION

- **Sensation** is the raw sensory data while **perception** is how the brain interprets that data.
- Our brain cannot attend to all the information in the environment, so it selects what is regarded as important at the time.
- Just because a teacher says something doesn't mean that the student interpreted the words in the way the teacher intended, or even that the student heard them at all.
- **Premature closing** happens when the brain decides that it already knows some information based on a few words or signals.
  - For instance, mentioning Piaget in my classes usually results in students assuming they already know what I am going to say.

## MEMORY

- The nature of memory is not well understood. There are numerous theories about whether it is chemical, electrical, holographic, etc.
- Damage to areas of the brain result in specific memory losses, but this doesn't mean that a particular type of memory is housed there.
- Direct stimulation of the brain during surgery shows that vivid memories still are housed in the brain even though we are not conscious of them.
- Concepts of short- and long-term memory are used to describe the phenomena of being able to remember a name or phone number for a few seconds and then 'forgetting' it.
  - It is not clear whether the issue is a failure to store the information, or an inability to retrieve it.
  - Strategies and effort are required to ensure that material can be retrieved later.

## Types of Memory

- The number of different types of memory depends on the specificity of criteria. For instance, sensory memory could be further divided to include hearing, smelling, touching, seeing, or tasting memories.
- The three most important types of memory for education are declarative, episodic, and procedural.
- Declarative, or semantic, includes facts abstract information such as dates, names, and theories.
    - This type of information is forgotten easily if not used and usually requires memory strategies for retrieval.
- Episodic memory involves the memory of intense personal experiences.
- Procedural memory usually means physical actions.
    - These actions make take some time to learn but they usually are not forgotten over time. Indeed, the process of reproducing the action becomes almost unconscious. Once you have learned to ride a bike, for instance, you will be able to ride one for the rest of your life even if you don't practise for years.
- Types of memory are not really rigid categories.

## Forgetting

- Chemical or biological decay of cells or cell structures has been proposed as a reason for forgetting.
- Some information may be forgotten because of repression, where the memory is pushed out of conscious awareness.
- Age is a critical factor as older people have more difficulty remembering recent information.
    - The reason for this could be biological or cognitive and varies from individual to individual.
    - Any deficit is improved by memory training.
- **Inhibition,** which occurs when one piece of information makes it difficult to retrieve other pieces, may be another reason people forget things.
    - **Proactive** inhibition is when information we have learned previously makes it difficult to learn new information.  _round world/is flat._
    - **Retroactive** inhibition occurs when information we are learning now causes us to forget information we have already learned. _- Calculatn._

## Remembering

- Events with high emotional impact are easy to remember.
- Rehearsal aids memory.

- People are more likely to remember what they were doing when they first heard about important events.
- **Facilitation** occurs when knowing one piece of information helps us remember another piece.
  - **Proactive** facilitation occurs when something we have learned helps us learn something new. _riding - bike/physics helps ride scooter_
  - **Retroactive** facilitation occurs when information we are learning now makes it easier for us to remember information we learned before. _peoples names._
- Control processes or memory strategies help us to remember information.
  - Examples of control processes include loci methods, where pieces of information are placed mentally in specific parts of a room. One example of control processes involves loci methods where bits of information are placed mentally in a fixed pattern around a room or building. For instance, the introduction to a speech could be placed mentally on the door to a room, the next part of the speech on the light switch, etc. Other examples of loci methods include developing acronyms, nonsense rhymes, associations, etc.
- Various forms of representing information, including visual and auditory constructions, improve memory. For example, a student might draw a map visually showing the relationships of different processes.
- Teachers need to recognize that humans learn in patterns or schemata rather than in a linear manner like a tape recorder.
- There is some evidence that improvements in general health, relaxation techniques, the use of music, and various visualization strategies improve remembering.

| Exercise 11–1 | **Piaget vs. The Mall** |

1. Think back to a topic, such as Piaget's theory, that you had to study for a recent test. List in point form as much information as you can about this concept.
2. Think back to a place, such as a mall, that you have visited only once in the last five years or so. List in point form as much information as you can about this place.
3. Was there any difference in the amount remembered? Why does this difference occur?

## Importance of Information Processing For Education

- Information processing concepts remind teachers that *how* information is presented is as important as the information itself.
- These concepts lead to the exploration of techniques to improve information processing.
- Information processing reinforces the concept of learning styles.

■ Information processing concepts help teachers to focus on the issue of specific learning difficulties as opposed to general statements about a student's inability to learn.

| Exercise 11–2 | **Thirty Days Have...** |
|---|---|

List all the strategies you know for remembering specific information. For example, most of us have a rhyme for remembering the number of days in a month. "Thirty days have September . . ."

## CONSTRUCTIVIST APPROACHES

■ Constructivist approaches are at the other end of the cognitive learning strategies continuum from information processing.

■ The constructivist approach sees humans as organizing information themselves to produce individual meaning.

■ Students must individually discover and transform knowledge.

■ Some approaches to constructivism stress the role of social context in producing meaning more than others.

■ All approaches see students as active learners.

■ Education must be learner-centred.

■ More information related to the constructivist approach to teaching is presented in the next chapter.

## COMPLEX COGNITIVE STRATEGIES

■ Both the information processing and constructivist approaches are interested in complex cognitive tasks such as learning a new concept, critical thinking, and problem solving.

■ Strategies for accomplishing these tasks must be taught and supported in the classroom.

  ▪ This includes concepts of reading such as highlighting, making notes, asking questions, etc.

  ▪ Various ways of organizing information including use of colour and sound, concept organizers, mind maps, etc., are seen as important.

■ Blocks to problem solving must be examined and removed. Usually these blocks are the result of rigidity in approach to concepts or tools.

■ Development of both expert teachers and students requires learning material thoroughly, being emotionally involved, and focusing effort.

  ▪ This leads to a depth of knowledge that results in many routines becoming automatic, with the resultant release of energy for creativity.

■ Expansion of metacognitive skills or the ability to monitor and alter our thinking processes is an important part of constructivism.

## CASE 11-1: PAY ATTENTION

Catherine thought that a name change would be a good idea. "Pay Attention would be more appropriate," she mused. "Everyone is always calling me that anyway."

"Active little baby," was a comment her parents heard quite a bit. Usually it was accompanied by a strained smile as a host nervously watched to make sure that Catherine wasn't climbing on the fridge or investigating the dresser drawers in the bedroom. Her parents noticed that they often got invited to go for walks or to have a picnic as opposed to having a visit with friends in their homes.

Catherine was learning that some people seemed to be angry a lot when she was around. Mrs. Hancyk next door had told her firmly a number of times to stay out of her backyard and not to climb the cherry tree. She had even complained to Catherine's mother, and Catherine had been threatened with dire but undefined punishment if she ever went in the yard again.

Staying out of high places — including trees — probably would have been a good idea. When she was three, Catherine broke her arm when she tried to fly off the garage roof. A tumble from the top of the swing set in the park resulted in a broken leg a year later. This time the family doctor warned her sternly about climbing up on things. "You'll break your head next time," he scolded.

Catherine found the idea of breaking your head kind of funny and a bit interesting. "I wonder what it's like to break your head," she thought.

The early school years hadn't been too bad. Teachers didn't seem to mind Catherine's continuous exploration of the classroom or her jumps in interest from a book, to the window, to who was going to the washroom. Often the teachers would ask her to come and sit by them at story time or would ask her to return to her desk or group. Catherine never put much importance on these events and indeed, liked to be asked to sit by the teacher.

The change really came in Grade 3. For some reason the teacher that year seemed to get very upset with Catherine's constant roaming. "Sit in your chair like a good girl," seemed to be the teacher's constant refrain. For the first time, Catherine began to feel that she was different, that there was something wrong with her. This feeling was reinforced when her parents came back from a meeting with the teacher looking very worried and started to talk to Catherine about some medicine she might need.

Even now, years later, Catherine could remember the medicine and how it made her feel. She had been able to sit in her chair as the teacher wanted and her parents seemed happier with her report cards. She valued the feelings of greater acceptance by the adults in her life, but she also felt that in some way she was not really herself. Some part of her always rebelled at the idea of taking medicine when she wasn't sick.

On her 14th birthday she refused to take her medicine. During the following two decades she rejected all pleadings, reasoned arguments, and threats trying to change her stance. It had been far from smooth sailing; school had been a series of stops and starts with alternate schools and correspondence classes finally being the only way she could complete high school. Her work life had been a series of abandoned jobs and projects. She started them all with the best of intentions, but soon would feel an anxiety, a need to move or to do something else.

Recently she had been watching a series of television shows about famous explorers. Actually she was amazed to find that she had managed to see all five shows on five consecutive weeks. "Must have really caught my interest," she mused. "I wonder what those explorers were like when they weren't out exploring? Too bad they didn't cover any female explorers. There must have been some."

## Discussion Questions

1. When is the use of drugs for controlling behaviour justified?
2. Do explorers make good farmers?

## CASE 11-2: ASK ME ABOUT 'THE HAWK'

Doug Lee was a fountain of information on popular North American musicians; his favourite was Ronnie Hawkins. If you wanted to know anything about The Hawk, Doug was the person to ask. Often he told you without being asked. Other students regarded him as a bit eccentric, but also respected his depth of knowledge. Teachers often tried to stump him with questions about drummers in obscure bands or the name of a songwriter. Doug loved both the attention and the respect his interest brought him.

Too bad that wasn't the case in Biology. Actually, too bad that wasn't the case in all his classes, but Biology was the worst. He could understand the concepts and even enjoyed learning about them; the problem came with exams. He read his notes over and over and looked at the chapters in the textbook until the words swam in front of him. It didn't seem to help that much. He just couldn't seem to answer the questions the teacher asked. There was so much information in his head. Why didn't the teacher just ask him to write some of it down? Actually sometimes he did just write some of it down, in the hope that the teacher would give him some marks for effort even though the information was not related to the question.

## Discussion Questions

1. Why could Doug remember so much about musicians and not be able to do well on his exams?
2. What might be some approaches a teacher could take to help Doug study?

## CASE 11-3: GOOD ENOUGH FOR YOU

"Cullen marches to a different drummer," explained his father. He wasn't actually sure that the cliché was true in his son's case, but he felt he had to justify Cullen's unorthodox behaviour to the other fathers. Their children had all gone on to university or to a career in the trades. Sometimes he thought his son was heading some place and other times he thought Cullen was just goofing around.

Cullen's grandparents had immigrated to Canada after World War I and had worked very hard to establish a small construction business in the city. Cullen's father had started to work in the business when he as ten; there never was any question that he would work like his father, expand the business even more and establish a family. No one even thought to ask him what he wanted to do, or paid the slightest attention to his various interests. Success was a matter of hard work and constant vigilance. Dreams and ideas were just woolgathering, an occupation for those who didn't have enough discipline and drive to own sheep.

Cullen's father had managed to develop his early interest in jazz as a hobby. The hobby was limited to collecting a few CD's however. He never had time to continue beyond the one year of piano lessons, and his fingers were too stiff from the years in construction to even considering playing an instrument now. Years earlier he had slipped a mention of jazz into conversations with a couple of friends but they had responded with looks of incomprehension or quick put-downs of the music. As a result, his interest remained his own secret.

Teachers always had difficulty labeling Cullen's behaviour. Some claimed that he was a thoughtful student who often came up with his own ideas about particular concepts; others complained about his failure to understand this or that piece of literature or scientific principle. His seesawing grades reflected this confusion about his behaviour. They also mirrored his father's feelings about Cullen's apparent lack of direction.

Cullen seemed to be most happy when he could graze through different books, web sites, magazines, and a variety of other media. This was supplemented by apparently random visits to different areas of the city and conversations with almost anyone and anybody. He sometimes hung out with kids on the street, but the next day might be seen talking to a business person, a street vendor, a bookstore owner, or a computer repair technician. The funny thing was that everyone seemed willing to talk to him. They seemed to find his questions and comments an interesting break in their busy lives.

"Perhaps he'll get something figured out," mused his father. "I sure don't know what the future holds but I know it won't be like the old days. If all else fails, I probably can find a job for him some place in construction."

## Discussion Questions

1. If it was good enough for me, why can't it be good enough for you?
2. If the past is not going to be the future, what must parents and teachers do to support young people?
3. Do you think that educators truly believe that students must construct their own knowledge?

## CASE 11-4: NOTES AS RAT'S NEST

High School and university were relatively easy for Francesca. Sure she complained like the others, but she had to admit to herself that she often skipped her university classes if there was something more interesting to do. She also managed to write her papers without outlines, and studied only the night before for exams. She just seemed to know how to organize her time and material in a manner that was most efficient, and that gained the greatest amount of credit from her teachers. Francesca knew that a few of the other students in her classes had difficulties because of disabilities or other demands on their time. Most of the students who complained about the amount of work or who did poorly on exams drew little sympathy from her, however. They were dismissed as being whiners, lazy, or not really interested in university.

Now a teacher herself, Francesca used the same relatively unconscious efficiency to prepare materials for her classes. She had a variety of overheads, videos, and short activities to involve her students. No one was going to be bored in her class. She asked questions during her class and scheduled a quiz every second Friday to ensure that students were keeping up and to find out if any students were having difficulties.

One of her Grade 10 Biology classes represented a typical cross-section of her students. Three or four students didn't seem to be interested in the content but were not disruptive and so did not represent a management problem to her. When she asked them questions, they seemed to know the answers, but didn't offer any elaboration or seem to have much interest in pursuing a topic on their own. Most of the other students seemed to be paying attention and a few responded quite enthusiastically to her questions during class.

Francesca was shocked with the results of the first quiz, one that she thought was quite easy. The three or four students who seemed to be present in body only got low B's and seemed perfectly happy with these marks, even though it was now quite evident to Francesca that they could have done a lot better if they had worked a bit harder. About a third of the class were in the high B or A range and obviously were not having much difficulty with the class. The rest were distributed through the B's and C's; a few even managed to fail, including a student who seemed to be so involved in the class. This upset Francesca as it was not clear to her why everyone should not have done very well on her quiz. She took the failure of some of the students as a personal insult. Their answers were so mixed up and incomplete, it was almost like these students had missed most of the classes even though this was not the case. What had happened?

On the bottom of their quizzes Francesca had asked the students who failed to meet her after class with their notebooks. Three of them came on time although only two had their notebooks. One student was looking for his Biology notes; it seemed they were mixed in his Social Studies notes as he kept his notes organized by day rather than topic. The student later told Francesca that this was so he would only have to carry one notebook at a time. A couple of students didn't come at all. One of them later told her that he had not read the quiz when he got it back and so had not seen Francesca's note.

When she finally did see all of their notes, Francesca was amazed at the lack of organization. Some students had written down what appeared to be random words. When she asked about the words, the students said they seemed important at the time although they no longer knew why they had written them. Another student had everything Francesca had written on the board carefully recorded, but one day's notes ran into another in a continuous stream. None of the students had taken any steps to improve their notes on a second reading.

Studying seemed to be even more haphazard. A couple of students read their notes over and over, but the rest didn't seem to have any idea how they studied. Two said they didn't study because they had found it to be a waste of time. They didn't know what was going to be asked so how could they study? None of them had thought about other ways to approach their note taking and studying. Francesca wondered how common this approach was even among the students who had done a little better on the quiz.

## Discussion Questions

1. What assumptions was Francesca making concerning the way students record their notes and study?

2. What would be some steps she could take now?

# chapter twelve

# Mastery, Direct, and Constructivist Approaches

## TEACHING/LEARNING STRATEGIES

Academic writers have developed many different, supposedly unique, classifications of teaching behaviours. However, most of these classifications involve very subtle distinctions — too subtle to be recognized in classroom application. In addition, approaches to teaching blend together, with any one approach containing components of other approaches. While divisions may be somewhat arbitrary, any presentation of material requires that the information be structured so that it has some logical flow: a complex concept cannot be 'downloaded' in one burst of data with all the inter-relationships immediately obvious.

- This chapter explores mastery learning, direct instruction and constructivist approaches to teaching.
- Chapter 13 covers differentiated, group/cooperative, and brain-based methods of teaching.
- All of the materials related to educational philosophy, developmental theories, approaches to learning, and information processing already covered directly affect all methods of teaching.

## LESSON PLANNING

- Lesson planning is the cornerstone of all approaches to teaching. Sometimes teachers misuse particular approaches to teaching — such as discovery learning — to hide the fact that they have not done the proper lesson planning.

- Lesson planning includes the big picture, the overall approach we are going to take to a class, unit, or year, and the details of particular classes.

- Lesson planning always involves stating learning outcomes, activities or experiences planned for the class, methods of instruction, times, materials needed, and methods of evaluation.

## TRANSFER OF LEARNING

- Transfer of learning is an essential issue in any form of instruction. **Transfer of learning** refers to taking knowledge and skills learned in one context, and using them in another.

- We generally have to overlearn the material in one context before it can be transferred.

- Students are able to transfer learning more easily to real world contexts if the teacher makes the connection obvious while the material is being learned.

  - This usually has the added advantage of providing increased motivation for students to learn the material in the first place.

## LEARNING OUTCOMES

- Authors and instructors use many different terms to refer to the concept of learning outcomes.

  - Goals, objectives, outcomes, targets, expected learning outcomes, and prescribed learning outcomes are some common ones.

  - Sometimes I have my students make a table of the different words their instructors use for the same concept.

- Regardless of the words employed, the underlying logic is to define clearly what we are trying to do and then to measure whether or not we did this.

- General categories cannot be measured and so it is impossible to know if they have been met.

- Sometimes teachers go to the other extreme and list 2000 specific outcomes for a short class. This is a useless process since there will not be time to measure each of these outcomes.

- Probably the best approach involves two steps:

  1. Write out a small number of general expected outcomes or objectives for the class or unit. This will give your class an overall direction.

  2. For each of these general objectives write 4 or 5 specific, measurable outcomes (who, what, when, how much). There is no need to write them down if you are not going to measure them.

■ I must emphasize a fundamental weakness in the whole concept of objectives/outcomes as the concept usually is applied in education. In fact, teachers have no control over what the students will do. As a result, teachers should not evaluate their own performances based only on their students' performances. Measures of student performance reflect student knowledge and understanding; they may have little to say about teachers.

■ Objectives usually are written in terms of categories in the cognitive, affective, and/or psychomotor domains of learning.

■ The main categories of the cognitive domain (Bloom's Taxonomy) are knowledge, comprehension, application, analysis, synthesis, and evaluation.

■ The main categories of the affective domain (Krathwohl's Taxonomy) are receiving, responding, valuing, organization, and value or value complex.

■ The main categories of the psychomotor domain (Simpson's Taxonomy) are perception, set, guided response, mechanism, complex overt response, adaptation, and origination.

## THE MASTERY LEARNING APPROACH TO TEACHING

■ In the Mastery Learning approach, the teacher breaks concepts into small skills or areas of study.

■ Each area must be mastered before a student can move on.

■ Mastery usually means a score of 80 percent or better.

■ Students who attain mastery may be given enrichment activities if they have to wait for other students in the class to complete the area of study.

■ Other students may need extra help to reach mastery.

  ■ Often there is a problem of providing resources for this extra help.

  ■ Providing these resources may involve additional staff or material resources.

■ Mastery Learning means that students are not left trying to learn new material before they have satisfactorily learned earlier material.

## THE DIRECT INSTRUCTION APPROACH TO TEACHING

## Purpose

■ Direct Instruction is the fastest and most effective way for humans to learn a fixed body of information. This is particularly true if the information is of a basic nature and can be taught in a step-by-step manner.

■ Direct Instruction makes maximum use of a teacher's greater understanding of a field or concept.

■ Direct Instruction decreases the possibility of students' failing to grasp the important basic structure of an area of knowledge.

## Difficulty

- The basic difficulty with direct instruction is that human beings are not good at faithfully recording and understanding or giving meaning to large amounts of information.
  - We are not tape recorders or computers.
- This difficulty in understanding and giving meaning to data means that it is necessary to take steps to assist students in learning materials taught by direct instruction.
  - These steps are part of lesson planning.
- An additional issue with Direct Instruction is that it does not fit present academic interests in teaching strategies. This means that student teachers may not understand its value and will not be prepared to implement it effectively.

## Components

The components of a direct instruction approach to teaching will vary from teacher-to-teacher and concept-to-concept. Good use of the approach usually requires that teachers include seven components, described below.

1. Provide a mental set. This involves stating the learning outcomes for the unit, or otherwise orienting students.
2. Review prerequisites. This could be an activity, a class discussion, a worksheet, a short lecture or some combination of these.
3. Present new material. The teacher must decide which of a variety of techniques is the best approach to cover new material. Straight lectures, unless they are quite short, usually are not as effective as presentations that use multiple formats.
4. Devise learning probes. This can involve, for example, general questions to the whole class, questions to particular individuals, or thought experiments. One way to quiz the whole class quickly is to ask a question with a 'yes or no' answer. Thumbs up if you think the answer is yes and thumbs down if you think it is no; thumbs horizontal if you don't know.
5. Arrange for independent practice. This occurs when students work by themselves or in groups to expand or apply the concept being taught.
   - Independent practice is crucial to anchor learning.
   - The teacher must make sure students have a basic understanding of the concept and provide clear instructions before students start their independent practice.
   - It is important to keep the time of independent practice relatively short.
6. Provide distributed learning and review material. Distributed learning could involve homework, larger projects, or other activities that generalize learning.
7. Assess performance and provide feedback. More material about assessment is provided in Chapter 17.
   - The above seven steps may occur many times during a class period as each new sub-skill or section of material is presented.

# THE CONSTRUCTIVIST APPROACH TO TEACHING

## Overview

- There is no specific constructivist approach to teaching. As well as those that use the specific label constructivist, approaches such as discovery learning and problem solving approaches all share similar philosophies.
- Beneath these philosophies lie the concepts of Piaget and Vygotsky. These concepts were discussed in Chapters Five and Eleven.

## General Principles

- Rote learning is not meaningful and will not be retained or be useful in the development of more advanced concepts.
- For knowledge to be meaningful, students must find and test its basic patterns for themselves. Students must be active in transforming data into meaningful structures.
- Social contexts are very important in determining both the success and the eventual nature of this transformation.

## Guided vs. Unguided Transformations

- Sometimes unguided searching or problem solving is both practical and meaningful.
- Often as concepts become more complex and/or involve safety and other considerations, student activities must be guided by the teacher.

## Components

- Students are provided with complex problems or issues that have real possibilities for exploration.
  - Usually the teacher selects these problems or issues because he or she knows from experience, or from a mentor, that they have relevance for students at particular ages.
- Problems or issues are presented in multiple formats.
- Often scaffolding, in the form or questions, cues, support, or intermediate activities, is provided to help students explore.
- There is an understanding that the development of knowledge is a shared responsibility. Students are encouraged to explore issues with other students, and provided with social support in the form of teachers and mentors.
- Students are given opportunities to test their new understanding either through direct interactions with the environment, or through discussions with individuals who have a greater depth of understanding.

## CASE 12-1: DIVIDING BY FRACTIONS

"I don't really understand how to do this problem," whined one of the students in Wendy Kulai's Grade 10 Math class. Others in the class picked up the whine and added their claims of lack of understanding.

"Well, it's really just dividing by a fraction," Wendy explained.

"How can you divide by a fraction?" responded the student. "I thought fractions already were division."

Wendy realized that she would have to go over the concept of dividing by fractions, a concept that the students in her class should have learned in earlier grades. Later in the staff lounge she complained about the amount of time she had to spend covering material the students should already know. "You should see some of the spellings I get," commented the English teacher. "And it's students who have been in our system for years."

### Discussion Questions

1. Why do students not know simple skills supposedly covered in other years?

2. What approaches might help to alleviate this problem?

3. Why are these approaches not used more often?

## CASE 12-2: BUT I MAKE IT SO CLEAR

Mr. Johnson has taught Grade 11 Biology for 8 years. Each of his classes contains a great deal of carefully prepared content. Reading a specific number of pages from the text is usually the assigned homework. He tries to cover an individual topic each day using a course timetable that he developed in the first couple of years. He doesn't share this timetable with the class, as he doesn't want them to get confused and start reading about future topics before he has a chance to provide the proper foundation. He has prepared overheads of his material and follows what he sees as a logical progression in each class. Students take notes from the board and the overheads. When they are asked for comments or questions, there usually is no response. They also are asked to summarize the main points from the text for themselves as homework, and to be ready with any questions they have at the start of the next class. There are always a few questions from the text on quizzes to ensure that students have done their reading homework.

Mr. Johnson is frustrated, though, because several students never seem to do well on his quizzes. Indeed, from time to time almost all of the class manages to misunderstand concepts that were presented in a very clear manner. Even those students who do well in the class complained about the amount of time they have to spend memorizing notes. Mr. Johnson can't think of any way he can make the information clearer.

### Discussion Questions

1. What are some reasons that Mr. Johnson's clear, logical approach to teaching might not help his students learn the concepts involved?

2. What are students missing when they do not have the course timetable?

## CASE 12-3: OUR TEACHER DOESN'T DO IT THAT WAY ⸺

Linda Sam was hoping the phone wouldn't ring that Friday. She already had worked as a Teacher-on-Call (TOC) for three days that week and had a whole list of personal errands to run during the day before she picked up her son after preschool. Getting him ready in a hurry each of the three mornings had been an added strain. She had to take him to her sister who in turn took him to the preschool when it opened. Fortunately, being a TOC meant that she could leave the school right after classes and get to the preschool before closing time. It also meant that she usually did not have a lot of work in the evening.

The clock was approaching 7:30 am and she began to relax a bit. "Look's like no calls to-day," she thought. Just then the phone rang. Maybe it was her sister asking if she was coming over early. No such luck; it was the TOC Service wondering if she wanted to sub for a Grade 7 teacher who couldn't come in for some reason. Linda always accepted these calls as she felt it built her reputation as a TOC who could be counted on to work. It was unusual to have so many calls by the first of October, however.

The usual mad mix of washing, dressing, eating, and driving followed as she got everything organized. "I'm probably the only person on earth who brushes her teeth and eats breakfast at the same time," she mused. "Seems to be a nice symmetry about it."

Linda had taught at the school two or three times in the past month but had never subbed for this particular teacher, so she didn't know what to expect. She was a few minutes late getting there, and the vice-principal already was explaining to the class that their teacher was ill and that they would have Ms. Sam today. She was used to being regarded as both a curiosity and prey by students who learned that they were going to get a sub. "Never show them any fear," she remembered a principal telling her on one of her first TOC experiences. She found the daybook that the classroom teacher kept; it had a list of the students and a few brief notes about material the teacher planned to cover. Not much to go on, but Linda was used to improvising on a limited theme. There always were students who were willing to tell her the correct way to do things if she went too far off the rails.

Later that afternoon the principal came in and asked Linda to come to her office at the end of classes. When they met, the principal asked Linda if she would be willing to sub for the classroom teacher for the next week. Linda followed her plan of always being available and agreed, while at the same time thinking of all the work she would have to do on the weekend. She asked the principal what had happened to the classroom teacher and was told only that he was sick. When Linda wondered if she could phone him at home to get some information about his plans for the class, the principal responded, "That probably would not be a good idea at this time. He is quite sick. Besides, I am sure that he left most of his plans in the classroom." Linda was about to say that she didn't see any plans but hesitated because she did not want to get the teacher into trouble.

The principal went on to explain that the classroom teacher felt that students should be allowed to explore issues for themselves and develop their own ideas and concepts. While the principal had some reservations about this approach, she felt it was worth a try for at least for the first few weeks. She and the teacher had planned to review the whole process at the end of the October but didn't know if that would be possible now because of the teacher's sickness. Since the end of the month was three weeks away, Linda asked if she was going to be subbing for that long. The principal replied that she didn't know for sure since she didn't know the extent of the problem. "We've had three or four subs in for that teacher in the past month," she stated. "They were fine but I had excellent reports about you the times you worked her and so I asked for you in particular this time."

Over the weekend Linda pulled together units she had prepared for other Grade 7 classes and even went out to a local office supply store to photocopy some handouts and worksheets for Monday. A couple of the worksheets involved a series of math, science, and language arts activities to help her gauge where the students were in the Grade 7 material. She also planned to teach a unit in science and use a small experiment that had worked well in other classes.

After an initial hesitation, most of the students started completing the worksheets. A few complained that they were working on their own projects and their teacher had told them they could continue. Linda responded that they would talk about the projects when the worksheets were completed. The students grumbled but started. "Are these for marks," one of them demanded.

"No, just for me to see how you are doing," Linda responded.

"Then they don't really count," the student responded somewhat snidely.

"That's right," said Linda. "There just to help me see where I should start teaching."

After the students had completed their worksheets Linda started to talk to them about the projects they had been doing. "Our teacher lets us work on what we're interested in," indignantly stated the student who had raised the issue.

"Yes, but what were you supposed to be doing?" asked Linda. "Do you have any outlines or plans for these projects?"

"Sure we do," responded the student.

"Great," said Linda. "Perhaps you could all get your outlines organized a bit and give them to me before noon."

While the students were working on their outlines, Linda had a quick look at their worksheets. She was concerned to find that the students did not understand many of the concepts they should have covered in September. Actually, they seemed to know a few concepts quite well but others not at all. Her thoughts about this were interrupted by arguments in a couple of the groups who presumably had been working on projects about exactly what they were supposed to be doing.

Over the lunch break Linda had a quick look at the project outlines. A few groups were working on interesting topics, but most of the projects didn't seem to have any particular focus. Indeed, in a couple of cases they didn't have anything to do with the Grade 7 curriculum. Three or four groups had been looking at a series of topics that had no obvious connection. Linda didn't understand what this was all about and wasn't sure how to proceed.

Her whole concern was sent in an entirely new direction right after lunch. One of the students at the back of the class piped up with, "You know, our teacher went crazy." This sparked an argument in the class with some of the students saying that their teacher just got a bit upset sometimes and others saying that they should not be talking about him at all.

Linda was thrown for a loop by this information, but said that she was sure the teacher would be better soon and that they should get on with their class. She immediately started on her science unit by putting up a transparency with an overview of the unit. She was surprised to see the students just sitting there without making any effort to take notes. When she mentioned that they might want to write some of the concepts down, several students responded that this was not the way their teacher did it and that he had told them they would not have any tests so there was no need to write down anything.

"Well, I don't know what your teacher said," Linda responded. "I may be here for a few days and I plan to have a quiz on Friday about what we cover in class. I also would like to talk to each of your groups about their projects." This produced an elaborate scene of students wearily and noisily getting out their notebooks. A few muttered about this not being what their teacher wanted them to do.

After classes Linda went directly to the principal's office. The principal confirmed the classroom teacher was having some difficulties with depression and that it was not clear when he would be back. The principal also acknowledged that the class had lacked a bit of direction because of the number of subs and because she had not wanted to confront the teacher about his approach.

## Discussion Questions

1. What are some of the reasons that the classroom teacher might have used his approach to teaching?
2. What are some of the advantages and disadvantages of the teacher's approach?
3. What do you think Linda should do now?

## CASE 12-4: WHICH WAY WILL THE BALLOONS GO?

The students in Aaron's class had been working on the nature of air in their science unit. He had been teaching this unit for about two weeks and was almost ready to move on to something else. The students had learned about the composition of air, the concept of atmosphere, and had been introduced to the nature of and reasons for wind. One day they had built kites and flown them in the schoolyard. Another day they had performed some experiments to show the effects of air pressure. Most of the students predicted that water would run out of a glass when it was inverted in a pan of water. They were surprised to find that most of the water stayed in the glass in a column above the surface of the water in the tray. Aaron went on from there to introduce the concept of air pressure and its effects on the world around them.

As one of the concluding activities for his unit, he planned to cover convection currents and their role in weather and cloud formation as well as the movement of air within the room. He was explaining that warm air rises while cooler air sinks when he used the concept of lighter air instead of warmer air. One of his students put up her hand and asked, "How can air be lighter or heavier. Air just floats; it doesn't have any weight."

Aaron tried to explain that air has mass and as a result, also has weight, the same as any other material on earth. He mentioned the idea of air pressure again to reinforce the idea of weight, but the students seemed to be having difficulty with the idea of air having weight. He thought about a demonstration he could do to help the students understand and after class set up an apparatus to be used the next day. He filled one balloon with ordinary air and left the other deflated. He attached one of the balloons to each end of a meter stick and put a string in the middle. He left the apparatus overnight so that there would be no concern about the temperature of the air in the blown up balloon being any different from room temperature.

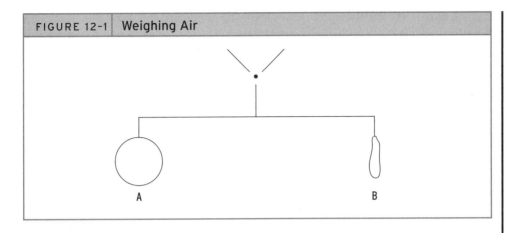

FIGURE 12-1 | Weighing Air

A          B

The next day he held the apparatus up and asked the students what would happen when he let the ruler go and held it only by the string in the centre. Would Balloon A sink or rise? Would Balloon B sink or rise? Would the ruler stay horizontal? A few students thought A would sink while a few others thought B would sink. Some students thought the ruler would stay level. The majority of students admitted that they had no idea. Even when he asked the students who thought they knew the answer to explain their reasoning, he found that they could not say much more than they just felt their answer was correct. Then he released the ruler and held the apparatus only by the central string.

## Discussion Questions

1. Why were the students having so much trouble with the concept of air having mass or weight?
2. What did Aaron hope would happen with his demonstration?
3. What do you think happened to the balloons in the demonstration? Try the experiment.

## CASE 12-5: NO CRITICISM ALLOWED

The phone rang in Rajinder Dhillon's classroom during the middle of the first period. Rajinder's stomach knotted with anxiety. The principal had insisted that no calls be put through to teachers during class periods unless there was an emergency. Rajinder was concerned that his wife or one of his three children had been hurt. He was planning the steps he would need to cover his class and deal with the emergency as he picked up the phone.

"Good morning, Rajinder," said the principal. "Can you come down to my office during the lunch break?"

"Well I had hoped to get some worksheets run off for one of my afternoon classes. Can it wait until after school?"

"One of the parents is complaining a bit about something you covered in your class. We need to talk about it as soon as possible," responded the principal.

The phone call left Rajinder badly shaken; he completed the rest of his morning's classes on automatic pilot. He always found it amazing that he could continue to teach as if nothing were the matter while his mind and emotions were swirling with anxiety. The walk to the principal's office seemed to be down a long corridor that took only seconds to cover. The look of concern that the school secretary gave him when he entered the office only increased his discomfort.

"Come in Rajinder," said the principal. "I'm sorry to have to interrupt your lunch period but this issue is getting out of hand and we have to deal with it right away. I have had phone calls from both the radio and TV stations. The school superintendent also let me know that she wants the issue to go away now."

"What is going on?" asked Rajinder. "I thought there was just some complaint from a parent. We all get those from time to time."

"This is more than the usual complaint. The parent claimed that you have been teaching things against her religion in your class and she thinks this is totally inappropriate and unprofessional. It seems she also has gone to the media with her complaint."

"I haven't been teaching anything about religions," declared Rajinder. "And if I were, I certainly know enough not to speak negatively about anyone's religion in today's climate."

"Well, something definitely has happened and I need to get the story straight. I don't want this issue to get all over the news and have a whole bunch of other parents calling me. Outline for me what you have been doing and where anyone might have got the idea that you were teaching anything about religion."

Rajinder explained that his Grade 12 Social Studies class had been working on the development and influence of different social service institutions in Europe. He had taught about schools, hospitals, and social services agencies. He had mentioned that the church had a large role in setting these up but had placed all of the emphasis on the role and importance of these institutions. He then had allowed the students to work in groups to further their understanding of other agencies that were of interest to them. Some had picked The Red Cross or St. John's Ambulance. A few had been interested in the development of organizations like the YMCA and the YWCA. Each group then made a 15-minute presentation to the class.

Two groups had explored topics that might be considered a bit controversial. One had looked at the Suffragettes Movement while the other had been interested in a relatively small religious group that had immigrated to Canada. Both presentations had mentioned the opposition of some of the churches to these groups. Rajinder hadn't thought much about their presentations since what they said was completely true and besides, their comments had been made as historical fact rather than with any real sense of criticism, certainly not any sense of criticism of present day churches.

"I guess I'll just have to apologize and hope that satisfies everyone," said the principal with a sigh.

Rajinder was stunned that even a modest effort to allow students to explore issues on their own could lead to such a storm. "What would happen if I really allowed them to question things?" he wondered.

## Discussion Questions

1. Do you think Rajinder was justified in allowing the students to explore the roles of social agencies on their own?
2. Was the parent justified in complaining?
3. Do you feel that the principal's decision to apologize was appropriate?
4. What do teachers and parents often assume will happen when they say they support the concept of students developing concepts for themselves?

# Differentiated Instruction, Group/Cooperative Learning, and Brain-Based Approaches

The existence of homogeneous classrooms is an underlying assumption of many books and discussions of teaching practices. The presenters fail to recognize or ignore the fact that Grade 5 or Grade 9 or Grade 12 classes do not exist. These designations serve for administrative efficiency only; they do not reflect the experience of the classroom teacher.

| Exercise 13-1 | **Which Grade?** |
| --- | --- |
| Ask teachers for copies of student work from their classrooms. Post the material on a bulletin board and then | rate the grade level of the students in terms of their actual performance. |

- The above exercise reflects differences in performance but there are many other factors that differentiate students.
  - Some of these, such as culture, interests, and preferred learning styles, have been discussed already in Chapter Eight.

■ Teacher practices must reflect the varied nature of the classroom if all of the students are to obtain the maximum benefit from their school experience.

# DIFFERENTIATED INSTRUCTION

Differentiated Instruction (Tomlinson, 1995) is a teaching strategy that attempts to deal with the high levels of diversity in a typical classroom.

## Criteria of Differentiated Instruction

■ Differentiated Instruction is proactive.
  ■ Teachers recognize that they will have individual differences in their class and plan for this.
■ Differentiated Instruction concentrates on the interests and needs of individual students.
■ Different approaches to all aspects of the instructional process are used rather than more or less of a single activity.
■ Individual, group, and whole class activities are combined to give a feeling of flow or movement.

## Conditions That Do Not Reflect Differentiated Instruction

■ Differentiated Instruction does not imply individualized instruction.
  ■ Individualized Instruction quickly leads to chaos and teacher burnout.
■ Students are not grouped by ability or other characteristic for any length of time.
  ■ Students might be in one group for an activity, then in another or working by themselves.
  ■ The dangers of homogeneous grouping of students are discussed later in this chapter.
■ Students are not receiving more or less of the same material.
  ■ It is not a matter of asking the gifted students more advanced questions and leaving the simple knowledge questions for those who are having more difficulty with the class material.

## General Rules

■ All the general rules of good teaching such as having clear objectives and proper lesson planning apply to Differentiated Instruction.
■ All students must be involved in lessons and given opportunities to construct meaning from their experiences.
■ As in other approaches, there should be avenues for students to explore topics in their own way and according to their own interests.

## Managing The Differentiated Classroom

- All of the learning environment and classroom management concepts and strategies discussed in Chapters 15 and 16 apply to the Differentiated classroom.
- Group activities in Differentiated Instruction follow the same guidelines as discussed below under Group/Cooperative Learning.
- Home-based whole class activities are required at the beginning and end of class.
  - Whole class sessions are required at the beginning and end of class to introduce class objectives and to reinforce learning.
  - Home-based sessions often are needed to hand out supplies and to clean up.

## Instructional Strategies

- Differentiated Instruction uses a broad variety of instructional strategies.
  - Examples of strategies include contracts, either individual or group projects, learning centres, and the use of mentors.
  - The strategy employed depends on the needs of particular students and the nature of the concepts being taught.
- Differentiated Instruction encourages *compacting*, or having teachers state clearly the essential concepts that have to be covered, and then evaluating students as to how they understand these concepts.
  - This approach allows students who already know the concepts to move on, and indicates to other students what they have to know to complete a unit or topic satisfactorily.
- Differentiated Instruction encourages teachers to look at multiple approaches to assessment including the possibilities of different approaches and criteria for different students.
  - Particular emphasis is placed on grading students on their ability to reach their own goals rather than in competition to other students.

## GROUP/COOPERATIVE LEARNING

## Arguments For Individual vs. Group Activities

- Debating the pros and cons of individual versus group activities can help to highlight the strengths and weaknesses of both positions.
- It is important to get beyond 'it's the real world' and 'well, we all have to work together' bumper stickers.
- Either an individual or a group approach tends to be the flavour of the day.
  - Positions often are accompanied by buzzwords that ignore all kinds of political, economic, and historical factors.

## Balance In Teaching

- The teacher is at the pivotal point among hundreds of different concepts about the nature of the world and the best way to help young people prepare for future life while meeting present needs. The balance point is always intuitive rather than rational.

## Practices Used To Group Students

### Grouping Across the School or School District

- The grouping of students according to various characteristics such as ability or interests into different classes or schools is called **streaming**.
- Districts and schools have to be very careful that streaming does not lead to schools and classes that have fewer resources, are labeled as having lower standards than others, or reflect a particular economic or cultural bias.
- On the other hand, this grouping may be the best way to provide specialized programs that meet student requirements and reflect the economic realities of later work life.

### Grouping Within A Class

- Homogeneous ability grouping sometimes is necessary to meet individual needs.
  - The teacher needs to provide situations where all individuals can succeed.
  - Class, district, and provincial exams limit a teacher's ability to do this as there is one standard for all.
  - Homogeneous ability grouping should be limited to specific activities and not be a continuous condition of the class.
- Heterogeneous ability groupings are best for increasing the level of questioning among students and helping students come to understand that all people have differing abilities.
  - The teacher needs to ensure that all students participate, and that no students are being harassed.
  - Students should not be involved in roles that place stress on them — group discipline, teaching, etc. These are the tasks teachers are paid to do.
  - More advanced students are not 'teacher's little helpers'.

### Age Grouping

- Social grading mandates that students be kept with their age peers. The result is still a broad range of abilities in the class.
- A few school districts are experimenting with more of a family approach, where students stay with the same teachers for a number of years and each class reflects a range of ages.
  - These approaches represent aspects of a return to the one-room school.

## Gender Balance

- Usually it is better to have all one sex in a group or a balance of females and males.

## Self-Chosen Groups

- Allowing students to choose their own group often leads to difficulties.
  - Some students have difficulty finding a group.
  - There is a broad range of abilities and behaviours in groups.
- On the other hand, sometimes students have situations and interests that support their forming a group of their own.

## Flexible Arrangements

- Most teachers use some type of flexible arrangement.
  - Students move from one type of grouping to another depending on their needs.

# Group Activities

## Active Games

- The group has to work together to accomplish some goal.
  - There needs to be a balance in the teams with everyone participating.
  - Games can be arranged so that higher levels of participation result in higher scores.
- Groups in older classes can develop their own games and then play those from other groups.
- CAUTION: A lot of the cooperative education material uses the concept of teams competing. This can defeat the purpose for me. Perhaps the problem is the teacher's fear of not being able to motivate students without some type of competition. Learning is its own reward; students who see an opportunity to succeed in learning will be motivated.

## Research Projects

- Research projects require students to develop reports on particular topics.
- The topic needs to be carefully defined.
- Students probably will need the project to be developed in stages with the teacher checking each stage.
  - Vision, goal(s), plan, literature review, practical experiences, presentation, evaluation, etc., are examples of stages.
  - Usually it is best to have a time limit for each day or phase of a project, especially for younger students.

- It also may be necessary to have students show who is doing what as part of the plan.
- The teacher needs to ensure that everyone is participating.
- There usually needs to be a variety of projects so resources are not exhausted.
- Projects need to be cleared with other teachers and resource people if it is expected that they will be involved.

## Expert Systems

- Expert systems are similar to research projects except that presentations are made to the whole class.
  - Other students may or may not be responsible for material covered in terms of exams or other forms of evaluation.

## Jigsaw Classroom

- A jigsaw approach is similar to the use of expert systems, except that each group is given an aspect of a particular area for class presentation.
- The whole picture emerges when all presentations made.
- Teachers may need to summarize and integrate.
- A jigsaw approach also can be used within the group when each member of group is made responsible for a particular area.

## Discussion Groups

- Discussion groups are useful for exploring subjective or affective issues.
- Discussion groups also are useful for difficult topics if students are able to arrive at a deeper understanding.
- Discussion groups give a broader view of the topic and are good for examining issues in different contexts.
- Any group discussions require a specific focus and time limit.

## Evaluation

- One approach to the evaluation of group projects involves having one evaluation for the whole group.
  - In this case, it may be necessary to find a way of giving members an opportunity to say that someone didn't participate, and prorating that person's mark if this is found to be true.
- Other approaches include interviews of individual members, a jigsaw format for the project, or a quiz written by each student.

# BRAIN-BASED APPROACHES

While many methods of teaching claim to be brain-based, only a few have come to be associated with the approach. Some of these approaches are founded on knowledge about the brain, while others use bits of brain research to support a particular educational theory. Even in the best of cases, the use of brain research to support approaches to education needs to be viewed with caution.

- All brain-based approaches emphasize the growing importance of brain research in education.
- Tony Buzan, Renate and Geoffrey Caine, Leslie Hart, and Eric Jensen probably are the best respected and recognized names in the area.
  - Gardner's concept of Multiple Intelligences sometimes also is considered as part of brain-based learning.
- Leslie Hart (1983) developed the Proster Theory to emphasize the brain's tendency to detect and learn patterns as opposed to a linear string of information.
  - Proster is a compression of the two words program and structure.
- Tony Buzan, in a series of ten programs for BBC television in 1974, brought together several approaches to learning that helped students do a number of academic tasks more efficiently and effectively. The concepts included improved methods of reading and writing, information about memory and memory techniques, and mind maps.
- Books such as Don Campbell's *The Mozart Effect* have alerted educators to the importance of auditory and other stimulation to brain function. This is true even though there is some debate as to the actual nature and extent of this role.
- Eric Jensen probably has had the most influential voice in integrating and explaining brain-based learning principles to the classroom teacher.
- Caine and Caine outlined their 12 principles of brain-based learning in 1998; they modify them slightly on their 2001 web site. These principles, as available on their web site, are:

  1. The brain is a living, complex dynamic system.
  2. The brain/mind is social.
  3. The search for meaning is innate.
  4. The search for meaning occurs through patterning.
  5. Emotions are critical to patterning.
  6. The brain processes parts and wholes simultaneously.
  7. Learning involves both focused attention and peripheral perception.
  8. Learning always involves conscious and unconscious processes.
  9. Memory is organized in both a spatial and a rote manner.
  10. Learning is developmental.
  11. Complex learning is increased by challenge and limited by threat or fear.
  12. Every brain is unique.

## CASE 13-1: VIEW FROM THE HEIGHTS

City Heights School was built in the late 1800s on a 'mountain' near the principal residential area of the small town and now overlooks the surrounding mid-sized urban area. Some in the community say the old school should be closed and the land sold for condominium development. Proceeds from the sale of the school property could be used to build a more modern school, with funds left over for other projects. Many families have a long connection with the school however — some families have attended the school for five generations. These families loudly support the school and strongly resist any moves to close it.

The view from the school is spectacular. Mind you, some might smile a bit at the idea of the school being on a mountain, but it certainly is the highest point of land around. The history of the community can be seen from the school parking lot. In one direction there are the older homes of long-time residents, beautiful older buildings with large lots and big shade trees. Some of the homes look a bit run-down but most are well maintained and speak of both wealth and stability.

Views in two other directions consist of recent housing developments. Some of the new homes obviously are very expensive while others are more modest. In both cases there is a feeling of newness and change. Names on the small stores in these neighbourhoods indicate the variety of cultural backgrounds of the people living in the surrounding communities.

Sprawling, flat-roofed industrial buildings along with a few high smokestacks dominate the final direction. While some might find this landscape not as attractive as the other three, it is this area that produces the work and income that support the whole city. Houses can be seen sprinkled among the factories. There is an enormous variation in the architecture and level of upkeep of these homes. Some families prefer to live in the industrial area while others use the less expensive homes here as stepping-stones to the new residential developments.

Antonio Frattaroli was a student at City Heights many years ago. At the time his family lived in the industrial area although they moved to a new home in one of the suburbs after Antonio left for university. Antonio finished his Education program twelve years ago and taught in three schools since then. He saw the job of principal at City Heights advertised in a teachers' magazine, applied, and was hired immediately. He was a bit uneasy about coming back to a school where he had been a student, but both he and his wife thought his former hometown would be an excellent place to raise their young family.

Four months into his new job, Antonio realized that City Heights now was not the City Heights he remembered. Over the past few years, teachers at the school tried to cope with the change by taking a number of organized and ad hoc approaches to dealing with the variety of student backgrounds and needs. Unfortunately these approaches had lacked a unifying philosophy. The result was confusion in both the school and the community and a growing number of complaints. Antonio used his experience in other schools as well as some of the material he had been reading about structuring school programs to best meet the needs of all students in an attempt to articulate City Heights' new educational direction for parents, teachers, and students.

Last Friday he had a very difficult meeting with a delegation from some of the community leaders, the people who had been such strong supporters of keeping the school open. They felt City Heights had drifted far from the type of school they remembered and valued; they also pointed out several times that Antonio had done very well by the way schools were 'supposed' to be. This delegation wanted Antonio to give more structure to the classroom and to provide parents with a better understanding of what to expect on a day-to-day basis. They felt teachers should be able to give parents an outline of what was going to be taught during the week and what homework could be expected. They used all of the arguments about the importance of being able to read and write correctly, the existence of provincial exams, the necessity of students learning good work habits, etc. Antonio told the group he appreciated their input and agreed with most of their concerns. He told them he would be willing to give a complete report on the school's direction to any interested parent or person in the community at the next parent-teacher meeting in three weeks. The delegation agreed to this although they emphasized that they were expecting some answers and not just a bunch of education jargon.

After the meeting Antonio was left wondering how he could demonstrate some of the issues confronted by teachers each day so that more people in the community would understand the issues involved in planning a program. One idea that came to mind involved calculating the average number of students that were away from classes each day for a variety of reasons. He would need many more points, however, to demonstrate why the one-size-fits-all approach to the classroom would not work very well in today's school.

## Discussion Questions

1.  What types of issues must Antonio deal with as he plans future directions for the school?
2.  What are some of the factors related to the students' needs that teachers must consider in any classroom on any given day in the school?
3.  What ways could Antonio use to demonstrate these factors to community leaders and parents?
4.  What different types of approaches to teaching might he develop to try and meet student needs?

## CASE 13-2: TEACHER CRISIS

Ms. Gunderson is at the end of her 15th year of teaching. She is preparing for her yearly evaluation and discussion of next year's teaching assignments with her principal, and is using this meeting to review her career. Ms. Gunderson was born in 1967 and grew up in a small town in the interior of British Columbia. She had a stable family background that included a large extended family, regular attendance at church, and many community social events. Her father worked in logging while her mother worked on a part-time basis in a local clothing store. Neither of her parents had been to university and both viewed education in a very instrumental way: if it helped find or keep work, it was good. Her family was loving but did not discuss issues at a very emotional level.

Ms. Gunderson always did well in her classes and found school to be a place of refuge. She studied her notes carefully, wrote her papers in a diligent manner, and behaved well in class. Positive comments were the norm on her report card.

A wedding in her church and two children followed graduation from the Faculty of Education at a nearby university. She was a Teacher-on-Call (TOC) for four years but has been on a full-time contract teaching Grade 10 literature in a nearby town for the past 11 years. Life has been very busy with the demands of work, home, and family. Two years ago her father died suddenly. She was completely unprepared for the tremendous feelings of loss she experienced. Her father had always been a stoic person, with her mother being the one who dealt with most of the social or emotional issues in the family.

Ms. Gunderson's teaching career has not been what she expected. There are rewards of course, but many students do not respond to her classes; indeed, some students are even hostile. She has tried everything to make the students excited about the literature curriculum, but most just do the minimum and sit behind their books. In the last five years there have been more and more behavioural problems, and the range of student abilities seems to be expanding. Ms. Gunderson is considering asking for a leave for the next year or even changing careers. Her job pays a good salary and has excellent benefits though, and she thinks that somehow there might be an answer to her crisis.

## Discussion Questions

1.  Do Ms. Gunderson's experiences correspond to those of most of her students?
2.  What kind or kinds of classrooms would Ms. Gunderson have done well in as a student?
3.  What types of changes may she need to make in her approaches to teaching?

## CASE 13-3:  YOU'RE NOT IN OUR GROUP

Andrew Urbanski moved from a large city to a small town to be able to buy a home that he and his wife would enjoy and to raise his family. He found a job easily at the local high school, although the principal warned him that the views and behaviours of students might be different from what he had experienced in a big city. Andrew said that he was sure this was true and that it probably would be a good thing.

Andrew was a strong believer in the use of group activities to accomplish learning objectives. At first, the students in his class were hesitant about working together. They gave the usual objections such as that somebody might not work in the group, or that it was not fair for everyone to get the same mark. Andrew agreed that these were legitimate issues but that group activities would only be a part of the class mark. Besides, it had been his experience that most students worked well in groups.

He allowed the students to choose their own groups for the first few activities. Most of the students formed the same groups each time, although there was some movement with four or five individuals that seemed to be having trouble deciding on a group. Most of the groups worked together quite well, although there were a few students who tended to do far more talking about outside activities than working.

"For this activity I am going to assign you to groups," stated Andrew one Wednesday morning. The whole room became silent as they absorbed this and waited for the names of their groups.

"Can I work with my usual group instead?" asked one student.

"Not this time," Andrew responded. "I think you would benefit from an opportunity to work with other people."

There were mutters from other students. Some made exaggerated and groaning motions as they moved to another place in the classroom. Others sat and waited for their group to come to them. In a couple of cases this turned into a real power struggle and Andrew had to intervene to tell the students where the group was meeting. Gradually the groups got down to work and it seemed like the new arrangement was going to work better than the self-chosen groups. A couple of the more active students were out of their seats quite a bit but this was normal for them. He was a little bit concerned that Cheri, a shy and thoughtful student, was sitting on the outside of her group. He asked the group to move their chairs so Cheri could be in the circle.

The next morning Andrew noticed that Cheri was missing from her group. When he asked the group, they responded, "I guess she is just sick or something." He noticed that there seemed to be a little smirk on some of the members of the group however, and wondered what was going on. Cheri didn't show up on Friday either, and Andrew decided that he would phone her home if she wasn't back by Monday. Students being sick or away always was a problem, but in this case Cheri would miss the whole group activity if she was not back soon.

On Monday evening Andrew phoned Cheri's home. Her father answered and Andrew asked about Cheri. "Well, it's kind of embarrassing Mr. Urbanski," responded Cheri's father. "She said she was sick on Thursday but I didn't think there was too much wrong with her. I ask if she wanted to go to the doctor but she said it was just the flu and she would be better by the weekend. When I got back from work today though, I found out that she still hadn't gone to school. I didn't accept the sick excuse and asked her what was going on."

"What did she say?" asked Andrew.

"Well, this is the embarrassing part," responded the father. "It seems that a couple of the kids in that group you put her in have been teasing her a bit."

Andrew was shocked by this information. He hadn't noticed any teasing and would have put an end to it as soon as he had noticed anything. He explained this to Cheri's father and asked what kinds of teasing behaviours were involved.

"Actually it really is more than teasing," responded the father who now seemed to be getting angry. "It seems that a couple of members of her group told her that they didn't want her in their group and that she should stay away. Apparently one of them even phoned later in the day and called Cheri a bunch of names and told her that she was stupid and they didn't want to have to be with her. I don't know what's going on but actually it's got me pretty upset."

## Discussion Questions

1. What were the advantages and disadvantages of using the self-chosen groups?
2. How might Andrew have reduced the students' concerns about marks while working in groups?
3. What steps should Andrew have taken before he assigned students to groups?
4. What do you think he should do now?

## CASE 13-4: A SERIOUS ILLNESS

Gregory Shechtman had been one of those students teachers love to have in their classes. There were frequent comments in the staff room about Gregory's academic ability and his leadership roles in the classes. Gregory always was receiving one or more certificates at Awards Night, and often was the student chosen to introduce guest speakers or to make some short speech at assemblies.

In April of last year, Gregory was diagnosed with a very serious illness. His teacher and the principal agreed that he already had met the learning objectives for the year or could be expected to do so quickly when he recovered, so they passed him to the next grade. Unfortunately, Gregory and his family learned in September of this year that Gregory probably was not going to recover and most likely had less than a year to live.

Gregory's mother approached the principal of the school to ask that Gregory be allowed to return to the school, recognizing that he would have to be away from time to time for treatment and that eventually he would be unable to continue. She wanted Gregory's life to be as normal as possible considering the circumstances and for him to be with his peers.

The principal approached Jodee Yudkin, the teacher of the grade Gregory would have been in normally, and discussed the situation with her. Jodee was apprehensive but also felt a great deal of empathy for Gregory and agreed to have him in her class. She explained to the class that Gregory was coming back and asked them to help Gregory catch up on any work he had missed. She also told the class that they should be prepared for the fact that Gregory's sickness may have changed him somewhat. This did not seem to be a concern to any of the students; indeed, they all seemed anxious to have Gregory back and a few students even argued over where he should sit.

Neither Jodee nor the class was prepared for the changes in Gregory. The physical differences were the first thing that the students noticed. All activity and conversation stopped and everyone stared at the bald, pale child. Jodee recovered almost immediately and hurried over the welcome Gregory to the class. By the time she had finished some of the students had come up to greet Gregory. He was shown his seat in the class and more students smiled at him; someone started a round of applause and the others joined in.

After everyone had settled down, Jodee did a review of the material they had been covering and gave the students a couple of worksheets to do. This really was not a break from routine as her usual procedure was to cover some new material and then give the students a series of exercises or some activity to do. She went to Gregory's desk to help him but soon found that she would have to do quite a bit of remedial work with Gregory. She was going to have to run one class for Gregory and one class for the rest of the students until she could get him up to the level of the class. Over the next week she found this split approach very draining. She also noticed that Gregory would get restless when she was teaching the rest of the class and she often had to have the other students working longer on exercises or worksheets than she would have preferred. Progress was being made though, and now she sometimes could teach a topic so that everyone could participate. It looked like she might be able to get back to a regular classroom routine soon. These expectations were dashed when she learned that Gregory would have to be away for a week while he took some more treatments.

When Gregory came back on the next Wednesday, it was obvious that the treatments had drained him both physically and mentally. Jodee found that he tired quickly and that he could not catch up on all the topics they had covered in the time he had been away while still learning new material. Some other approach was needed.

## Discussion Questions

1.  What are some of the assumptions that underlie Jodee's present approach to teaching?
2.  What do you think of Jodee's decision to run one class for Gregory and another for the rest of the students?
3.  What steps might Jodee take to help Gregory when he came back the second time?
4.  Who else in the class might benefit from the steps you developed in #3?

## REFERENCES

### Brain-Based Learning

### Tony Buzan

Any of Tony Buzan's books such as:
Buzan, T. (1982). *Use your head*. London: BBC Books.

Tony Buzan Web Site: http://www.mind-map.com

### Renate and Geoffrey Caine

Caine, R. & Caine, G. (1998). Building a bridge between neurosciences and education: Cautions and possibilities. *NASSP Bulletin*, *82*(598), 1-6.

Renate Nummela Caine & Geoffrey Caine Web Site: http://www.cainelearning.com

### Leslie Hart

Hart, L.A. (1983). *Human brain and human learning*. New York: Longman Inc.

### Eric Jensen

Jensen, E. (1996). *Brain-based learning*. Del Mar, CA: Turning Point Publishing.

Jensen Learning Centre: http://www.jlcbrain.com

### Mozart Effect

Campbell, D. (1997). The Mozart Effect: Tapping the power of music to heal the body, strengthen the mind, and unlock the creative spirit. New York: Avon Books.

Mozart Effect Web Site: http://www.mozarteffect.com

### Differentiated Instruction

Tomlinson, C.A. (1995). *How to differentiate instruction in mixed-ability classrooms*. Alexandria, VA: Association for Supervision and Curriculum Development.

# chapter fourteen

# Emotions, Stress, and Motivation

## EMOTIONS

### Nature

- Emotions are biological responses to a perceived internal or external environment.
- Emotions have both genetic and environmental influences.

### Steam Engine Model of Emotions

- The steam engine model claims emotional pressure builds up and has to be released.
  - The model is perhaps useful as a metaphor in some cases, since the effects of emotional states do accumulate.
- The steam engine model of emotions has little validity today, but it is one that many people implicitly believe.

### Chemicals and the Brain

- Various hormones and other chemicals accompany emotions.

- Emotional feelings are registered in particular areas of our brain as covered in Chapter Four.
- The cerebral cortex interprets the meaning of these feelings based on perceptions, past experience, and usual thought patterns.
- It is not clear whether hormones produce feelings, or whether they are the result of particular thought patterns resulting from an internal or external perception.

## Genetic and Environmental Influences

- As is the case with almost every aspect of human nature, our emotional responses to situations are influenced by both genetic and environmental conditions.
- Genetic influences on psychological states such as our temperament were discussed in Chapter Three.
- Environmental influences such as the presence or absence of a trusted adult, our perception of our ability to control the situation, and social conditioning also influence our emotional reactions.

## Emotions as Information

- Emotions are felt much more intensely than thoughts because they involve the whole body.
  - As a consequence, young people in particular may pay much more attention to how they are feeling than to any intellectual information.
- On the other hand, because emotions are not thoughts, we may fail to recognize the very valuable information emotions carry.
- We need an appropriate vocabulary to understand information from emotions.
  - Sometimes people's emotional vocabularies are very limited and so they can interrupt and explain their feelings in only very imprecise ways.

## Authentic and Inauthentic Emotions

- Authentic emotions are the result of our moment-to-moment experience.
- Inauthentic emotions are the result of deliberately induced mental states.
  - Inauthentic emotional states are induced by choosing inappropriate external stimulation such as drugs, and deliberate or compulsive thinking patterns.
  - Inauthentic emotions separate us from the ability to experience authentic emotions.

## Emotions and Negative Feeling States

- While all authentic emotions are valid, some lead to feeling states that are uncomfortable and disruptive to the individual and to society.
- Persistent anchoring in negative feeling states without taking positive action results in diminished life satisfaction, and may also lead to very destructive behaviours.

## Emotions and Behaviour

- Sometimes emotional states are used as an excuse for behaviour.
  - "I hit that person because he or she ticked me off."
- Students need help in giving up this almost external view of control of their behaviour and accepting more responsibility for what they do.
- As teachers, we need a good concept of our own boundaries so that we may tell people we accept their right to their emotions, but will not accept certain behaviours directed toward others or us.
- We can help our students practise attention and understanding versus impulsive action.
- We also can help our students learn skillful ways of dealing with emotional states.
  - This concept is discussed in more detail under the section on stress later in this chapter.

## Emotions and Long Term Health

- The relationship between emotional states and long-term health is not as clear as the popular media sometimes indicates.
  - There probably is no such a thing as a 'cancer personality' for instance.
- On the other hand, those experiencing emotional crises are more likely to have accidents and suffer from diseases than those who are not experiencing crises.
- In any case, our emotional states strongly influence our level of satisfaction with our lives.

## Emotional Quotient

- Various authors such as Daniel Goleman have promoted the concept of an emotional intelligence with its Emotional Quotient, or EQ, to balance the concept of Intelligence Quotient of IQ.
  - Different tests are available to measure EQ.
  - Anecdotal evidence is provided to support the idea that EQ is at least as important as IQ in determining success.
  - Sometimes the impression is left that EQ and IQ are mutually exclusive, although this is not the case.

## GLASSER'S CHOICE THEORY

William Glasser's Choice Theory of total behaviour is one of the more interesting approaches for teachers to consider in relation to emotions. A basic outline of his theory is introduced here and will be discussed again in terms of classroom management.

- All emotions are behaviours. The purpose of behaviours is to satisfy genetically determined needs.

- Our genetic needs are survival, belonging, power, fun, and freedom.

- Our behaviours are designed to meet our needs, not necessarily to please others.

- When we first experience a need, we put a 'picture' or perception in our mind of what or who meets that need.

- If we experience the need again, we check to see if the environment conforms to our 'picture' of how our need is satisfied. If the environment has the correct 'picture' we are satisfied; if not, we behave to try to correct the situation.

- Our total behaviour involves acting, thinking, feeling, and changes in physiology.

- All aspects of total behaviour should be considered as verbs in the sense that they all are actions including feeling. A more accurate way to describe depression, for instance, is depressing.

- Sometimes our behaviours are effective and we feel relief. However, those behaviours may not be helpful to society or healthy for us.

- Sometimes our behaviours are ineffective or anti-social and our crisis continues or even deepens.

- When our behaviours are not effective or are anti-social, the two aspects of behaviour that we have the most control over are first acting and then thinking. We have little control over feelings and even less over physiology.

- Changing our emotional world, then, is accomplished by changing our behaviour and our thinking patterns.

- Depth psychology may help us understand the basis of our emotional behaviours and the needs we are trying to meet with them, but the decision to change emoting behaviour is a conscious decision.

- Glasser's Choice Theory then sees emotions as one aspect of total behaviour designed to meet genetic needs. Feelings are chosen behaviours and can be changed by altering the way we act and think.

## YOUTH AND STRESS

### The Nature of Stress

- One view of stress claims that it is the body's non-specific response to any demand placed on it.
  - In this view, stress can be either positive or negative depending on the situation.

- A more common view of stress sees it as an adaptive response in which the body prepares to deal with a threatening situation, the 'fight or flight' response.
  - This event can be real or imagined.

- At least part of the confusion arises from combining the pleasant feelings of positive events with the stress we feel because of the change involved.

- While stress includes diseases, injuries, etc., this chapter is concerned with psychological stress of a negative nature.

## The Body's Reactions to Stress

- When confronted by a threatening situation our body prepares for survival by increasing heart rate and blood pressure, changing blood flow to make it more accessible to muscles, decreasing immune response, etc.
- From an educational point of view, one of the most important changes involves blood flow in the brain. As stress increases, blood flow increases in the brain stem and midbrain and decreases in the cortex.
  - Actions become more instinctive or deeply learned.
  - There is less possibility for learning or creativity.

## Signs of Stress in Youth

- In addition to increased difficulties in learning, some of the more common signs of stress in young people are listed below.
  - Performance declines.
  - The student exhibits age regression.
  - The student may experience a number of pains and illness including headache, indigestion, and colds.
  - Sleep patterns may be disrupted.
  - Accidents may occur more frequently.

## Stress Scale for Youth

- Stress scales are one tool researchers use to rate the relative stress effects of different events in our lives.
- Part of a stress scale for young people is given in Table 14–1 below.

| TABLE 14-1 | Stress Scale for Young People |
|---|---|
| **Life Event** | **Stress Value** |
| Death of Parent | 100 |
| Death of a Sibling | 95 |
| Divorce/Separation | 86 |
| Break Up With Boy/Girl Friend | 60 |
| Flunking a Grade in School | 45 |

| Exercise 14–1 | **Your Own Stress Scale** |
| --- | --- |

1. Brainstorm a list of stressful events that might happen to young people.

2. Have each person rate this list of events for their level of stress, with 100 being the most stressful event that can be imagined, and 0 being no stress.

3. Calculate an average value for each item for the whole class.

4. You now have a stress scale for your class. Perhaps you can check your ratings by having another class rate your list.

## Helping students Deal With Stress

- Classroom changes that help reduce student stress include providing variety in activities, promoting an atmosphere of acceptance, and reducing the costs of errors.

- Physical actions that reduce stress include stretching, controlled breathing activities, and attention to diet.

- Cognitive activities that reduce stress include discussions about stress, visualization routines, examination of underlying beliefs about the world, and stress mapping.

  - Albert Ellis' Rational Emotive Behavior Therapy (originally Rational Emotive Therapy) is a particularly good approach to examination of beliefs about the world.

| Exercise 14–2 | **Stress Mapping** |
| --- | --- |

A relatively simple approach to stress mapping involves a table with three columns. In the first column divide your waking hours into 30-minute blocks. Then at 30-minute intervals, note what you are doing in the second column. In the third column, rate your level of stress at that time from 1 to 5, with 1 being very low stress and 5 being a very high level. At the end of the week look for groupings of time and/or activities where you experienced low levels of stress and other groupings where you experienced high levels of stress. You now have a stress map for the week.

## FLOW

- Flow, a concept developed by Mihaly Csikszentmihalyi, has close ties to stress.

- Flow postulates that some tasks exceed our ability and we experience anxiety. In other cases our ability exceeds task difficulty and we experience boredom.

- When task difficulty and ability match, especially when both are high, flow is experienced.

- Under conditions of flow people experience deep enjoyment and happiness. They do not tire very easily and often do not experience the passage of time.

| Exercise 14–3 | Flow |
|---|---|

1. List any activities that cause you to experience a sense of flow. What are the conditions of this activity that lead to this feeling?

2. Pick another activity in which you definitely do not experience flow and examine what it would take to make that activity a flow experience.

## MOTIVATION

### The Concept of Motivation

- **Motivation** refers to an emotional and cognitive mental state that energizes, directs, and maintains behaviour.
- Motivation is one of those concepts that seems easy to understand at first, but that becomes very difficult to define in specific ways, or to implement with specific strategies leading to expected outcomes.
- Motivation is an internal state that students develop themselves. The best that teachers can do is to provide conditions that might be expected to help develop and maintain motivation.

### Intrinsic vs. Extrinsic Motivation

- **Extrinsic** motivation refers to the desire to increase or decrease behaviours based on the presence of rewards or punishments.
- **Intrinsic** motivation refers to the desire to increase or decrease behaviours for the sake of the behaviour itself.
- From a behaviourist perspective, all motivation is extrinsic.
  - Any appearance of intrinsic motivation is due to previous extrinsic motivation to perform the behaviour.
  - It would be impossible to prove that a person had never received a reward for doing a behaviour at some time in the past.
  - To avoid a continuous loop of argument, perhaps a better approach is to say that at this time people might engage in behaviours for intrinsic reasons.
- Another interesting debate over the years has been whether or not people are intrinsically motivated to engage in behaviours that are socially and personally beneficial.

### Humanistic Approaches to Motivation

- Humanistic perspectives of motivation stress concepts of choice, personal growth, and the positive qualities of humans.
- Whole person development and individual experience are very important.

- Human freedom and choice are critical. People have enormous potential for growth.
- Maslow's Hierarchy of Needs is one example of humanistic approaches to psychology. Stages of the Hierarchy are physiological, safety, belonging, esteem, and self-actualization needs.
  - Victor Frankl (discussed in Chapter Six) raised concerns about a strict interpretation of Maslow's Hierarchy. Frankl pointed out that he saw high levels of self-actualized behaviour under the extreme deprivation of concentration camps.
  - Later in life Maslow added Transpersonal Psychology as an additional component of his approach.
- Carl Rogers, with his client-centred therapy and unconditional approval concepts, was another important contributor to the humanistic approach to psychology.
- The role of humanistic concepts in developing classroom learning environments is discussed in Chapter 15.

## Cognitive Approaches to Motivation

- Cognitive approaches emphasize the ways people's thinking patterns influence their motivation.
- Attributions, efficacy, locus of control, and self-monitoring procedures all are part of the cognitive approach.
- Many of these concepts were discussed in Chapter Six.

## Expectancy-Valence Model of Motivation

- **Expectancy** refers to what is regarded as likely to happen. Expectancy does not equal want; we may have lots of wants we don't expect to satisfy.
- The expectancy or expectancy-valence approach to motivation says that motivation to pursue a goal is the product of expectations about success and the value placed on success.
- Expectancy Motivation = Perceived Probably of Success x Value I Place On Success (M = PV).
- Teachers can influence expectancy motivation by helping students change one or both of the factors involved.

## Achievement vs. Affiliation Motivation

- Those with high levels of achievement motivation are likely to behave in ways to meet goals, while those with high levels of affiliation motivation are more likely to engage in behaviours only because of the opportunity to be with friends.

## GOAL STRUCTURES

- **Learning** or **mastery** goals refer to the desire to gain competency in some activity.

- **Performance** goals refer to the desire to have some particular outcome or judgment by others.

- People with performance (outcome) goals become frustrated more easily than those with learning or mastery goals.

- People with performance goals lose motivation as soon as the goal is reached, while those with learning goals tend to continue in the activity.

- People who are sensitive to failure tend to set easy or unrealistic goals.

## CASE 14-1: IT JUST SEEMS TO BUILD UP

Alison Lau was parked in her usual place on the bench by the principal's office and it was only a bit after 10 on a Monday morning. "What on earth could she have done in 90 minutes?" sighed Ms. Meikle. "It's mornings like this that make me wish I was back with a Grade 5 class."

Ms. Meikle went past Alison to a desk covered in phone messages, letters from parents, and a seemingly endless series of memos and reports from this or that official; people who didn't seem to have anything else to do than demand answers to meaningless questions or outline suggestions for restructuring that anyone with a bit of real experience would recognize as nonsense. She had to remind herself at moments like this why she had chosen to become a principal. Alison represented one of the reasons for her choice.

Ms. Meikle recalled her previous meetings with Alison. Now in a Grade 6 class composed of students with a variety of cultural and language backgrounds, Alison had come to the school early in the Spring of last year. Right from the first she had a lot of difficulty with her academic work; initially this was attributed to her difficulty understanding English. Her teacher made every effort to help Alison, including asking another student to work with Alison. There was some improvement in performance but not enough to justify completely her moving on with her classmates. Ms. Meikle and the teacher decided to allow her to continue with her class and to monitor the situation closely in Grade 6.

The situation became much more difficult right from September. Alison's language skills had improved to the point where her understanding was on a par with many students in the class. On the other hand, her performance in many of her academic subjects remained well behind the rest of the class. Alison increasingly had become frustrated with her work and with school in general. She disrupted her teacher and lashed out both verbally and physically at other students. Saying she was unpopular was a big understatement.

After the last time Alison was in her office, Ms. Meikle had called the child's mother. The women was upset and embarrassed at being called by the principal, but also was relieved to have someone to talk to about Alison. "She often becomes very angry at home," the mother explained. "She hits her sister and storms out of the room whenever I try to talk to her. I don't know what to do."

Ms. Meikle and Alison's mother discussed these angry outbursts in more detail trying to determine their cause. "I don't know," stated the mother. "She just seems to have the anger build up in her and then she starts hitting and shouting."

As Ms. Meikle considered how she would deal with Alison this time, she began to wonder if there were not some basic concepts regarding emotions that she needed to consider. Certainly more needed to be done to help Alison than just trying to eliminate situations that might cause her to become angry; the world was full of such situations for everyone.

## Discussion Questions

1. What basic model of emotions were Ms. Meikle and Alison's mother using?
2. What are some of the essential weaknesses of this model?
3. What are some approaches Ms. Meikle might take to help Alison deal with an emotion that everyone experiences?

## CASE 14-2:  THE DEMON RUM

Royce had started to drink when he as a young child. Of course, all children tried to sneak a drink at parties when the adults weren't looking and some parents allow their children a drink of wine from time to time. The situation was different for Royce, however. He went to considerable effort to check glasses and bottles at parties for any leftover booze. Before long, the pursuit of alcohol became his main purpose at social events. His parents did not pay very much attention to his behaviour; the fact that he usually fell asleep after drinking helped to disguise his situation.

By the time Royce was a teenager he had a serious drinking problem. The ingenuity he displayed to obtain alcohol would have resulted in acclaim by his community if it had only been directed in more approved ways. Unfortunately, the result of all this effort was a steadily declining school performance and ever increasing difficulties with family, school, peers, and law enforcement officers. Royce was receiving community recognition all right, but also its condemnation.

Royce didn't care. School was stupid and his parents had a bunch of silly rules only meant to control him. They were all a bunch of losers. Besides, he felt a lot better when he drank; otherwise the world was a boring, depressing place.

## Discussion Questions

1. What role did alcohol serve in Royce's life?
2. Are all emotions valid?
3. What are the relationships between drugs and emotions?

## CASE 14-3:  DEPRESSION OR DEPRESSING?

First week in February, Third Year. Cullen felt like someone had dropped him in a dark hole and nobody was looking for him. Even his parents hadn't e-mailed him in a couple of weeks and they were supposed to care. He thought about calling them, but it just seemed to be too much effort and what could they do anyway?

Actually, everything had been pretty good until about a year ago. He always had a bit of a bleak outlook on life and maybe used this to get attention and to allow for outbursts of temper. His girlfriend seemed to take it all in stride and try to lift his spirits. He had no other close friends and only a few acquaintances from the odd pick-up game of basketball whenever he wandered over to the court. Last January, though, his girlfriend had come back from a holiday in the south with some friends and phoned to say she had found some-one else and didn't want to see Cullen any more.

Cullen couldn't believe that she would abandon him like that. He needed her and she had let him down. Maybe she just didn't understand. He phoned her late the next evening to explain how much he needed her, apologize for some of the rotten things he had said, and remind her of the good times they had listening to some of his CDs and talking about things in his room. She listened for a few minutes and then said she had to go. The next time he phoned, her roommate said that Cullen's former girlfriend did not want to speak to him again.

Cullen didn't know how he had got through the next year. Everything seemed so diffi-cult. After a few weeks nobody wanted to listen to his problems; some of his acquaintances were so unfeeling as to suggest that Cullen 'get over it'. While his parents were not so blunt, they did seem to be more likely to cut his discussion of difficulties short with requests that he get some help from medical services. A couple of months ago he had gone to see a doctor and been given a prescription for an antidepressant. Over the last two months he had started to feel a little better but still often lamented the loss of his girlfriend and the boring nature of his classes.

One of his professors noticed Cullen's lack of response in class and asked him if he was feeling all right. Cullen told him he was a bit depressed and the professor suggested he visit the counselling office at the university, pointing out that Cullen he could see someone for a few visits as part of his student fee. Cullen didn't expect too much but decided he had nothing to loose by giving counselling a try. Maybe it could fix what was wrong with him.

His first meeting with a counsellor started pretty much as he expected. The counsellor explained the nature of the university's counselling service and asked Cullen some general questions about his present activities. Cullen answered her questions in a brief manner and then started talking about his former girlfriend; he even threw in a bit about his childhood because he felt the counsellor would want to know. The counsellor cut this monologue short however, and went back to relationships and activities in Cullen's present life. Cullen explained that he was depressed because his girlfriend had left him.

"So the event that you are depressing about relates to the breakup of your relationship with your girlfriend over a year ago?" the counsellor asked.

Cullen noted the unusual use of 'depressing' but responded that the end of his relation-ship was what caused most of his depression.

"Is there any possibility that you can re-establish your relationship?" the counsellor asked.

"No," responded Cullen. "My girlfriend said she didn't want me calling her and besides, she is involved with someone else now."

"Then depressing is not going to help you with your former girlfriend," the counsellor stated. "Do you think it will help you establish any new relationships?"

Cullen was becoming angry at this point. "I don't know what you are talking about. You seem to be saying that I am deliberately causing my depression and saying that I am depressing. How is that going to help?"

The counsellor explained that Cullen might want to consider whether emotions were feelings that just happened to people, or whether they had some control over them. At the time, Cullen thought that people causing their own emotions was a particularly stupid idea. After he had calmed down for a couple of days, he gave the matter more serious thought.

## Discussion Questions

1.  What do you feel were the factors behind Cullen's depression?
2.  What types of rewards was Cullen getting for depressing?
3.  What does Glasser's Choice Theory say about how Cullen might change his feelings?

## CASE 14-4: WHAT DIFFERENCE DOES SCHOOL MAKE?

Keri always had her nose in some magazine that supposedly described incidents in the exciting lives of some entertainment personality. She dreamed about being an entertainer and living a whirlwind life of performances and public events. "I know it's hard to become an big entertainer," she explained in an exasperated tone to her father. "You know I am taking all kinds of dance and acting classes. Last year I even had a part in Oak Ridge Junior High's theatre revue. The teacher said I was really good."

Keri's father bit his tongue to keep from saying that the teacher said this to all the people in the performance. He was very worried about Keri's schoolwork. Keri always had to work hard to pass her grades but since Grade Eight her willingness to do this seemed to be declining. Last year at the end of Grade Nine most of Keri's marks had been in the C range and her father suspected that some of her teachers had stretched the criteria quite a bit to even give her a C.

When Keri's father spoke to her about her marks, Keri had dismissed the importance of the whole issue. "I don't care about school," she had explained. "As soon as I am old enough I'm going to do what I really want."

## Discussion Questions

1.  What are some of the reasons that Keri claims to be not interested in school?
2.  What two factors might her father and her teachers attempt to influence to improve Keri's motivation to do better in school?

## REFERENCES

### Choice Theory

Glasser and Choice Theory: http://www.wglasser.com or http://www. wglasserinst.com.

### Emotional Quotient

Goleman, D. (1994). *Emotional intelligence: Why it can matter more than IQ*. New York: Bantam Books.

### Flow

Csikszentmihalyi, M. (1990). *Flow: The psychology of optimal experience*. New York: Harper & Row.

# chapter fifteen

# Learning Environments and Learned Difficulties

## LEARNING ENVIRONMENTS

Effective teaching and management strategies are very important in assisting student learning. Equally important factors are the emotional and physical nature of the learning environment. Teacher expectations, student and teacher anxiety, motivation, incentives for learning, and a clear understanding of the learning environment are crucial for effective teaching.

## GENERAL SETTING

- The classroom is a box in which you as the teacher and some 20 to 30 other people are trying to meet a variety of needs while attempting to learn some prescribed bits of information with your progress being evaluated by a number of outside individuals and groups.

- Because there is very little that is natural about the situation, our instinctive behaviours and reactions usually do not apply. A previously learned group of skilled behaviours is required.

## Multi-Dimensional

- Initially teachers may think of the classroom as only being a place where teacher and students interact to learn a certain amount of material.
- Actually, there are many 'parallel universes' in the classroom.
  - Students bring their personal universes to the classroom and often are more involved with that universe than they are with what the teacher is doing.
  - Students are very aware of each other and often are more involved in those interactions than they are with the teacher.
  - Teachers themselves also are involved in many dimensions of the classroom including their personal lives and other issues within the school or community.
- Teachers might think of themselves as artists finding patterns in chaos, or conductors producing music from a bunch of people with noisemakers.

## Nature of Events

- Many events are occurring in a classroom simultaneously.
- Events occur very quickly and in an unpredictable manner.
  - One moment you're discussing models of the atom, and the next moment two students are arguing about something that happened yesterday.
- There is little or no privacy in the classroom. Students are able to watch teachers compose themselves to deal with some new event.
- All student and teacher behaviours have a history.
  - Any comment to a student, for instance, will be judged in terms of previous comments.

## With-It-Ness

- Teachers need to be aware of all that is going on in the classroom, including Rebecca's attempts to pass notes when she thinks she is not being watched.
- Nervousness causes the teacher to have a very narrow focus and to be almost completely unaware of what is going on with students.
- Usually the teacher needs to 'ignore' most student behaviours; otherwise the whole class period will be spent commenting on this or that behaviour.
  - One reason to intervene involves behaviours that present barriers to learning.
  - Physical and emotional safety also are large factors in deciding when to intervene.
- Over time, teachers learn a balance between ignoring and intervening.
- While all this is going on, teachers also must maintain a strong bond with their students.

## Physical Space

- Arrangement of desks, chairs, and other components of the classroom goes a long way in determining the types of interactions that occur in the space.

- There is no ideal arrangement; learning goals determine how the classroom is structured.
- Most classrooms are pretty sterile spaces that promote a certain feeling of disconnection and boredom.
  - Teachers can strive to overcome this by personalizing the classroom to fit their particular subject and style.
  - Personalizing does not mean confusion. Most students learn better in an atmosphere that has both beauty and simplicity.
- The classroom space should be organized and free of clutter. There should be space for individual and group work.
- The classroom space should include elements that show the space is both the teacher's and the students'.
- There is no way that you are going to get an ideal classroom. You have to do the best you can with what you have. Perhaps there is a more efficient and productive way to organize the space than has been in use in the past.

# CRITICAL INSTRUCTIONAL FACTORS

## General Principles

- Students need appropriate learning tasks and systematic instructional procedures.
- Students must be given sufficient time to become involved in their learning.
  - Moving quickly from one topic to another leaves students disoriented and disconnected from the material.
- Students need an opportunity to apply and generalize what they have learned.
- Students and teacher must monitor progress through effective and authentic evaluation.
- Solutions rather than failures need to be recognized and an emphasis placed on success.
- Students must be helped to learn to make good behavioural choices.

## Lesson Planning

- Lesson planning is one of the most important components of a positive learning environment.
- Students need to feel that the teacher knows what is going on; they will benefit from the details of the plan being made available to them.
- Clear long- and short-term goals communicated to students will provide a thread of order in what seems to them to be a bit of data selected from a seeming endless ocean of such data.

## Instructional Strategies for Assisting Students

- Controlling complexity of tasks is a very effective method of assisting students. This can be done in the following ways.

  1. Reduce the number of requirements in any particular activity.
  2. Increase the size and clarity of instructions.
     - Use bigger writing and more white space to reduce both board and handout load.
     - Employ colours to make information stand out.
  3. Provide more time for students to complete activities and answer questions.
  4. Reduce the cost of mistakes.
     - Use self-checking as much as possible.
     - Encourage experimentation.
     - Reduce public identification of mistakes.
     - Programmed instruction, where students can work at their own pace and self-correct, helps some students.
     - Appropriate CAL (Computer Assisted Learning) sometimes proves helpful.
  5. Encourage a relaxed working atmosphere.
     - Use a workshop approach versus direct teaching.
     - Include a games approach where error is just part of the game.
     - Break routine with changes of pace and relaxation exercises.
  6. Provide immediate and private evidence of performance.
  7. Use activities where success is inherent.
     - Asking a child to draw a wiggly line they like, or to choose an adjective to describe water, means that success is inherent.

## TEACHER EXPECTATIONS AND BEHAVIOUR

- It is important for teachers to talk about solutions rather than problems, and to provide students with visions of success.
  - "What would success look like to you, Lucinda?"
- Teachers shouldn't concentrate on diagnosis, causes, or blaming, but instead should provide an encouraging, forward-looking atmosphere.
  - Beware of even labels such as low self-esteem.
  - Find new, non-dysfunctional labels for situations. All problems have many different explanations.
  - Develop new, creative, fun explanations.
- A constructive, conversational way of talking, with time for students to respond, helps to reduce tensions in the classroom.
- Reducing unnecessary distinctions based on academic performance helps to treat all students equally.

■ I would stay away from randomly calling on students to answer questions as a form of evaluation. You may be evaluating stress level only. This does not mean that randomly calling on students should not be used at all. It can be a good classroom management technique and students can be given the option of 'passing' if they don't want to or can't answer.

## LEARNED DIFFICULTIES

Variations in learning based on issues such as intelligence, creativity, learning styles, language, and culture were examined in Chapters Six and Seven. Many learning difficulties, however, are actually *learned* difficulties — unique ways students have learned to deal with the stress resulting from conditions in their school and home lives (Tinney & Tinney, 1990).

## Basic Principles of Learned Behaviours Concept

■ Many learning problems are learned problems that develop very early in children's lives.

■ These learned ways of behaving represent children's individual attempts to deal with the stresses in their homes and schools.

■ Children's learned problems are the result of patterns of behaviours they have adopted to deal with the fear caused by threats to their identity from their environment.

■ These patterns of behaviour reduce students' abilities to learn because the behaviours usually result in lack of focus on the tasks required of them.

■ Students with these types of learned problems often will demonstrate attention and competency for tasks that they select; unfortunately, society often does not value these activities.

■ Parents, teachers, and specialists need to place less emphasis on the diagnosis and remediation of supposed learning problems and focus more on teaching in diverse and supportive ways that allow students to demonstrate their abilities and achieve success.

## Behavioural Evidence of a Problem

■ Student behaviour can be used as evidence of a learning or learned problem. These behaviours can be divided arbitrarily into three categories, keeping in mind that these categories overlap and students may exhibit behaviours in more than one category.

■ **Controlling behaviours** are the most obvious indications of student problems. Examples of controlling behaviours include being one or more of active, aggressive, bullying, excitable, impulsive, hostile, loud, and unpredictable.

■ **Compliance behaviours** may go unnoticed or not be dealt with because of more immediate pressures on the teacher. Examples of compliance behaviours include being one or more of dependent, helpless, fearful, ritualistic, and solitary or seeking confirmation, nurturing, protection, reassurance, and safety. Students who use compliance behaviours to deal with stress also may avoid challenge, evaluation, newness, and questions.

■ **Indifference behaviours** are more noticeable than compliance behaviours but also can be disregarded by the teacher because of more immediate pressures. Examples of indifference behaviours include being one or more of confused, disorganized, disinterested, forgetful, humourous, preoccupied, and unmotivated. Students who use indifference behaviours to deal with their stress also may ignore demands, spend a lot of time fantasizing, and be indifferent to the consequences of their actions.

■ Teachers may reinforce all of these behaviours through their responses.

## Intentions Behind Behaviour

■ When students behave in inappropriate and ineffective ways, the teacher always should assume that students are trying to meet their needs and to protect their integrity.

■ Teachers should not assume that students understand what is required and are deliberately choosing not to behave. Most of the choices students make are rapid and automatic, and most frequently come from anxiety and confusion.

| Exercise 15–1 | Most Upsetting Behaviour |
| --- | --- |

All of us tend to be upset by some behaviours and relatively unaffected by others. Behaviours that cause the most concern vary from individual to individual. Would you be most concerned about controlling, compliance, or indifference behaviours? Which specific behaviour would be the most upsetting? How would you feel if a student exhibited this behaviour? Why do you feel you would be concerned about this particular behaviour?

## HUMANISTIC APPROACHES TO THE CLASSROOM

Humanistic approaches to Psychology have contributed to our understanding of the importance of the classroom environment.

## General Principles

■ Teachers should allow students to choose what they want to learn whenever practical.

■ Teachers should treat students as a whole; teachers should 'see' all the important qualities of a person.

## Carl Rogers

■ Carl Rogers felt that significant learning occurs only if teachers adopt three specific attitudes.

1. Teachers are genuine and share their honest thoughts/feelings with students in a manner appropriate to their age and the maintenance of suitable emotional boundaries.

2. Teachers have unconditional positive regard for students in that they value and accept students by using an open, non-judgmental approach to teaching.

3. Teachers have empathy for students in the sense of being able to put themselves in the students' places and understanding their experience of the learning.

## Abraham Maslow

- Maslow's Hierarchy of Needs model reminds teachers that students have a variety of needs beyond basic survival and physiological needs.
  - Belonging, beauty, truth, justice, and the opportunity to come to understand themselves in an authentic manner all are important aspects of the classroom environment.
- On the other hand, people like Frankl clearly show that a challenge to basic needs does not excuse failure to behave in a higher order manner.

## QUALITY SCHOOLS

- The concept of Quality Schools was developed by William Glasser based on his Choice Theory and the Quality concepts of W. Edwards Deming.
- Choice Theory rather than external control psychology is the underlying basic philosophy.
- Emphasis is placed on education rather than schooling. **Education** refers to using knowledge that has real meaning and value for the student, while **schooling** refers to being forced to learn data that has no value for the student personally, and no value in the world outside the school.
- All students must do competent work before they are passed to another grade. Competent work refers to work at a B level in most schools. Students are not ranked by letter grades or other measures of academic performance.
- Schools wishing to be recognized as Quality Schools by the Glasser Institute must meet a list of criteria. Unfortunately, some schools and even school districts use the name 'Quality' without having any affiliation with the Institute.
- The William Glasser Institute has developed a rubric for measuring a school's progress toward becoming a Quality School. The rubric has the following six components.

1. Relationships are based in trust and respect.

2. There is measurable continuous improvement.

3. All students demonstrate competency.

4. Some students demonstrate quality or performance well beyond district competencies.

5. All students and staff know Choice Theory.

6. The school is a joyful place to be.

## CASE 15-1: THE YEARBOOK

"Well, I worked on the school yearbook when I was in junior high," stated Francine Steyn. It was only a little sentence made in the middle of a job interview. After the interview she was sure the principal would have hired her without any mention of the yearbook. Unfortunately, the statement had led inevitably to a question about Francine working with the Yearbook Committee for the next year. Francine really didn't know much about yearbooks; she had only helped select a few pictures in junior high. She felt trapped though, and responded that she would be glad to work with the committee.

The Yearbook Committee held their first meeting the second week of school. Talk about an enthusiastic group of students! Some members had been on the committee for two or three years. Last year's committee had chosen the editor and he and a couple of the committee members had worked on the yearbook over the summer. They seemed to have established an overall theme and developed a general layout. The other members of the committee agreed with the approach and Francine was very impressed with the commitment of at least the key committee members. Thoughts about working with the Yearbook Committee had made her very anxious but now she saw that they really didn't need her help all that much.

Gradually pictures, biographies, jokes, opinion pieces, and reminiscences were collected. Francine noticed that some of the opinion pieces had strong political overtones, but felt that this was a wonderful opportunity for students to develop critical thinking skills. She did object to a few of the jokes and the committee seemed to go along with her opinions without too much controversy. She also was concerned about a few of the pictures that were obviously inappropriate for publication; the photographers agreed to substitute others. Actually she was very impressed with the apparent willingness of committee members and the editor to accept her opinion.

In February the principal asked to meet with Francine to discuss the yearbook. He asked her to bring along any draft materials she had. Francine was a little bit annoyed at his request; she had the feeling that the principal regarded himself as having some sort of final authority over the contents of the publication even though he had not been involved in any aspect of its production.

The principal became more and more upset as he looked over the material Francine brought to the meeting. "Have you really thought about this material?" the principal asked. Francine could tell that he was trying to be diplomatic although the tight lines around his mouth and the anger in his voice negated any attempt at goodwill.

"Well, I didn't think it was my job to censor what the students were writing," explained Francine. "They are so enthusiastic and put so much effort into their work."

At this point the principal seemed to realize that Francine really was quite naïve both about the purpose of yearbooks, at least from the administration's point of view, and the somewhat devious agenda of at least some members of every Yearbook Committee. "Look at this picture of Mr. Linning," he demanded. "Do you see what is written on the board behind him? And how about the angle used to shoot the picture of Ms. Tomescu. Do you think these pictures were taken like this by accident?"

Francine knew that the people who had taken the pictures were good photographers and probably intended for the pictures to be as they were. "Well, I could ask them to take these pictures again," she said weakly.

"The two pictures are not the issue," explained the principal. "People in several other pictures are making obscene gestures and many of the jokes have double meanings. You have to be aware of what the students are doing. Usually they're not being mean but part of the game for them involves trying to see how far they can go without getting caught."

Francine was torn between defending the Yearbook Committee and anger at being tricked. She decided to raise some good features of the material by praising the critical thought that had gone into the articles.

"That's another thing," explained the principal. "The Yearbook is not a place for critical articles about the school, society, or anything else. It represents the school in the community and serves as source of memories for students years after they have graduated."

## Discussion Questions

1. Why was Ms. Steyn not aware of what the students were doing with the yearbook?
2. Why did the students include some of the materials they did for use in the yearbook?
3. What do you think of the principal's views of a yearbook?

## CASE 15-2: OCEAN'S CONFUSION

Ocean was a source of frustration for all of his teachers. Ms. Tolonen sighed as she saw him slouched in his chair with his eyes closed. She had tried every trick she could think of to involve him in the class but he always responded with claims of confusion and lack of interest. He managed to pass his courses though; indeed, his ability to get the lowest mark possible without actually failing drew her admiration. It was like watching a famous comic negotiate a dangerous cliff.

Ocean's parents claimed that initially he had really liked school and had done quite well in his early classes. There were some difficulties with math and his reading was a bit behind some of the other students, but his parents felt that he could be very successful if he just applied himself to his work.

His present behaviour started to manifest in Grade 5. According to his parents, Ocean had a great teacher that year who constantly told Ocean that he could do better if he just focused more and worked a bit harder. Ocean actually seemed to do worse that year; maybe it was just because the work was becoming a bit more difficult. That year there also were frequent arguments between his parents and a move from an area of the city where he felt safe with his friends to one where he didn't know anyone and where groups of older kids made even a trip to the corner store a potential minefield.

Most of the other students in Ms. Tolonen's Grade 10 English class seemed to understand what she wanted them to do, and even showed sparks of interest and excitement from time to time. Not so with Ocean. She had just asked the students to take out the novel they had been working on and to answer some questions on a worksheet she had given them. Ocean was looking in his backpack for something. Ms. Tolonen went over to his desk to see what was going on.

"Can't you find your novel?" asked Ms. Tolonen.

"Got it now," Ocean replied as he pulled the book through a pile of clothes, pieces of paper, candy wrappers, and other indistinguishable articles.

"Good. Now you can start to fill in the worksheet."

"Do you have a pencil I could borrow? I can't seem to find mine," Ocean responded.

With another sigh Ms. Tolonen got him a pencil and went on around the class to see how the other students were doing. A few minutes later she was dismayed to see that Ocean had not started yet. Indeed he seemed to be moving his worksheet and book around on his desk as if he were trying to solve some jigsaw puzzle.

"Is everything alright?" Ms Tolonen asked.

"I don't know what I am supposed to do," responded Ocean.

This kind of confused behaviour tended to drive Ms. Tolonen up the wall, especially when it came from a student that she had just seen after school yesterday write out the directions for accessing a music site on the internet. "I wish he would apply some of that interest to his school work," she thought.

## Discussion Questions

1. Do you think that Ocean may have some learning difficulties?
2. If he has learning difficulties, do they explain his performance in school?
3. If not, why does he perform at such a low level?
4. What might Ms. Tolonen do to help?

## CASE 15-3: HIGH PERFORMANCE OR ELSE

The School Board knew they had to do something about Bayview High. While there was a lot of rhetoric about provincial exam marks only being one measure of a school's performance, the Board knew that the graduating class from the school had done much poorer than students from other high schools in the district. Claims about other benefits of going to Bayview tended to be negated by stories of bullying, vandalism to the school, and the highest dropout rate in the district. The Board decided to go outside the district and bring in a principal with a reputation for cleaning up schools from another area of the province.

Mr. Siegler arrived at Bayview with considerable fanfare. There were several articles in local newspapers and a national radio station interviewed him on its morning program. The School Board let District officials know that what Mr. Siegler wanted, Mr. Siegler got — no waiting six months for maintenance or equipment.

Changes occurred immediately. Some of them were cosmetic involving such things as coats of paint, repairs to windows that hadn't opened in years, replacing cinder walkways with cement, and planting trees in front of the school. Others involved a systematic enforcement of rules related to attendance, bullying, drugs, and other behaviours that didn't show the proper respect. Indeed 'respect' became the catchword for all kinds of decisions about behaviour and performance.

Teachers were told bluntly what was expected of them. Failure to improve student performance would result in negative performance evaluations and strong encouragements to change careers or move to another school. The principal let it be known that he was setting the rules and that if anyone didn't like it, they could talk to District officials. Since everyone knew the officials would support the principal, this wasn't a valid option.

Improvements in student performance and public support for the school occurred over the next year. In the second year, marks of graduating students equaled the district average and by the third year those students writing provincial exams were performing well above average. Discipline problems also had declined dramatically in the school and Mr. Siegler was being feted by community organizations for the miracle he had performed.

There were some clouds in the clear sky of acclaim, however. The school dropout rate actually had gotten a bit worse. Many felt that this was just due to those students who knew they couldn't compete in the school quitting or going to an easier school. It was their problem if they couldn't measure up. However, a couple of cultural groups were claiming that their kids were much more likely to drop out of school than kids were from other groups.

These same cultural groups complained that their students were much more likely to be punished by the rigid enforcement of rules. There wasn't anything wrong with the rules themselves; it was just the way they were being interpreted. For instance, bullying didn't mean the same thing to all people. Hitting someone in a violent way definitely was bullying, but was the same true for calling a friend 'musclehead'? Skill in trading these types of comments actually was valued by some people.

Some of the people who held strong views about the nature of education also were concerned. They felt that Mr. Siegler's model of a school had overtones of a boot camp, and wondered if even those who were doing well in the school were being well served by this approach. There was no denying the improvement in the school on many fronts. The question really was whether the improvements could be obtained by other approaches without the downsides of Mr. Siegler's method.

## Discussion Questions

1. What might be some of the reasons that Bayview High was having difficulties in the first place?
2. What are the positive features of Mr. Siegler's method of turning Bayview High around?
3. What changes would you make to Mr. Siegler's approach to deal with some of the difficulties still present in the school?
4. Could your changes have been made right from the start or was Mr. Siegler's approach a necessary first step?

# REFERENCES

## Learned Difficulties

Tinney, R., & Tinney, M.A. (1990). *Changing ineffective learning behaviours: Instructional/Interactional strategies*. Victoria, BC: Department of Psychological Foundations in Education, University of Victoria.

## Quality Schools

Deming, W. E. (1986). *Out of the crisis*. Cambridge, MA: Massachusetts Institute of Technology, Center for Advanced Engineering Study.

Glasser, W. (1990). *Quality schools: Managing students without coercion*. New York: HarperPerennial.

Glasser, W. (1998). *Choice psychology: A new psychology of personal freedom*. New York: HarperPerennial.

Glasser and Choice Theory Web Site: http://www.wglasser.com or http://www. wglasserinst.com.

# chapter sixteen

# Classroom Management

Chapter 15 dealt with conditions in the classroom environment that influence learning. This chapter is a continuation of the concepts in Chapter 15, but with more of an emphasis on understanding, preventing, and responding to student misbehaviours.

## GENERAL PRINCIPLES

### Being Real

- All students will misbehave at some time.
- Statements such as, "You just need to have respect" represent either a fundamental misunderstanding about human behaviour or an attempt to repress the anxiety that results from thinking about student misbehaviour.
  - Respect is, of course, a fundamental component of teaching but must be based on the potential of students and not on unreasonable expectations for continuous appropriate behaviour.

## Charity and Empathy

- Students will misbehave, as will teachers.
  - Most of these misbehaviours will be relatively minor, have no long-term consequences, and can be dealt with using strategies discussed in this chapter.
  - On rare occasions, misbehaviours may be so physically or emotionally damaging or so disruptive that the teacher and school administration have no choice but to take the appropriate steps to ensure it never happens again.
- All of us will have a bad day, month, year, or perhaps even decade.
- The difference between a 'good' student or teacher and a 'bad' one may be a matter of events outside the person's control.
- Empathy and charity are more powerful than righteousness.

## Courage

- Being a teacher takes great courage.
- Teachers continuously are confronted by academic, behavioural, and personal challenges.
- There is little acknowledgement of success but much criticism of any misstep some one thinks a teacher has taken.

## THE 'GREAT TEACHER' MYTH OF CLASSROOM MANAGEMENT

- The 'Great Teacher' myth of classroom management promotes the idea that effective management is the result of some unique genetic or personality trait.
  - 'Great teachers' presumably can manage any classroom based on their mere presence in the classroom.
  - Even if this myth were true, other teachers have to manage the thousands of classrooms in a province.
- Effective classroom management really involves a combination of attitude, knowledge, and skills that can be learned, recognizing that this learning may involve more effort for some than for others.
- All of us need to improve our abilities to deal with our own emotional issues.

## GOALS OF CLASSROOM MANAGEMENT

- Effective approaches to classroom management allow students to spend more time on learning activities.
- In addition, the possibility of serious behavioural problems developing is reduced.

## MANAGEMENT VS. DISCIPLINE

- The need for discipline represents a failure of management, which in turn often represents a lesson planning failure.
  - This failure is not necessarily the teacher's 'fault': students choose their behaviours for a variety of reasons, many of which have little to do with the teacher.
- Teachers need to have a number of strategies for dealing with situations that are moving from management to discipline issues.
  - These strategies need to be learned to the point that they can be implemented automatically in a disruptive emotional climate.
  - Student teachers on a practicum should discuss appropriate strategies with their sponsor teacher to ensure understanding and preferably congruity with previous practice in the classroom.
- There is no simple trick for dealing with classroom management problems.

## Expectations and Rules

- Teacher and school expectations and rules must be clear to students.
- Consequences of not meeting expectations or breaking rules must be specified and enforced.
- Broad general statements about desired behaviours may be valuable as themes but do not provide the specifics that many students require.
- Classroom meetings are very useful for developing classroom rules provided students understand that they and the teacher are governed by a variety of rules and standards mandated by the school district, laws, and various provincial or federal legislation.
- Appropriate and systematic rewards for meeting expectations and obeying rules are much more effective than consequences for not doing so.

## Behavioural Choices

- Students must be helped to understand that behaviour is a personal choice.
  - This is especially important in a media climate full of people describing their behaviour as being someone else's fault.
- Teachers need to show students how they can and do show effort and self-control.
- Students can be encouraged to work together to solve behavioural problems.

## CLASSROOM MANAGEMENT STRATEGIES

### Approaches to Teaching

- **Authoritative** styles of teaching combine a caring attitude and considerable discussion with clear limits on behaviour, and are the most effective approaches to teaching.
- **Authoritarian** and **permissive** styles of teaching result in more behavioural problems and less student learning.

- Authoritarian styles of teaching involve an emphasis on rules and control while permissive styles provide a lot of student autonomy but little structure. Both of these approaches to teaching result in more behavioural problems and less student learning than is the case with authoritative styles.
- Providing variety in classroom activities, and using more desired class activities as rewards for completing less desired ones, help to reduce disruptions.
- Teachers need to have a classroom management plan with different types of interventions and consequences. Sending a student to the office every time there is a problem is ineffective; it also annoys the vice-principal or principal.
- Management interventions may be of a minor nature that do not disrupt the flow of teaching, or may involve strategies that involve stopping instruction to deal with the misbehaviour.

## Minor Interventions

- Minor interventions include walking around the class, standing near a student.
- Non-verbal signals often are effective.
  - Examples include smiling, frowning, shaking head, staring, moving a hand in a downward patting motion, and turning to face a student.
- Asking a student a question that follows from what is being discussed serves to bring the student's attention back on task and alert others that they also may be asked.
- Embedded commands such as, "When we all have our books out, we will..." can serve to tell students what needs to be done without disruption.
- Sometimes teachers will arrange private signals for a particular student. This helps the student recognize that an inappropriate behaviour is starting without others in the class being aware of the interaction.

## More Disruptive Interventions

- Sometimes minor interventions will not be enough to stop a misbehaviour and the teacher will have to stop the class to deal with the issue involved.
- More disruptive interventions involve being specific and concrete about inappropriate behaviour, appropriate questioning, mini-counselling, implementing consequences, changing a student's placement, or even removing a student from the class.

## Classroom Management Bumps

- In their 1994 book, *Classroom Management: A Thinking Caring Approach*, Barrie Bennett and Peter Smilanch conceptualized the move from least disruptive to most disruptive management strategies as a series of management bumps.

  Bump 1 – Low Key Response.

  Bump 2 – Squaring Off.

  Bump 3 – Either/Or Choices.

Bump 4 – Implied Choice.

Bump 5 – Move to Power by Student.

Bump 6 – Informal Logical Contracts.

Bump 7 – Formal Contracts

Bump 8 – In-School Suspension

Bump 9 – Out-of-School Suspension

■ Each of these bumps has a group of possible behaviours by the teacher.

## Choice of Strategy

■ A variety of factors will influence a teacher's decision about which strategy to use in a particular situation.

■ All misbehaviours have a particular intensity and occur in the context of student, teacher, and the present environment as well as the history of the class.

| Exercise 16–1 | The Management List |
|---|---|

In groups of three or four brainstorm all the strategies you can remember being used by your teachers in the past. Rate them from least to most effective.

## MISBEHAVIOUR THEORIES

Misbehaviours are actions that have both cause and purpose for the person performing them; they are not random or meaningless events. The Choice Theory of William Glasser and the Goals of Misbehaviour approach of Alfred Adler, particularly as developed by Don Dinkmeyer and Gary McKay, are two models of misbehaviour that help explain why these inappropriate actions occur.

## Glasser's Choice Theory

■ Glasser's Choice Theory was covered in Chapter 14 and his concept of Quality Schools was reviewed in Chapter 15.

■ Glasser's basic premise is that all behaviours, including emotional behaviours, are chosen to meet basic genetic needs. The only exceptions to this are rare medical conditions that make choice impossible.

■ Behaviour involves the four components of acting, thinking, feeling, and changes in physiology.

■ The teacher's role is to help students learn to make responsible choices.

■ Glasser encourages teachers to give up external control psychology completely. Criticizing, rewarding, blaming, threatening, and punishing language meant to control the behaviour of others is replaced with language meant to work out differences and help students make choices that are effective for them.

- Creativity often is required to find solutions to conflict.
- Choice always is exercised within a reality. This reality includes school rules, laws, political and economic climate, and general safety.
- The teacher also has choices and can decide not to interact with a student until the student decides to act in a manner that is acceptable to the teacher.
- Teachers can help students choose effective behaviours by employing the following strategies.
  1. Maintain as much flexibility as reality allows.
  2. Point out choices to students.
  3. Establish a set of appropriate rules in collaboration with the students (the classroom meeting).
  4. Stress the students' responsibility to make appropriate choices, as they must ultimately live with the consequences of their behaviour.
  5. Never accept excuses for inappropriate behaviour.
  6. Have students make value judgments about their inappropriate behaviour.
  7. Work with students to find alternatives to their misbehaviour.
  8. Set up consequences for both appropriate and inappropriate behaviour.
  9. Establish a system of classroom meetings during which solutions to class problems are sought. Fault-finding and blame-placing are not allowed. Sometimes meetings are not appropriate.
- Teachers should avoid trying to discuss a situation when the student is upset, or implying that decisions are final.

| Exercise 16–2 | **Role-Play A Meeting** |
|---|---|
| In groups of four or five, role-play a classroom meeting to establish conditions and rules for a classroom. Give each person in the group a chance to be Chair | with the others being students. Each time the Chair changes, discuss how the process is going and what steps are necessary to reach the best outcome possible. |

## Alfred Adler (Dinkmeyer and McKay)

Like Glasser, Adler believed that all behaviour is purposeful. Misbehaviour is the result of the child's mistaken assumptions about the way to gain status and find a place in the world and in the classroom. If teachers are not able to identify the student's aim, they will reinforce the inappropriate behaviour.

## Goals of Misbehaviour

- According to Alder as developed by Dinkmeyer and McKay, the four primary goals of misbehaviour are the need for attention, the need for power or control, revenge, and assumed helplessness or inadequacy.

- Three additional goals for misbehaviour common to teenagers in particular are excitement, peer acceptance, and superiority.

## Types of Misbehaviours

- Typical types of misbehaviours for attention-getting include:
  - disrupting the classroom;
  - asking for favours;
  - tattling on one another;
  - refusing or being slow to work;
  - requesting help when help is not needed.
- Typical types of misbehaviours for power or control include:
  - arguing;
  - contradicting;
  - throwing temper tantrums;
  - defying the teacher;
  - lying;
  - attempting to upset the teacher.
- Typical types of misbehaviours for seeking revenge include:
  - acting in cruel, violent ways;
  - justifying misbehaviour;
  - feeling others out to get them;
  - needing to retaliate.
- Typical types of misbehaviours for helplessness or inadequacy include:
  - withdrawing from situations where they assume their inadequacy will be obvious;
  - needing to convince the teacher of their disability so they can be left alone.
- Typical types of misbehaviours for seeking excitement include:
  - avoiding routine;
  - being interested in drugs, promiscuous sex, etc.;
  - repeating claims of being bored.
- Typical types of misbehaviours for seeking peer acceptance include:
  - constantly looking to peers for approval.

- Typical types of misbehaviours for seeking superiority include:
  - constantly stressing one's own achievements;
  - negating the achievements of others.

## Identification of Student's Mistaken Goals by Teacher Responses

- Sometimes it is hard to discern what mistaken goal students are trying to accomplish by their behaviours.
- One indication of students' goals is our own emotional reaction to their behaviour as explained in Table 16-1.

| TABLE 16-1 | Teacher Reactions to Misbehaviours |
|---|---|
| **Student Goal** | **Usual Teacher Reactions** |
| Attention Getting | Annoyance |
| Power | Anger, Desire to Fight Back |
| Revenge | Feeling Hurt and Angry, Justifying |
| Inadequacy | Despair |
| Excitement | Nervousness, Anger, Hurt |
| Peer Acceptance | Worry, Disapproval |
| Superiority | Frustration, Inadequacy |

## Appropriate Responses to Misbehaviours

- Appropriate specific responses to student misbehaviours are given in Table 16-2.

| TABLE 16-2 | Teacher Reactions to Misbehaviours |
|---|---|
| **Student Goal** | **Appropriate Responses** |
| Attention Getting | Ignoring, Rewarding Appropriate, Behaviours |
| Power | Withdrawing, Defining Boundaries, Using 'I' Statements. |
| Revenge | Building Trust, Not Getting Hooked |
| Inadequacy | Avoiding Pity or Criticism, Building Success |
| Excitement | Providing Positive Outlets, Sharing Your Excitements |
| Peer Acceptance | New Peers, Rewarding Success |
| Superiority | Unconditional Approval, Humility, Social Responsibility |

## General Reactions to Misbehaviours

- Adler had two general reactions to misbehaviour: encouragement and consequences.
- Teachers encourage students by accepting all students as worthwhile regardless of their behaviour.
  - Teachers must help students develop their capabilities and potentialities.
  - Teachers should use words and actions that emphasize effort and improvement rather than outcome.
  - Encouragement should come during task and not only at completion. This approach promotes enjoyment in doing the task.
- Two types of consequences for our actions are natural and logical.
  - Natural consequences are those experiences that are a direct result of one's behaviour. For example, drinking too much coffee can lead to the 'jitters'.
  - Logical consequences are the result of breaking rules and are arranged by the teacher, administration, class meeting, etc. Consequences of both appropriate and inappropriate behaviours need to be explained and understood. Some form of contract often is used.

## Cautions in Using the Adlerian Approach

- The goals of misbehaviour are not always obvious. For instance, a student may show inadequacy as a form of revenge.
- Adler's approach is not mechanical. It is not a case of "the student did that, therefore I do this". Wisdom is involved.
- The process works best in an atmosphere of adult maturity. The adult must be emotionally strong enough to help students deal with the mistaken ways they are trying to reach goals.

| Exercise 16–3 | Worst Misbehaviour |
|---|---|

Which of the above goals of misbehaviours as explained by Adler would be the most difficult for you to handle? Why would this goal be difficult for you? What can you do to learn to deal professionally with the misbehaviours that result from a student having this goal?

## AGGRESSION

- Violence is becoming an increasing concern in schools.
  - Students, teachers, and parents all report increased levels of aggression and increased fear about being the victim of aggression.

- The nature of aggression in the school also may be changing.
  - Violence seems to be more random, a spur-of-the-moment reaction to some minor situation or need for excitement.
  - Temporary groupings of students are more likely to be the instigator of violence.
  - Use of weapons is becoming more common.
  - More teachers are reporting violent, physical attacks directed against them, their families, and their property.
- Teachers need to think about ways they would deal with aggressive acts by students.
  - Teachers need to appear calm.
  - Teachers should make every attempt not to escalate the situation.
  - Sometimes the situation can be downplayed and dealt with after a cooling-off period.
  - Other times the teacher will have to ask the offending student to leave the class, send another student for help, or get all of the other students out of the classroom.
- The safety of other students and personnel over-ride every other issue.
  - Only in the most rare of circumstances, when there appears to be no other alternative to avoid injury, would a teacher try to control a student physically.
- Schools and classrooms should implement one of a number of conflict resolution programs available to help students learn to resolve disagreements in a non-violent manner.
- Care needs to be taken with zero tolerance programs unless the behaviours which lead to mandated penalties are specifically described, and are illegal or involve a significant danger of severe injury.

| Exercise 16–4 | **Responses to Student Aggression** |
|---|---|

With three or four other students brainstorm a few situations that a classroom teacher might reasonably be expected to encounter. Develop possible strategies for dealing with these situations.

## BEHAVIOUR MODIFICATION PLAN

A **behaviour modification plan** is a very specific way of dealing with an undesired behaviour or a closely related group of undesired behaviours.

## Basic Principle

- The most important aspect of behaviour management involves ensuring that the student also is committed to behavioural change.
- Students are responsible for their own decisions and actions, even if these actions and decisions will lead to difficulties.
- Teachers do not have the right to manipulate students.

## Observation of Behaviour

- It is very important that teachers observe behaviours along with their antecedent conditions and consequences rather than use labels.
- This observation refers to both inappropriate and appropriate behaviours.
  - Catching the student behaving in suitable ways will go a long way in deciding what intervention strategy would be most effective.

## Development of Plan

- A specific description of the misbehaviour or misbehaviours is required. The student should be able to identify and describe these misbehaviours.
- Detailed information as to the frequency, duration, and timing of these behaviours is needed to provide a baseline.
- The teacher then discusses the advantages and disadvantages of the misbehaviour with the student.
- If the student wants to change, the teacher needs to elicit or provide alternatives for the misbehaviour.

## The Plan

- The details of the plan needs to be developed with the student.
- At this point, the student and teacher must agree as to whether it would be better to punish the problem behaviour, or reward an incompatible positive behaviour, or some combination. Whichever approach is taken, records must be kept and displayed so that both the teacher and student can see any changes.
- Sometimes students who are committed to a behavioural change can manage their own behaviour modification. Self-reward and punishment seem to be as, or more, effective than an external monitor.
- The teacher needs to encourage the student to stick with the plan.

## CASE 16-1: LACK OF RESPECT

Alexandra Lehrer felt that all the discussions of classroom management in her professional year were a waste of time and somewhat offensive. They smacked to her of social control, manipulation, and even brainwashing. Perhaps the 'nice' methods were even more insidious. After all, a person could understand if someone was forcing them to do something but might not recognize the manipulation involved if a teacher were using some type of sophisticated behaviour management approach.

Respect of others from everyone was all that was required. Teachers built this feeling of respect in their classrooms through their positive feelings for their students, and through providing a safe, interesting place for students to be. Sure a student might get a little rambunctious from time to time, but this was easily dealt with and did not require any management technique. She remembered her years as a day camp leader; all the kids loved her and wanted to be in her group. The few behavioural incidents that occurred during a summer were dealt with easily through calling the child's name or asking everyone to pay attention. Nothing 'drastic' was required.

Alexandra's practicum report praised her enthusiasm and preparation. It mentioned that she had some difficulty with classroom management, though. Alexandra attributed these difficulties to the atmosphere that already existed in the class. Her sponsor teacher was quite strict and the students merely were letting off a bit of steam when Alexandra took over the class.

The first few months of Alexandra's teaching career seemed to confirm her views about classroom management. All of her Grade 8 students seemed to love her and other teachers commented on the excitement her students had about being in Alexandra's class. Problems among students were few and were stopped by Alexandra referring to the RESPECT FOR OTHERS poster at the front of the room. This saying replaced the list of classroom rules found in other rooms, and provided a sort of affirmation that was the foundation for all aspects of the class. Alexandra clearly let it be known that she was disappointed if a student failed to show the proper respect to others.

On the first Tuesday in November at 11:15 Alexandra felt that her students were very involved in their projects and that this might be a good time to go down to the office to prepare a handout for the afternoon. She had never left the class for more than a few minutes before, but felt that it was a measure of her respect for her students that she could leave them alone to continue their work. She told the students she would be back in about 15 minutes and asked them to continue working. When she came back at 11:30 the classroom looked like a bomb had hit it.

Lunch bags and books littered the floor and two of the desks were knocked over. A window at the back was cracked, apparently unintentionally when a lunch pail had been shoved against it. When she opened the door, four or five students seemed to be engaged in some combination of dodge ball and tag. A few others were running up and down between desks; the rest watched the whole performance or chatted with their neighbours. Actually, except for the broken window, no serious damage had been done. The students were right when they claimed they had just been fooling around a bit after they got their work done. Alexandra recognized the truth of these statements but could not help feeling that the students had betrayed her. "How could they behave like this after all our discussions about respect?" she lamented.

## Discussion Questions

1. What are some of the issues that underlie the issue of classroom management as manipulation?
2. What are some steps that Alexandra should have taken in addition to her emphasis on respect?
3. Was Alexandra engaged in a form of manipulation herself?

## CASE 16-2: TOO QUIET TO TEACH

The class clapped and cheered as Mira led them through the Grade 4 game she had developed as part of her teaching portfolio. Her energy and enthusiasm, combined with a smile that seemed to include the whole world, made her a favourite with her Professional Year colleagues. "I wish I had a personality like that," sighed John Yang. "My students are going to find me about as exciting as watching paint dry."

Indeed, when John came to make his presentation there were none of the laughs and foot stomping that had accompanied Mira's. He was very aware of the attention his audience focused on him and noticed that some were even taking notes. He wished though that he had some good joke or maybe a daring action to end his material. It would be nice to hear the cheers.

John knew that his lesson plans had more than enough detail and that he had plenty of activities to help students understand the concepts involved. He looked forward to almost all aspects of teaching; it really was only the issue of classroom management that filled him with anxiety. He felt that he wasn't very dynamic and knew that he could never maintain some type of act to make him appear exciting. Students were going to interpret his quiet nature as being a weakness and misbehave. He just didn't have a dynamic enough personality to project an atmosphere of control.

### Discussion Questions

1. How important is personality in classroom management?
2. Is John correct in his assumption that a dynamic personality projecting an atmosphere of control is the basis of classroom management?
3. What does John need to know to improve his opinion of his abilities to manage a class?

## CASE 16-3: THE CLASS MEETING

What a great workshop! Miles really had not been looking forward to the Professional Day workshop that Friday and actually had been thinking about phoning in sick so that he would have a long weekend. The principal's stressing of the value of the workshop, combined with Miles' desire for a full-time contract next year, ruled out the 'sick' option.

As part of a whole new approach to classroom management, the workshop presenter had stressed the value of class meetings. Miles really liked the idea of the meetings and thought they might be a solution to the dilemma he had been experiencing: maintaining a respect for rule in his classroom while still having students like him as a teacher. Too often he had found himself criticizing or ridiculing a student for some misbehaviour. The students usually responded with frustration and some mumbled justification. Classroom meetings might be just the answer. He would try them at his first class on Monday.

When his students first heard that they were to establish the rules for the class and the consequences for breaking rules, they thought Miles was kidding them somehow. He had never seemed to be much interested in their opinions before. When he assured the students that he wanted them to have a meeting to develop classroom rules, and that one of them could chair the meeting, they responded with enthusiasm. Unfortunately, they also responded with confusion and the class was half over before a Chair for the meeting could be chosen. The rest of the class was spent brainstorming a motley collection of rules and consequences that seemed to have little coherence or even possibility of implementation. Miles was very disappointed with the outcome of his new approach and decided not try it with any of his other classes. He didn't know what he could do now with this class since he couldn't just drop the whole issue the next time he met with them. "Another harebrained idea from consultants," he thought.

### Discussion Questions

1.  What were some of the problems with Miles' approach to classroom meetings?
2.  What initial steps should he have taken before launching into a full meeting?

## CASE 16-4: WHY IS SHE DOING THIS?

"This is just the last straw," thought Helina Bartkowski. Now the little paperweight that she got on her trip to Europe after her first year of teaching was gone. She really loved that little paperweight. It reminded her so much of that summer: no classes, no homework to mark, and a bit of money that should have gone to pay off more of her student loan. She often told students stories about buildings and people she had seen on the trip, omitting the meeting of her partner at that train station.

While everyone looked confused and innocent when she mentioned the loss of the paperweight, Helina knew who had taken it. It was the same student who had been the bane of her existence all September. Right from the first day of class Helina had felt a lot of animosity from Carol, a student who had appeared on her class list just at the beginning of the year. It was amazing that such a young child could combine an aggressive stare and smirk at the same time. Carol had insisted on mispronouncing Helina's last name; the smirk and the checking with other students to see the result showed that the behaviour was deliberate. Carol had managed to break the pencil sharpener, tear one of Helina's favourite posters, and spill a glass of water across Helina's desk ruining a card from her father. All of these had been 'accidents' according to Carol, but Helina was sure they were deliberate and was becoming increasingly angry and hurt by this behaviour.

Helina had tried every strategy she knew to reduce the friction between herself and Carol. She even had asked Carol if there was something that Helina could change to make Carol feel more welcomed in the class. "I don't think there is anything YOU can do," responded Carol with a big emphasis on the 'you'. "Older people just don't like me very much."

The loss of the paperweight made Helina realize that she had to try to find out why Carol seemed to be so determined to torment her. For the first time she really paid attention to the fact that the family name listed for contact information was not the same as Carol's on her student file. When Helina phoned the number and explained some of her concerns about Carol, she learned that Carol's guardian also was having the same or worse kinds of difficulties with her and really didn't know what to do.

Carol's guardians were looking after Carol until her parents could come to some resolution of financial and personal problems in their relationship. They had thought it would be better for Carol to live some place else while her parents were going through this diffi-cult time and had asked Carol's aunt to look after her for the time being. The guardians had three other children of their own and really did not have the energy to look after another child but didn't think they could refuse the request for help.

Carol's harassment of her cousins and the general disruption she had caused in their household was forcing the guardians to ask her parents to take Carol back unless some way could be found to stop the misbehaviours soon.

## Discussion Questions

1. Why were Helina's classroom rules ineffective in controlling Carol's behaviours?

2. What type(s) of misbehaviours was Carol engaged in?

3. What do you feel was her goal or goals for these misbehaviours?

4. What actions might Helina consider to start improving Carol's attitude and behaviours?

## REFERENCES

### Adlerian Concepts of Misbehaviour

Dreikurs, R. & Soltz, V. (1964). *Children: The challenge*. New York: Hawthorn/Dutton.

Dinkmeyer, D. & McKay, G. (1983). *The parent's guide: Systematic training for effective parenting*. Circle Pines, MN: American Guidance Service.

### Management Bumps

Bennett, B. and Smilanich, P. (1994). *Classroom management: A thinking and caring approach*. Ajax, ON: VISUTronX, Bookation Inc.

# chapter seventeen

# Assessment and Evaluation

## HISTORY OF EVALUATION

The first **measurement**, or process of obtaining quantitative data about a person's performance, and **assessment,** or appraisal of performance from a variety of both qualitative and quantitative data, took place for the Civil Service in China starting about 2000 BCE. The resultant **evaluations,** or decisions based on the measurements and assessments, were used to try and obtain the best people for the civil service.

- U.S. Civil Service exams started in 1871.
- IQ tests started about 1900.
- Various types of occupational and selection testing also started about 1900.

## MISUSES OF EVALUATION

- All uses of evaluation involve the potential for misuse.
- Most misuses are unintended, but the consequences are real.
  - All evaluations inherently possess biases from the worldviews and values held by those responsible for the evaluations.

- Examples of biases included cultural and language differences.
- Biases result in some students being perceived as having lower abilities than is really the case, while other students appear to excel when that also may not be the case.
- From time to time, forms of evaluations also have been used intentionally to cause individuals or groups to have difficulty meeting some criteria.
  - An example of this would be a strength requirement for a career when the career really does not require it and it is known that females will have more difficulty meeting the criteria.
  - Another example would be finger dexterity requirements that are deliberately meant to make it more difficult for males.

# DEFINITIONS

## Critical Distinctions

- While there are many terms used in assessment and evaluation to denote differing approaches or theoretical positions, four of the most important are static, dynamic, contextualized, and decontextualized.
- **Static assessment** occurs when there is no interaction between the person being assessed and the assessor or other people. This is the case in most types of exams and is even more so in some of the standardized assessments discussed later.
- **Dynamic assessment** means that interactions between the person being tested and the tester, as well as perhaps of other people, can occur.
  - This type of assessment is far more likely to give a realistic understanding of a person's abilities and potential because any confusion can be cleared up and prompts can help overcome temporary and minor misconceptions.
- **Contextualized assessment** occurs in a context where the assessment conditions are clear to the person doing the testing, and are most consistent with the context in which the material was learned.
  - Assessments carried out in the classroom with the teacher present and in conditions similar to regular classroom practice are examples of contextualized assessment.
- **Decontextualized assessment** occurs when the work being assessed was produced in conditions that are not considered by the person doing the assessment.
  - Homework is an example of decontextualized assessment. The teacher has no idea who actually did the work and under what conditions.
  - Marking homework from all students in the same way does not consider the vast differences in home environment.

## Authenticity, Reliability, Validity

- **Authentic assessment** stresses the use of tasks and settings that duplicate real life situations.

- Authentic assessment might require students to obtain information from appropriate foreign language texts to complete a task such as ordering a meal in a restaurant. In their ordinary life students are not often asked to stop everything and fill in a series of blank spaces with a specific word, a much less authentic form of assessment.
- Authentic assessment is really a form of validity but has come to be considered as a separate issue.
- **Reliability** is a measure of consistency from one assessment to another.
  - Reliability does not indicate that something is true, but the concept of being true has no meaning without reliability.
- **Validity** is the extent to which assessments are appropriate and meaningful for making decisions or evaluations.
- There are several forms of reliability and validity but they all have the same underlying meaning.

## Objective, Subjective, Formative, Summative

- An **objective** evaluation is one where there is no possibility of bias or other emotional factors influencing the evaluator's decision.
  - True/False exams are often presented as objective.
- **Subjective** evaluations are open to personal bias.
  - Performance evaluations have a high level of subjectivity.
- The relationship between objectivity and subjectivity is not as clear as it seems, however. Someone chose the content of a true/false exam and even the type of test was chosen. On the other hand, some evaluators may be quite objective in their performance evaluation.
- The critical factor in **formative** evaluation is that both the teacher and the students have an opportunity to learn from any areas of weakness without any significant affect on a final grade.
- **Summative** evaluation occurs when the grade obtained is the final one for that section and there is no opportunity to learn the material again.

## PRIOR LEARNING ASSESSMENT

- **Prior learning assessment** has become increasingly important in situations such as when a student moves to a new school from an educational program that is significantly different from the new one, or when a more mature student wants to claim personal experience and training as being worthy of credit in an educational institution.
- In addition to regular students coming here from other countries, this issue arises when adults return to school or university after some time in a career, or when a professional person in one country applies for certification in Canada.
- There are three ways of assessing prior learning.

1. Demonstrations of achievements through portfolios, employment records, etc may be used.

2. Students may try to demonstrate how a course they have already taken is equivalent to one they now are being asked to take.

3. Standardized and challenge exams may be used to show proficiency.

## EVALUATION PLANNING

■ Some of the reasons for evaluation are to help our teaching, improve decision making in terms of selection and placement of students, and to report to students and their parents.

■ In addition to the above factors, assessments have to be feasible and reportable.

  ▪ Video taping the class everyday as a form of assessment would be neither feasible nor reportable.

■ Teachers have to decide when they are going to do their assessments, what types of assessment are going to be done, and how these materials can be collected, stored, and returned to students.

■ The criteria of each assessment and its weighting in terms of a final grade must be decided and communicated to students.

■ The amount of input students will have in terms of the above factors must be decided.

■ Because the classroom has students of differing abilities, cultures, languages, learning preferences, etc, a variety of approaches to assessment is required.

## STANDARDIZED ASSESSMENT

■ **Standardized assessments** usually involve mass-produced materials that are used for people over a school district, a province, or a country.

■ The conditions for doing the assessment are supposed to be the same for everyone.

■ **Criterion referenced** assessments determine the quality of the student's performance by comparing it to some predetermined standards.

■ **Norm referenced** assessments determine the quality of the student's performance by comparing it to the performance of others, particularly those in some norm group.

■ While much is made sometimes of the difference between criterion and norm referenced standardized assessment, in practice they tend to amount to the same thing.

  ▪ The criteria were established based on some concept of expected behaviour for students at that grade, a sort of virtual norm group.

■ Scores from standardized assessments often are reported in terms of percentile rank, age equivalent, or grade equivalent.

■ Standardized assessments are particularly useful in determining how a group of children are doing or how a program is working. Their value may decline quite dramatically for a particular individual whose reality is different from that of the norm group or where conditions are different from those anticipated when the standardized assessment was developed.

- There is increasing concern that any standardized assessment used to evaluate individual students be designed to look more at learning *potential* rather than at level of *achievement*.

## STATISTICS

- A basic understanding of a few statistical concepts is essential for teachers, especially those dealing with any students who may have standardized test results.
- Statistics is merely a language for describing large amounts of data.
- One form of statistics uses graphic presentations of various forms.
- Another form of statistics uses various types of mathematical calculations.
- Two of the most important concepts in statistics involve average values and spread.
- The various forms of **average** are *mean,* or the sum of scores divided by the number of scores, *median,* or the central value in an order distribution of scores, and *mode,* or most frequent score.
- The **range,** or highest minus lowest score, is one of the simplest ways of describing the spread of a sample of data. The range does have the weakness of giving too much importance to extreme data.
- **Standard deviation** is a calculated measure of dispersion that takes into account how often a score occurs.

## CLASSROOM ASSESSMENTS/EVALUATIONS

### Observation of Students and Interviews

Advantages

- Notes from observation and interviews allow the teacher to give context and meaning to student behaviour.
- Observation and interviews may be less threatening to students than other forms of assessment.

Disadvantages

- Observations and interviews may be seen as being subject to bias.
- Observation of students and interviews take a great deal of time, especially when the need to get notes into some type of logical form is considered.

### Testing

Methods

- There are several approaches to testing including true/false, fill-in the blanks, multiple choice, matching, short answer, and essay.

- Each has its strengths and weaknesses.
- Each requires the instructor to understand the types of errors both instructors and students typically make in the different types of tests.

## General Principles

- Do the test yourself before you give it to students.
- Place a line for the student's name and any general instructions at the top of the first page.
- Usually pages should be numbered and stapled together. Ask everyone if they have the right number of pages.
- Make the test as graphically pleasing as possible.
- Group similar types of test questions together and then use some type of logical progression of questions within each category.
- Carefully determine the number of questions that should be on the test based on the level of students and the type of questions being asked.
- Encourage students to ask you quietly for help if there is something they do not understand.

## Marking and Returning Tests

- Use a marking guide for all questions. This is particularly important for short answer and essay questions.
- For short answer and essay questions it usually is better to mark the same question for everyone and then move on to the next question.
- Try not to look at student names when you start marking.
- Use a method of returning tests that does not indicate the students' performances.
- Put the student's mark so that other students cannot see it.

## Test Analysis

- After students have written the test it is necessary to find out if there were any questions that were confusing, any content areas that seem to be weak, and any difficulties that particular students are having.
- One way to do this is to ask students. This provides some valuable information, although you must recognize that students are more inclined to concentrate on perceived shortcomings of the test than they are on their own performance.
- The grade spread can be used to determine if the test was too easy or too hard.
- A table such as the one below can be constructed based on the students' answers. Choose a level that you would consider satisfactory for the questions, for instance 80 percent correct. Give any answers that meet this level a '+' on the table. Other answers receive a '−'. Construct the following table.

| TABLE 17-1 | Exam Questions Analysis Questions | | | | | |
|---|---|---|---|---|---|---|
| Questions | | | | | | |
| Students | 1 | 2 | 3 | 4 | 5 | Etc |
| Lori | + | + | − | + | + | |
| Pedro | + | − | − | + | + | |
| Sangai | − | − | − | − | + | |

- From this table we can see that there is some problem with question #3 and all students understand question #5. Lori is doing very well while Sangai is having some difficulty with the majority of the class content.

## Helping Students with Tests

- There are a variety of ways that teachers can help students with tests.
- Care in the initial presentation of material helps students organize their notes and determine what is important to know.
- Students and teacher can work together to brainstorm study and exam-writing skills.
- Teachers can help students interpret their marks in a realistic manner. A mark of less than 100 percent does not mean a lifetime of terrible consequences.
- Teachers and students can work together to develop strategies to reduce anxiety.
- Teachers can let students know that they are sympathetic to the problems students are having and will make allowances in times of personal crises.

| Exercise 17–1 | The Nonsense Exam |
|---|---|

One of the ways to learn about the difficulties in writing exams is to try deliberately to produce an exam that appears on the surface to be fine, but that closer examination shows to be either complete nonsense or impossible to complete. Work with two or three others to write exam questions and instructions that have completely unintended errors. An example of such a question is:

The number of bones in the human hand is:

a) Less than 50.

b) Less than 20.

c) Less than 10.

An exam students brought to me last year asked them to complete as many questions as they could in the time available, but then told them marks would be taken off for any spelling or grammar errors. I have asked students to answer a question and then given them the answer two questions later.

## Problem Solving and Diagnostic Assessment

- **Diagnostic assessment** does not refer to clinical diagnosis, but rather to obtaining information about a student's ability to understand a conceptual problem
- Problem solving and diagnostic assessment have the same underlying logic. Both attempt to determine the strategies students are using to solve conceptual problems and analyse these strategies to learn about fundamental misconceptions in understanding and application.
- There are four steps in problem solving or diagnostic assessment.
  1. Define the essential nature of conceptual problem.
  2. Define the nature of the steps a student must go through to understand the problem.
  3. Design an assessment tool for each of these steps.
  4. Order the assessment tools in the order needed to confront the problem.

## Project Assessment

### Types of Projects and Related Issues

- Projects include everything from the familiar research papers, lab reports, journals, and craft projects to many types of media productions.
- Projects always involve concerns about storage and display.
- Teachers have to be very careful about the marking of projects, particularly those that go beyond the usual research report.
  - Students are very ego-involved in their work and tend to be more affected by evaluations than would be the case for tests.
  - Student work must not be defaced with red ink comments.
  - Any comments should be placed so other individuals or groups looking at the project cannot see them.
- As is the case in all assessments, the conditions of assessment need to be clear to students.
- A **rubric** or scoring guide usually is required project evaluation.
- Case studies could be either projects or performances.

## Performance Assessment

- Performances can range from short role plays through relatively brief class presentations to full recitals or plays.
- Students are even more ego-involved than is the case for projects.
- Performances are very public.
- While performances are the least concrete of all forms of assessment, they often leave the greatest impression on the participants, the audience, and the teacher.

- Teachers must make the criteria for evaluation of the performance as clear as possible and then use those criteria.
- Rubrics also can be used for performance assessment.
- Peer or self-evaluations must meet the conditions discussed below.

## Group Assessment

- Concepts related to group assessment were discussed in Chapter 13.

## Peer and Self Evaluations

### Peer Evaluations

- Great care must be exercised in the use of peer evaluations.
  - Peer evaluations are very open to the social dynamics of the classroom.
- There must be a strong feeling of trust in the group and a shared commitment to excellence.
- Even with the feelings of trust and commitment, teachers usually should limit peer evaluations to statements of two likes and a wish.

### Self Evaluations

- While student self-assessments usually should not be used for grading, they are a very valuable source of information for the teacher.
- Approaches to self-assessment include questionnaires, skills inventories, and subject journals.
- Self-assessment allows students to be part of the educational process and gives them an opportunity to practice expressing ideas.
- Teachers also need to engage in a process of self-assessment or reflective teaching.

## PRINCIPLES OF GRADING

- Grades should relate only to academic performance. Any comments about social behaviour need to be kept separate.
- Grades need to have a close relationship to the objectives of the unit or course.
- Grades must be based on wide variety of valid and reliable data.
- Grades should be determined by a student's performance in relation to set criteria, instead of in comparison to other students.
  - Students should know as they go along how they are doing rather than finding out at the end of a term based on how well they did in relation to others.
- Marks and grades need to be kept in a manner that ensures student confidentiality.
  - Often computers are used to store marks and these files may be exchanged with a central office.

- Password protection and maybe encryption are required to ensure that students, other school employees, and visitors do not have access to these files.

## REPORTING TO PARENTS

### Report Cards

- Most school districts require a certain number of report cards in a specific format be sent to parents each term or year.
- Report cards must indicate to parents how their child is doing in terms of the objectives of the course and generally expected outcomes for students of that grade.
  - Many parents will access Ministry of Education web sites to determine what is to be covered in a particular grade.

### Parent Teacher Meetings

- Teachers should try to make parents as comfortable as possible. This will mean signs of respect such as proper seating.
- Often the whole school will hold parent nights at the same time. Beverages, food, and babysitting are services that should be considered.
  - Some school may have translators available to help parents communicate with teachers.
- Teachers should have materials ready to show parents.
- If the student is present, a teacher might consider allowing the student to chair the meeting.

### Informal Contact

- Teachers will be involved in a number of informal contacts with parents ranging from phone calls to random encounters.
- If any significant information is discussed, the teacher should record the discussion in a journal.
- Teachers should try to mention student achievements rather than concentrating on difficulties.

### Awkward Situations

- Teachers encounter a number of awkward situations in their dealings with parents.
- One of the most important of these revolves around the issue of custody and authority.
  - Teachers must respect any conditions of custody that are communicated to them.
  - Where conditions are not known but their existence is suspected, teachers must make an effort to find out about custody arrangements.

- Sometimes parents are very confrontational and the teacher must not get drawn into a conflict with the parent.
- Sometimes parents behave in totally inappropriate ways and the teacher must have clear boundaries as to what is acceptable and what will not be tolerated.
  - Parents may come to meetings or to the classroom under the influence of alcohol or drugs.
  - Parents may make comments to you or to students that are not acceptable and that cannot be dismissed as merely a misunderstanding.

## CASE 17-1: GOOD CONNECTIONS

Peter, a non-tenured faculty member, was in the second year of teaching a basic science course in the Faculty of Arts and Science. When he took attendance he noticed that the name of one of the students, Mary Grauso, was familiar but thought no more about it. By the midpoint of the course he noted that Mary was doing very poorly. She had failed her midterm and had done a very poor job preparing her lab reports. Peter also noted that Mary often was absent from class.

One morning Peter got a phone message from the Dean to please come and see him on Tuesday morning. Peter was nervous at the meeting. The Dean was very pleasant, however, and in the course of the conversation asked Peter about the progress of Mary Grauso. The Dean pointed out that Mary was the daughter of a prominent Board of Governors member and that Peter should do everything he could to ensure that Mary passed. Peter didn't respond other than to thank the Dean for his interest.

A week later Peter learned that the Dean was helping Mary and two of her friends with the subject matter in his course. In addition to help with content, the Dean had given Mary access to copies of old exams that were on the office computer.

### Discussion Questions

1. What are some of the conceptual issues that cause concern about the Dean's behaviour?
2. Was Mary guilty of any misbehaviour?
3. What do you think Peter should do now?

## CASE 17-2: CHANGING A MARK

The one-year appointment meant that Kiran finally had a chance to teach her own Grade 10 science class and the opportunity really to make a difference. In addition to teaching her classes and labs, Kiran had taken a very active interest in the role of women in science and had tried to emphasize the role of females in science during her classes. Having her own class meant that she could implement some of the concepts she knew helped women like science.

Shura was a student in Kiran's class. She did reasonably well in quizzes or multiple-choice exams, usually getting a B or B+. Unfortunately, she got a D with the final major assignment, which was worth 60 percent of the class mark. The result would be that Shura would get a C for the course, not enough to get into the honours program for the next year.

Shura came to see Kiran and told her that she was having a lot of problems in her life. She wanted Kiran to change the weighting of her assignments so she would obtain more value for the quizzes and less for the major assignment. This would result in Shura getting a B- for the course, the minimum requirement for the honours program.

## Discussion Questions

1. What changes would you make in Kiran's evaluation plan for the course?
2. Do you feel that Kiran's attitudes influenced her marking in an unethical manner?
3. Regardless of your opinion in Question #2, do you think Kiran should change Shura's mark? Justify your answer.

## CASE 17-3: THE IRATE PARENT

Mr. Armstrong obviously was very angry. His language was controlled but the muscles of his face were drawn, he was leaning across the desk, and his eyes never seemed to blink. Ms. Buie was very uncomfortable. Usually she would not tolerate this type of behaviour from anyone, but this was her first experience with a very upset parent.

Ms. Buie had started to teach at Summerside High in September. It was her first full-time appointment and she was anxious to make a good impression. She had been a Teacher-on-Call (TOC) for the last two years and, while this had given her an opportunity to develop lesson plans and try units in different classes, she definitely did not want to go back to the uncertainty of not having a regular source of income.

Now it was the end of October. Last Wednesday, report cards had been sent home and tonight was an opportunity for parents to come and talk to the teachers. Mr. Armstrong was one of those parents, indeed one of the few fathers who had come. His daughter, Jennifer, was in Ms. Buie's Math 11 course and unfortunately had done very poorly on a midterm exam worth 40 percent of the final course mark. She had done well on a project but it was worth only 10 percent of the mark. Ms. Buie did not have any other indication of Jennifer's ability in the class.

"How is my daughter going to get a decent mark in your class now?" Mr. Armstrong demanded. "She wants to take Math 12 to get into Pharmacy and this mark will ruin her chances. Why did you make one exam worth so much? Can't you use something else for a bigger part of the mark?"

Ms. Buie did not have a good answer.

## Discussion Questions

1. What other types of evaluations might Ms. Buie have used?
2. What do you feel about her weighting and timing of marks?
3. What do you think Ms. Buie should do now?

## CASE 17-4: THE RIGHT NEIGHBOURHOOD

Jason Chauchard did quite well in all his subjects, but he lived for theatre. Since coming to Shoreline High two years ago in Grade 9, he had volunteered or been chosen for almost all of the backstage work involved in the twice-yearly performances put on by the school's Theatre Department. Like all of the students, he also played a part in the chorus for group dance numbers. This year he had a brief solo part in the Spring performance, and had received a resounding ovation from the audience along with a request from the Drama teacher that he be sure and return next year.

The principal was surprised to get a phone call from Jason's parents asking to have a meeting to discuss Jason's continuing at the school. Their concern revolved around the publication of Grade 12 Provincial marks that rated another high school in the area higher than Shoreline. Jason's parents wanted their son to get the best academic education possible, and were willing to move for his Grade 11 and 12 years so that Jason could go to the other school. Unfortunately, the other school did not have a theatre program and so they wanted to discuss what would be best for Jason before they finalized any move.

### Discussion Questions

1. What are some of the issues involved in Provincial Exams?
2. What types of courses usually have Grade 12 Provincial Exams?
3. How might the principal outline the pros and cons of any move for Jason's parents?

# chapter eighteen

# Controversies

'Experts' for thousands of years have debated the content, form, and purpose of education. Someone born 2000 years ago from Greece, Italy, or China could enter today's debates without missing a step. For the most part, they could even use the same language and concepts. This chapter presents a few of these debates.

- I cannot write about these controversies in a manner that everyone will accept as an objective presentation.

- In a general sense though, I feel that all of these issues are complex and that no single position or statement summarizes or resolves the issues involved.

- Perhaps a central issue is that schools, school boards, and ministries of education often act to please everyone and offend no one.

  - As a result, school life and programs become a mishmash of different concepts, and social festivals become bland, meaningless activities.

| Exercise 18–1 | **The Other Side** |
|---|---|

Take any issue related to education where you are convinced of your position and examine the other side carefully. Without dismissing the views of other people through the use of derogatory and simplistic labels, find out why they hold a view that is contrary to yours.

## WHO CONTROLS EDUCATION?

Control of the education process is probably the central issue in all education debates. Is education controlled by teachers, ministries of education, parents, students, business, or some other group? Each of these groups has members who have strong, definite positions, while others maintain softer positions and are more willing to consider several sides of an issue. The problem with softer positions is that eventually someone has to make a decision, and then the true positions of the people involved become more obvious.

### Approaches to Education

Closely related to the above debate is the issue of the approach to education that is most appropriate. For the sake of simplicity the approaches to education might be seen as along a continuum from completely child-centred to completely driven by a curriculum imposed by outside authorities.

Of course, the debate as to which approach is best, and the nature of any curriculum that is used, goes back to the question of who controls education.

### Approaches to Teaching

Once a decision is made about curriculum, decisions also have to be made about how the curriculum is taught.

- Is whole language, or phonics, the appropriate way to teach reading?
- Should students be learning to divide when calculators are available or should they be working on problem solving?
- Should a broad range of topics be taught or should we go back to basics?

| Exercise 18–2 | **It Sounded Like a Good Idea** |
|---|---|

Examine approaches to teaching a particular area that were popularized 20 years ago. Are they still be used? If not, why not? Why were they ever considered in the first place?

# STRUCTURE OF SCHOOLS

- Should there be high schools and elementary schools, elementary, middle, and high, or something else?
- Should big mega-schools be developed or should schools be kept small?
- Should schools run year round?
- What hours should schools operate?
- Is the factory model of the school with its bells and fixed timetable appropriate for young people, or even for educating students in the much-hyped 'New Millennium?'

## Vouchers

- Some feel parents should be given a voucher for the basic funding their school board receives from their province for each child. They could use this voucher for any educational program they think would be best for their children.
- Some oppose the voucher system because they feel it is undignified for schools to have to compete for students, or because they have job security, philosophical or political reasons for opposing it.
  - Probably most people would dismiss these arguments as being far too self-serving.
- A voucher system does raise some very practical issues, however.
  - Do the schools that are being compared all have the same issues and resources?
  - Would all parents be able to take advantage of the voucher system?
  - What happens to the schools that are being abandoned? Do they keep getting worse?
  - What happens if thousands of students want to go to Fantastic High?

## Assessment

- Some of these issues are discussed in Chapter 17.
- Should there be provincial or even federal assessment of students?
- How should the results of provincial or federal assessment be used?
- Does the public have the right to see the results of provincial or federal assessments?
- Who should decide, and under what conditions, whether a child passes from one grade to another?

## Academic or Social Education

- Some people see the school's main purpose as being only academic education. They feel that teachers have no mandate to be involved in social education.
- At the opposite extreme, other groups stress the social role of education and are much more interested in discussing the latest social issue than they are in how to help children learn to read.

- Those that support the social purpose of schools sometimes try to use the schools to 'educate' students about their particular view of some social issue.

## Zero Tolerance

- **Zero tolerance** means a refusal to accept a particular behaviour, regardless of the circumstances or the extent of the behaviour.
- Schools sometimes are confronted by very serious situations that require strong action.
- At other times, schools appear to react with inordinate haste and in a very punitive manner to offences that most people would regard as minor or non-existent.
- Zero tolerance policies may serve to punish those who most need support in the school.
- Zero tolerance policies often are used to support the social positions of a particular group.

## Christmas or Winter Festival

- Public schools have students from a great variety of backgrounds.
- Over 3 in 4 Canadians say they are Christian but this proportion will not be consistent across schools.
- Schools and school districts have to decide how to handle the issue of holiday festivals that have religious overtones.

## WHO IS A TEACHER?

- This issue could become a very important one in education in the next 20 years.
- Teachers in the public school system in particular have to complete a certain approved education and be accepted for registration with one or more provincial bodies.
- Electronic education will involve people who do not have this background but who are developing and promoting education materials.
- The demand for more specific technical education will require that people with technical backgrounds enter education, even though they may not have taken the usual teacher education programs.
- The challenge to the accepted definition of teacher will parallel similar challenges in law and medicine.

## STREAMING, DESTREAMING, AND MAINSTREAMING

### Streaming and Destreaming

- **Streaming** means splitting the main river of the school into separate streams with areas of specialization such as academic, commercial, media, and technical.
  - This split occurs in all subjects including language arts and math.

- Students who are streamed into programs that do not meet university requirements have to upgrade if they want to go on to university.
- **Destreaming** means the stopping of streaming, especially for so-called academic courses.
- Debates about the assumed superiority of a university education versus the desire of many students to pursue other areas, and the need for skilled workers, underlie much of this debate.

## Mainstreaming

- **Mainstreaming** means the involvement of those with special needs in the regular school environment in a manner that is least restrictive to educational and social needs.
- Up until the last couple of years, any questioning of the concept of mainstreaming was seen as being inappropriate and was quickly dismissed with some platitude or accusation.
- Now there are more parents and teachers who feel that the whole issue needs to be revisited for some students.
- Two important questions are whether the student who is being mainstreamed is benefiting, and whether the educational and emotional needs of other students in the class are suffering.
- Lack of funding for extra staff and for training lie behind much of teacher frustration with the mainstreaming of some students.

## URBAN VS. RURAL

- Separation between rural and urban concerns and values is very important in Canada.
- Rural people feel powerless to deal with the political and social influence of the large urban population.
- Urban people often assume they understand rural issues because they like hiking or they belong to some ecology group.

## RACISM

- Issues of racism show every sign of becoming as important as gender issues have been over the past three or four decades.
- The definition of racism is subject to the kind of debate that characterized definitions of sexism in earlier times.
- Accusations of racism will lead to an examination and restructuring of many aspects of our culture.
- On the other hand, trivial or inaccurate accusations of racism also will be used to further the 'chilly climate' of the 1980s and 1990s that accusations of sexism produced.

## GENDER

The battle between the sexes has long been the basis of much literature and comment. Over the past 150 years in both North America and Europe, the battle has been drawn around political, economic, and family issues. In the last 30 or 40 years, the battle has resulted in a profound shift in the nature of family, work, and political structures. Almost every issue has been analysed in terms of sex or gender issues.

## Sexism

- Sexism is discrimination against an individual because of the person's sex.
- Charges and counter-charges of sexism have been a very common aspect of education since at least the 1960s.
- Often the charges reflect real and systemic concerns.
- Other times they were the result of superficial analysis.
  - If I believe something to be the truth, I always can find examples of it in a complex society.
- Sometimes charges of sexism result from individuals or groups trying to obtain an undeserved advantage.
- While it will be some time before an analysis can be done of the effects of charges of sexism, for the present these charges have done much to fuel fires of ill will between the sexes.

## Concern About Males

- Starting in the mid-1990s there has been a growing concern about the condition of males in our society.
- In schools the issues have revolved around the declining academic and social performance of males.
- Other issues include the higher rates of suicide for males than females, drug use by males, the disproportionate number of males that are in our criminal justice system, the lower life expectancy of males, and a variety of other social and health issues.
- Much of the present discussions from education and social work agencies that even touch on these issues claim any problems are the fault of the males themselves.
  - Apparently the argument of systemic discrimination that was used for females does not apply for males.
- It is going to be very hard for our society, particularly our schools and social work agencies, to deal with issues related to males.
  - Many males may already have lost faith in these agencies even if the agencies have started trying to deal with male concerns.

## Nature-Nurture

- The nature/nurture debate discussed in Chapter Three has been a prominent feature of the debate about gender.

- In the 1970s a particular definition of the concept of androgyny came to prominence. While **androgyny** means having characteristics of both female and male, the 1970s brought the idea of choosing which characteristics a person wanted and the understanding that any differences between females and males — other than the obvious biological ones — were the result of social conditioning.

- Scales were developed to measure the amount of male and female characteristics an individual exhibited.

- The way male and female characteristics were assigned was very sexist. For instance, self-reliance was seen as male, while yielding was seen as female. Being compassionate or tender was seen as being female, while aggression was seen as male.

## Sexism and Other Issues

- Concern about issues related to gender and sexism have overshadowed examination of many other social issues.

- Even where other social issues such as health or poverty have been examined, often the issue is shifted to one related to gender.

- There seems to be little understanding that the differences between other dichotomous divisions of the population, such as the poor and the wealthy or the sick and the well, probably are much greater than the differences between the sexes.

## SEXUAL ORIENTATION

- Educators have become increasingly concerned about the physical and mental health of those individuals who are not heterosexual.

- Beyond the health concerns, there also are issues related to the lack of other than heterosexual models and views in much of the education material.

- On the other hand, many cultural and religious groups have very strong views about sexual orientation and sometimes believe educators are promoting sexual orientations that are not acceptable to their culture or religion.

## MEDICAL PROCEDURES IN THE CLASSROOM

## Attention Deficit Hyperactivity Disorder (ADHD)

- According to Health Canada, prescriptions for Ritalin and the more powerful Dexedrine for young people increased by 456 percent between 1991 and 2001.
  - These drugs are given to students to control Attention Deficit Hyperactivity Disorder.

- Some students do much better academically when they are taking a drug such as Ritalin.
- While exact information is difficult to obtain, the number of students prescribed Ritalin varies dramatically from one area of the country to another.
  - On average, approximately eight to ten percent of Canadian students, mostly males, are on Ritalin or similar drugs.
- Young people are being kept on the drugs for longer times.
- These drugs, essentially a form of speed, are being bought and sold in the schools. They are legal with a prescription and easily available.
- Even though some students are helped academically, many people are suspicious about the underlying motivation of parents and teachers in encouraging the use of these drugs.
- The fact that experts seem to feel that more and more of these drugs are needed raises questions about the appropriateness of schools for young people.
  - Perhaps much of the behaviour that is labeled as hyperactive could just as easily be called normal or exploring.

## Other Medical Treatments

- In addition to Ritalin, students are being prescribed a variety of anti-depressants and other psychoactive drugs.
  - Teachers may be asked to oversee or even administer some of these drugs.
- Teachers may have to monitor students with chronic medical conditions and even supervise self-administered treatments.
- Special needs students may have medical conditions that have to be considered.
- Students with injuries or illnesses may require teacher help with treatment.
- Some parents might expect a teacher to make sure their children eat only particular foods or take their vitamin tablets.
- Parent or school expectations about teacher involvement in any medical treatments make many teachers uncomfortable.

## CONTROVERSIES AND TEACHERS

- Teachers who pursue an agenda to the detriment of some of their students are behaving in an unethical manner.
- Teachers must study a broad range of material related to some of these issues and try to engage in deep analyses of the issues.
- Teachers and the education system are targeted by a broad range of groups with particular interests who want the education system to promote their particular viewpoint.

## CASE 18-1: VOUCHERS

The Minister of Education was part of a new provincial government that had been elected with a large majority. Part of its mandate was to revitalize the education system. Over the past couple of years, the media and a large number of the public had been quite critical of the performance of students in the province's schools. The Minister had very strong opinions about the changes that were needed, but felt she needed support from some outside group or study. As a result, she commissioned an educational consulting company to study the provincial school system and make recommendations to her within six months.

When the report arrived, the Minister was pleased to see that it supported many of her views. The report gave some statistical analyses of public dissatisfaction and produced a list of recommendations. The concept of vouchers was a central theme for most of the recommendations. Parents were to be given a credit for the base amount that the province provided to the public school system for each child in the system. Parents would be able to use this voucher in whatever school they pleased.

The report predicted that the majority of teachers and some members of the public would oppose a voucher system, but that the majority of people supported this system. The report also predicted that some parents would move their children to private schools. This would not be a significant number, however, because the private school system did not have the resources or time to build new schools to accommodate large numbers of new students. Rather, school boards, principals and teachers would have to work within the public system to build programs that would attract parents and students. This would lead to a variety of new approaches, including a return by some schools to the traditional academic approaches that were thought to have served well in the past. Other schools would stress academic excellence, arts programs, student-centred experiences, web-based courses, etc. The Minister felt that the voucher system was the best way to revitalize the schools and was prepared to recommend this approach to cabinet.

### Discussion Questions

1. If you were the educational consulting company, what type of report would you submit to the Minister?

2. Do you think that the company's approach and conclusions are correct?

3. What are some issues that were not considered in the report?

## CASE 18-2: ZERO TOLERANCE

Fairmount Middle School had almost five hundred students from a variety of cultural backgrounds. Bullying was not a serious problem, but incidents of it were increasing. Teachers had observed more cases of name-calling and heckling on the playground, and parents were phoning with more complaints about their child being bullied. So far there had been no known cases of any physical violence other than a couple brief pushing matches. The principal wanted to 'nip the problem in the bud' and made the issue the main component of the school's next professional development day.

At the training event teachers and a guest speaker examined several anti-bullying programs that seemed to have been successful in other schools. In the end they chose sections from three different programs and added some ideas of their own. The emphasis was to be on education and prevention. The teachers recognized that incidents of bullying would still occur despite their program though, and discussed methods of dealing with these incidents for some time. In the end there was acceptance of a zero tolerance approach. A first offence of bullying would result automatically in a three-day in-school suspension; a second incident would lead to a week's out-of-school suspension. The teachers felt that any deviation from this policy invariably would lead to more exceptions and the eventual collapse of the policy. In addition to any aggressive physical contact, bullying also was to include emotional and psychological harassment.

## Discussion Questions

1. How would you define bullying? Do other students in your class agree with your definition?
2. What kinds of issues need to be considered in an anti-bullying education program for Fairmount?
3. What are possible concerns about the school's zero tolerance policy?

## CASE 18-3:  STREAMING

It wasn't so much that she hated school; at least hating implied some type of emotional response. Rather, school just left Joyce Chan feeling flat. It was like the jobs her parents wanted her to do at home; she could do them without difficulty but much preferred to avoid them if she could. In Grade 7, she momentarily attracted the attention of a high school student who was taking a technical program at a local high school. Before he decided that Joyce was just a kid, he outlined the different courses he was taking and his excitement about future employment possibilities. He never realized that Joyce was far more excited about the school program he was describing than she was about him.

Joyce immediately told her parents that she wanted to enter a technical program in High School. Her parents reacted with horror. Joyce expected this but thought the issue would be about a female choosing a technical career. She had marshaled all her arguments to counter this position, including the old standby that her parents didn't understand modern times. Because she knew that her parents realized she did not like school, she had not prepared for her parents' insistence that she get an academic education that qualified her for university.

## Discussion Questions

1. What arguments can you develop to support Joyce's decision to pursue a technical program?
2. What arguments can you develop to support her parents' position that Joyce should get an academic education that qualified her for university?
3. What is your position with regard to streaming?

# CASE 18-4: CONSIDERING MALES

Sarah Radyck recalled the 1960s as being such an exhilarating time to be in university. It seemed like a whole new world was being created right before people's eyes. Sarah had loved ever minute of it. She had been especially interested in the women's rights movement, and words like *gender, affirmative action, equality,* and *patriarchy* had taken a central place in her vocabulary. There were late night meetings where gender issues were hotly debated. Marches, publicity stunts, and sit-ins were planned in detail so as to appear spontaneous. Journalists, media personalities, and politicians loudly proclaimed their support for women's rights. Any counter positions were denounced and ridiculed.

In her second year, Sarah had to give more thought about what career she would practice after graduation. Many of her friends were talking about medicine and law. Journalism was a particularly hot choice. Sarah always had been drawn to teaching, however, and somewhat sheepishly said that she was going to be a teacher. "Boring," chimed those around her. "Teaching or nursing. Just like our Moms," snidely commented others.

Sarah justified her choice to her friends by stating that, "Teaching would allow me to influence young people. I think the only place we can really change opinions is with young people."

The school structure did not change easily. There were all these systems in place: curriculum guides, lists of recommended books to use in classes, principals who had old-fashioned views about what should be taught. Then there was just the sheer amount of work that had to be done. Teaching every day, marking, and meetings left little time to develop new curriculum ideas. Gradually things changed, however. More and more teachers entering the system were interested in issues related to females. Women's issues became common features in the media; more and more court cases supported women's rights. There was a lot of concern about females not doing well in math and science. The problem was seen as systemic rather than sex-related, and programs were developed to correct the situation.

By the mid-1980s Sarah was including more and more material specifically related to females in her curriculum. She included works by female writers and books that took a more female point of view. In discussions she encouraged her students to look at issues from a women's point of view. Sarah always was quite respectful of those who did not share her views though, and tried to see her role as teaching rather than preaching. Still, there was a fair amount of resistance. This resistance was balanced by the enthusiasm of some of the young women in her classes. "You're the greatest," they claimed. "You changed our lives. We really have come to see increased possibilities for women in your class. You make us feel so confident about our futures."

Sarah found these comments so rewarding. They more than made up for the ever-increasing stress of teaching. Any negative comments were easily dismissed as throwbacks to a previous time. By the early 1990s almost all of the students, both male and female, supported her position. They all could analyze situations based on feminist principles, and all seemed to support various types of rights for all kinds of people who were seen as marginalized. Empowerment became the code word that signified understanding of the basic power structure. Students regularly wrote letters of thanks to Sarah and praised her classes in the yearbook. She was asked to give talks at conferences and published a manual of teaching strategies that was strongly supported by the provincial teachers' federation.

Toward the end of the '90s, however, Sarah began to notice some data that she found disturbing. It seemed that males were having increasing difficulties, or at least that their difficulties were being noticed. There was a debate about whether the decline in school performance by males was real — some writers dismissed it as non-existent, while others said that any decline was due to the fact that boys were basically louts.

Sarah started to mention a few of these issues in her class. This always sparked a debate with many of the students countering any mention of males having difficulties with examples of how females were exploited. "Women only earn $0.65 or $0.75 or whatever figure was used for every $1 earned by males," was a common rejoinder. Statistics about much higher suicide rates in males were countered by comments about females being more likely to attempt suicide. Indeed Sarah noticed that any concerns expressed about males seemed always to be produce a series of 'Yeah, buts…'

From time to time though, Sarah brought in articles from the paper that mentioned difficulties that males were having. These usually were not well received by the class. In January a cartoon appeared on a notice board making fun of her. A group of students started a web site that quoted her as saying all kinds of things against females, none of them being true. The principal called her in for a meeting claiming that three of her students had written him a letter about her creating a hostile environment for women in her class. This criticism sickened Sarah. It seemed that everything she had spent her long career doing was being destroyed. "Why are they doing this to me?" she lamented to her partner. "I just thought we needed a bit of balance in the class."

## Discussion Questions

1. How could the concept of models be used to analyze Sarah's career and her present predicament?

2. By the mid-1990s, how could Sarah tell that she no longer was a pioneer in educational thinking?

3. What pressures will Sarah have to endure if she wants to deal with issues related to males in her classroom?

# chapter nineteen

# Alternative Schools and Organizations

Parents and students choose forms of education beyond the 'normal' public school systems for a variety of reasons.

- Sometimes parents are looking for a particular philosophy or a particular social context. Other times they are trying to avoid situations in the public school such as large class sizes, or social problems that are perceived as being more common in the public system.
  - Sometimes these requirements can be met within the public system, but occasionally only private or independent schools can or will meet their wants.
  - Independent or private schools that follow the provincial curriculum usually are eligible for at least a percentage of the provincial block funding that would be available to a public school.
  - In some provinces, Catholic schools are funded at the same rate as the public school system.

When most people think of education they imagine a classroom in a regular public school with the approaches and textbooks they remember from their childhood. In most cases now, even the so-called regular classroom is not the classroom of their childhood. In addition to the regular classroom though, there is a broad range of approaches to education used in Canada. Sometimes these additional approaches are called **alternative** schools although the word alternative tends to be used most commonly for schools that are designed to meet the needs of students with particular individual needs. This chapter examines a few of the more common options parents choose. The options have been chosen to give an idea of the breadth of choices rather than to focus on any particular theoretical basis for specific choices. The chapter has been organized so that alternative approaches found within the public system are discussed first, followed by approaches within either the public or the private, and then totally private approaches.

| Exercise 19–1 | 'Alternative' Schools |
|---|---|

Choose one of the alternative schools in your area and find out about its philosophy and approach. Usually this can be done without any special permission from a Human Subjects Committee at your college or university. While it would be nice to know why parents are sending their children to the school, any type of survey of parents probably is not possible without approval from the college or university.

## CHARTER SCHOOLS

- Charter schools are public schools that operate under a charter or contract approved by the local school board and the provincial ministry of education.
- Rather than it being the mandatory or catchment school for a particular area, students and their parents choose the school for its philosophy and approach to education.
- Generally, charter schools are governed by their own board and control their own staffing, budgeting, and programs.
- There is considerable variety in the mission statements of charter schools.
- Charter schools allow both parents and teachers a broader choice than is usually offered in the rest of the public system.
- Funding depends on a block grant per student, the same funding that is in place for other students in the public school system.
- No additional fees are charged and the provincial curriculum is used.
- Schools may have various interests and approaches ranging from teaching gifted and talented pupils, to students who are at risk, to using back-to-basics approaches. As a result, each charter school is unique.
- Charter schools must not practise any form of discrimination in terms of admission or program, although there will be limits based on available spaces and the type of programs or facilities that are available.
- A lottery system often is used to choose students for initial entry when there is more demand than spaces.

# HOME-SCHOOLING

- Parents home-school their children for a broad variety of reasons ranging from health and social concerns to pedagogical, political, and moral philosophies. For many, it is a combination of issues.

- Home-schooling is entirely legal provided an educational program actually is being offered, that the children are not just being required to work rather than attend school, and are not being abused in some manner.

- Parents are required to register their children with a local public or private school or with some other educational organization in the province such as a distance education centre.

- The local district superintendent is required to investigate if there is a report that a home-schooled student is not receiving an educational program. Any form of abuse, of course, must be reported, as is the case with all children.

- The local school or other educational organization receives a small portion of the block funding for a student for the home-schooled student, although what the school may do for that funding varies from district to district.

    - They usually loan educational resources that would be available to students in the school and provide some form of assessment, although the parent usually is free to reject the assessment.

- Some schools allow home-schooled students to participate in some school activities such as band or sports, although a fee may be charged.

- Approximately one to two percent of children in the country are home-schooled. The numbers are a bit hard to pin down because some parents do not register their children even though they are required to do so.

- The approach to education taken varies from parent to parent, with some following the provincial curriculum and others using a much more child-centred approach.

- Two issues of concern are socialization and continuing on to university or community college.

    - The issue of socialization usually is answered by pointing out that home-schooled children have a broader range of social experiences in their day than those in a school. They are involved with people of all ages and backgrounds in the community while school students are in a room with others of their age.

    - Parents of home-schooled children also raise the issue of bullying and other social problems in schools.

- The issue of post-secondary education is a little more difficult. Those home-schooled children who have not followed a provincial curriculum or written any school graduation exams may have more difficulty entering Canadian universities.

    - Electronic education makes many more graduation courses available through distance education.

    - Post secondary institutions all have a mature student designation.

    - American universities generally are more open to anyone who obtains satisfactory levels on entrance exams.

## SPECIALIZED SCHOOLS

■ Most urban centres have private and public schools that offer specialized programs.

■ Examples of such programs include those emphasizing ESL, sports, the arts, math/science, and special needs.

■ Public specialized schools receive block funding for each student, plus additional amounts for those with special needs designations.

■ Private specialized schools that follow the provincial curriculum are eligible for provincial funding at a percent of the funding for public schools, as is the case with other private or independent schools.

## RELIGIOUS SCHOOLS

■ Especially in larger urban areas, almost every religious group has its own school or schools.

■ Most religious schools accept students of other faiths.

■ The curriculum for religious schools varies, with some schools following the provincial curriculum and others having a unique curriculum.

■ Funding is an issue for many religious groups.

■ Parents place their children in religious schools for more reasons that just their belief in the religion of the school.

## PRIVATE ACADEMIC SCHOOLS

■ In addition to religious schools that are private, there are a large number of other private academic schools in most provinces.

■ These schools usually have their own Board and set their own curriculum.

■ Most of the non-religious and non-specialized private schools aim to provide a high level of academic education for parents who can afford their fees and think their children would benefit from the type of program offered in the school.

## THE MONTESSORI METHOD

Maria Montessori, the Italian educator who developed the educational approach that bears her name, was the first woman to graduate as a medical doctor in Italy when she did so in Rome in 1894. She started to work in the psychiatric clinic at the University of Rome where she became interested in the educational problems of children with mental retardation. Dr. Montessori continued this interest through an impressive career at the University of Rome and other educational institutions in Rome. She opened her first Casa dei Bambini (Children's House) in 1907 in a very low-income area of Rome, and spent the next four decades of her life opening other Montessori Schools and lecturing about her methods throughout Europe, India and the United States.

- One of the underlying assumptions of Montessori's approach is that children need to escape from the domination of parents and teachers so that children can be themselves without having to defend themselves against the intervention of adults

- Children are seen to pass through sensitive periods of development early in life.

- The Montessori Method emphasizes the use of simple concrete materials in helping children learn basic skills in mathematics, reading, etc.

  - Examples of these would be beads arranged in sequence to learn the basics of math and bits of wood to train eye movement for reading.

- Children spend a great deal of time exploring these concrete objects on their own rather than in a formal classroom structure.

- Education is seen as self-education as opposed to education by a teacher.

- Students work and the teacher watches, sometimes offering suggestions.

- Children acquire learning through the five senses.

  - Educational materials are very sensory.

- Beauty and orderliness are emphasized.

- The name Montessori is not trademarked, so virtually anyone could claim to be using a Montessori approach.

- Maria Montessori started the Association Montessori Internationale (AMI) in Amsterdam to protect her work.

- In 1997, 5000 American schools claimed to be using the Montessori Method.

  - Only about 20 percent of these belong to the two major sanctioning organizations: The American Montessori Society and the Association Montessori Internationale.

  - Only about 160 schools in the U.S. belong to AMI.

## WALDORF SCHOOLS

Waldorf Schools were developed in 1919 by Rudolf Steiner, an Austrian philosopher, scientist and artist. Actually, Steiner built his first school in 1913 in Switzerland, but the name Waldorf comes from a school he was asked to develop for the children of workers at the Waldorf-Astoria cigarette factory in Stuttgart, Germany in 1919. In a few years there were 1100 students at the school with hundreds more on a waiting list. There now are about 600 schools worldwide; most of the larger urban areas in Canada have a Waldorf School.

Steiner was one of those people who had some ideas that seemed interesting and worth pursuing, while some other ideas seemed so strange that many people rejected them outright. His philosophical and religious ideas are called anthroposophy and are not particularly relevant to this book. Waldorf Schools claim to be non-denominational, but many of the teachers will be interested in, if not supportive of, Steiner's philosophical concepts. The schools do tend to be religiously oriented in a generally Christian perspective.

Waldorf Schools and their founder have been a source of controversy since their beginning. Some of the charges against them have involved claims of occult beliefs. Charges of this type represent a complete lack of understanding of Steiner's philosophy. Other controversies have centred on the supposed separation of church and state in the U.S. where public school districts have experimented with Waldorf Schools. An organization called People for Legal and Nonsectarian Schools (PLANS) in the U.S. has been formed with the purpose of keeping Waldorf Schools out of the public system. PLANS' web site is given in the reference section at the end of this chapter.

The following overview attempts to separate Steiner's concepts of education from his cosmology. The resulting approaches to education are very interesting in terms of how children are viewed and how school is structured, especially in the early years.

- Waldorf Schools place considerable emphasis on their students imparting meaning to their lives on their own, rather than by impressing facts and concepts on the child from the outside.

- Development of the whole child, including academic, artistic, physical and social, is stressed.

- There is a strong emphasis on developing the creativity and imagination of children.

- A unique feature of most Waldorf schools is that a teacher stays with a student for a number of years.

- Steiner thought that children with mental disabilities needed to be treated with love and understanding so they could re-establish the self-confidence they had lost in their interactions with others.

## KUMON MATH AND READING CENTRES

The Kumon Math Program was developed in 1954 by a Japanese high school math teacher named Toru Kumon to help his son with math. It now is a franchise business. In 2001, Kumon Centres had 2.5 million students worldwide and offered programs in both math and reading.

- The Kumon Program is designed to increase math and reading comprehension.

- Kumon's Formula for success involves a diagnostic test, specialized materials, and a comfortable pace.

- Children start at a level where they can obtain 100 percent success.

- Students proceed in small steps with ample practice so they can achieve mastery.

- Students do not progress until they achieve 100% at their present level.

- The Kumon method has 6 steps:

  1. Visit a Kumon centre twice per week.

  2. Study for a short time with concentration.

  3. Develop self-confidence.

  4. Correct any mistakes.

  5. Record scores and monitor progress.

  6. Collect homework.

## SYLVAN LEARNING CENTERS

Sylvan Learning Centers originally were tutoring services established in 1979. It now is a franchise business with approximately 840 centres in North America, and 1000 in Europe.

- Sylvan Learning Centers advertise that they create confident, independent students through a process of assessment, personalized curriculum, positive reinforcement, and Mastery Learning.
- Mastery Learning is claimed as their approach but it has been advocated and used in many other contexts.
  - Mastery Learning at Sylvan means that students can use a skill three to five times with 80 to 100 percent accuracy
- Verbal and token rewards are given for success.
- Typical programs involve 50 to 100 hours of instruction on a two-to-four hours per week basis.
- Instruction typically is delivered in a small student-teacher ratio, one to three for example.
- Sylvan International Universities was launched in 1999 and had about 55,000 students in 2001.
  - In addition, Sylvan International Universities owns interests in other universities.
  - The goal is to create a network of universities throughout the world.
- Sylvan Ventures was launched in February 2000 to invest in companies bringing Internet technology to education.

## CASE 19-1: SHOULD WE HOME-SCHOOL?

Marie Bailes started to fall behind the other students in her class at about Grade 5. She managed to pass all her subjects for the next two years, but her report cards increasingly have expressed concerns about both her deteriorating work habits and her declining grades. This September she is to transfer to a local middle school, and her parents are very anxious about Marie's behaviour in a school with less structure and more demands. Marie's growing animosity toward school and the group of young people she has started to hang out with at a nearby mall heightens their anxiety. Marie's parents know that this group has a reputation among the other students as being the losers, even though the only reasons for this label seems to be that all the members of the group are having difficulty in school.

Last week in one of their frequent family discussions about Marie and school, the issue of home-schooling arose. Usually Marie sits in glum silence during these discussions and so her parents were startled when she responded with enthusiasm to this idea. Now her parents are in somewhat of a bind. They have not really considered home-schooling in any detail and are anxious about the whole idea. On the other hand, ruling it out without any further details might cause Marie to become even more negative, and also give her a club to hold over them in future discussions of her performance.

Another family in the neighbourhood has two children who are being home-schooled. These children are in the early elementary school years and one or other of the parents always seems to be available to look after the children's education. Marie's mother works full time in a government office and cannot be home during the day. Her father runs an accounting business from the family home. Although he is at home during the day, he has to see clients and prepare their business or personal financial statements. Neither of Marie's parents has any experience in teaching, nor, indeed, have they paid much attention to the whole area of education. They have no idea if they even could home-school Marie. Even if home-schooling were possible, where would they learn how and what to do?

## Discussion Questions

1. What are some of the arguments for and against home-schooling Marie in September?
2. Given that Marie's parents decide to home-school Marie, what are some of the initial steps they should take?

## CASE 19-2: WHICH APPROACH TO TAKE?

Vaneela Kumar truly was a unique child — just ask her parents. She was so enthusiastic about everything in her life, constantly exploring and learning. Of course, other adults saw her as another healthy and normal child although they were willing to grant that she somehow seemed more alive than most children. No one could resist her special charm.

Vaneela was so looking forward to starting school next year. She had been to a couple of events at the local public school and so had an image of a classroom and a teacher. Her parents, though, had been looking at a variety of alternative schools. Some of them seemed quite similar to the public school except that they usually had smaller class sizes and often had some underlying philosophy. Each had particular characteristics that seemed especially attractive. All charged modest fees to supplement the partial grants they received from the Ministry of Education.

One school in the community used approaches that were completely different from those of any of the other schools. It was very child-centered and emphasized the development of the total person. Vaneela's parents found some of the belief systems behind the school to be a bit unusual but they were assured that the students were not forced to learn these beliefs, nor were parents expected to support them. The Director pointed out that all teachers have belief systems although they usually do not state them. "Come and see our students," she said. "Only by seeing the kids can you make an informed decision."

Two visits to the schools left the Kumars very impressed. Each class had a small number of students who were so involved in what they were doing. The teachers did not appear to have any particular curriculum but rather were helping students explore areas of interest in more depth and from different approaches. Grades really indicated only age groupings rather than the completion of some set body of knowledge. Marks were meaningless since each child was involved in an individual exploration. Vaneela's parents found the school's approach appealed to deep feelings they had about the environment in which their child should grow up.

The Kumars did have a few concerns, however. Because the school did not receive any provincial funding, its fees were higher than other private schools. The school was several miles from the Kumar home, so Vaneela would have to be driven to school every day and would not be with her friends on the street. Then there was the issue of what would happen to Vaneela if she had to change schools or if she wanted to go on to further education. Since the school did not have regular grades, transferring to another institution might be difficult.

## Discussion Questions

1. What are the pros and cons of Vaneela going to the alternative school her parents like?
2. How important do you think it is that all students have the same curriculum?
3. What additional issues do you think Vaneela's parents should consider?

## CASE 19-3: WHERE TO TEACH?

There seemed to be lots of job possibilities, especially if he was willing to go on the Teacher-On-Call list for a short length of time. He could go to another province and find work or even to the States for a few years. The future looked pretty good to Mathew Caruana — just a matter of sending out a few resumés and finishing off the rest of his practicum.

The decision as to where to apply was not an easy one for Mathew, however. Applying to other parts of the country would give him an opportunity to travel and live in a new place. Moving to the United States or even to Europe seemed especially exciting. The only downside was that he knew eventually he wanted to live near his family, and moving away could mean that he would be behind his fellow students when he decided to return and was looking for a permanent contract.

Questions about teaching in the public school system at all were even more disconcerting. On his own time Mathew had visited several of the private and alternative schools in the area of the university, and was very impressed with many of their programs, although he really did not have time to examine their philosophies in detail. Class sizes were smaller and discipline problems seemed to be less. Of course, the pay also was less and he would not be part of contracts negotiated by a large Teachers' Union. What to do?

## Discussion Questions

1. What are some of the advantages and disadvantages of teaching in the public school system?
2. How important is the philosophy of a school to a teacher?
3. What other points do you think should be considered when Mathew thinks about his future as a teacher?

## REFERENCES

### Charter Schools

Birkett, F.A. (2000). *Charter schools: The parent's complete guide*. Roseville, CA: Prima Publishing.

Charter Schools Web Site: http://www.charterschools.ca

## Home-Schooling

Ishizuka, K. (2000). *The unofficial guide to homeschooling*. Foster City, CA: IDG Books Worldwide.

BC Ministry of Education Site for Homeschooling: http://www.bced.gov.bc.ca/homeschooling

BC Homeschool Association: http://www.bchomeschool.org

The Ontario Federation of Teaching Parents: http://www.ontariohomeschool.org

Saskatchewan Home-Based Educators: http://www.shbe.ca

## Kumon

Kumon: http://www.kumon.com

## Montessori

Montessori, M. (1967). *The absorbent mind*. New York: Holt, Reinhart and Winston.

Montessori, M. (1967). *Discovery of the child*. Notre Dame,IN: Fides Publishers.

American Montessori Foundation: http://www.montessori.org

Association Montessori Internationale: http://www.montessori-ami.org

## Sylvan

Sylvan Learning Centers: http://www.educate.com

Sylvan Learning Systems, Inc.: http://www.sylvan.net

## Waldorf Schools

Wilson, C. (1985). *Rudolf Steiner: The man and his vision*. Wellingborough, Northamptonshire, England: Aquarian Press.

PLANS: http://www.waldorfcritics.org

Steiner Schools in Australia: http://www.ozemail.com.au/~cromhale

Vancouver Waldorf School: http://www.vws.bc.ca

# chapter twenty

# Distance and Digital Education

At first, the meanings of both distance and digital education seem to be clear. However, closer examination demonstrates the turbulence that often results when an approach that originally was thought to have merely a specific use as an adjunct to an existing institution gradually becomes more and more broadly used. This is the case for both distance education and digital education.

- Distance education originally meant the development of programs for people who lived at a distance from bricks and mortar institutions or could not otherwise attend these institutions.
  - Now students could be residents at a university and taking distance education courses or they could be taking Grade 11 Physics at a local high school and Grade 12 English through a distance education program.
- Digital education also has undergone dramatic changes as the approach changes to meet demand and to make use of new technologies as they develop.
  - There is not even agreement on a name for the approach. Some of the names used are digital education, computer assisted instruction, electronically delivered education, and the trendy e-learning.

- Obviously distance and digital education are related, as distance education is more and more likely to include computers in its delivery.
- Electronic education, on the other hand often is offered through both distance education facilities *and* administrative structures.
  - In addition, computers are used in the traditional classroom and in access to media and web sites that are outside the usual purview of either distance or classroom based education.

If the relationship between distance and digital education might be thought of as a kind of middle ground in education, then the use of computers and other digital technologies in classrooms represents one end of the technology continuum, and virtual educational institutions represents the other end. This chapter examines all three situations starting with some general issues that are common to all of them. Underlying the whole chapter is the belief that the education system we have known for the last 150 years is going through a profound metamorphosis. The outcome will be a creature that bears little similarity to the present animal and one that we may not recognize for some time.

## GENERAL ISSUES

### Special Needs Students

- Some special needs students are attracted to the flexibility and convenience of distance education in its various forms.
- Their use of this approach, however, may threaten the emotional and social goals of mainstreaming.

### Social Development

- Schools place a lot of weight on social development, so any form of distance education or even use of computers in the classroom is challenged because it fails to promote social development.
  - This issue and others like it bring the whole issue of the role of schools into discussion.
- The controversy was discussed in more detail in relation to home-schooling in the last chapter.

### Training

- Much of the computer-based education used in schools as well as various forms of distance education have depended upon teachers who trained themselves, on their own time and at their own expense.
- Now the importance of digital media in education means that all teachers must be given the hundreds of hours of training that are required to become proficient with the media.

## Equipment

- As in the case of training, much of the early work in digital education depended upon teachers supplying equipment, or upon donations of used equipment.
- Lack of access to reasonably sophisticated equipment also is a problem in distance education, especially if students are expected to supply their own computers, etc.
- While provincial and federal governments comment more and more about the importance of computers and internet access for modern education, many students do not have access to this equipment in either their schools or homes.

## Teacher Time

- Teachers need time to prepare lessons and materials for digital education.
    - Teachers often are expected to do this work on top of regular classroom duties.
- Even when a teacher is solely responsible for electronic education, administrators may not understand the time that is required to produce materials.
- Sometimes grants are made available for the initial production of these materials. The problem comes when the materials have to be updated and teachers are expected to do this as part of their job. Administrators have little understanding of the hours involved.
- Production of a one-hour video involves much more time than preparing a one-hour lecture. More sophistication in presentation is expected. There is a record that people tend to look at more objectively and critically than they do a lecture or talk.
    - Also, the teacher is not moving around and interacting with the students so more actual content is needed.
    - Graphics have to be professional. Students will accept a Grade 2 drawing on the board but such a drawing looks very unprofessional in a video or manual.
- People expect their e-mails to be answered from any place at any time. Teachers, on other hand, have to ensure that work and home hours are separated.

## Intellectual Property Rights

- In a regular classroom situation a teacher's interactions with students is not recorded, and so there is little opportunity for another person to use the material again.
- Most teachers in a regular classroom would consider their notes and handouts to be their own, although this probably is not the case since they are employees of the school board.
    - The issue usually does not come up since teachers' classroom materials usually are not in a form that could be published.
- The issue does become important, however, when educational materials are published or recorded. Computer files sent from one computer to another can be considered to be published, and certainly there is a record of them beyond the author's computer.

- Teachers may feel they own published materials, especially if they have spent a great deal of their own time producing these materials and their names are on the finished product. Administration often views the materials as belonging to the institution.
- Loss of ownership affects the original authors in at least two ways.
  1. The materials are used either in recorded form or by another individual to teach a different course, without any input from or payment to the original authors.
  2. The original authors may no longer support positions originally espoused, and would like to change or upgrade the materials. This may not be possible.

## COMPUTERS IN THE CLASSROOM

### Controversies

- Some teachers are opposed to computer use in the classroom, especially at the early grades, because they feel it limits the student's ability to develop the academic and social skills that are necessary for later years.
  - Other teachers are opposed to computers on a philosophical basis because they feel it is an invasion of the corporate world into the classroom.
- There also are administrative issues related to computers in the school.
  - Some schools may expect teachers to maintain web sites where information about lessons, homework, and other class issues are maintained without the teacher being given any additional time for maintaining the web site.
  - Some teachers feel that the use of e-mail by parents to contact them is often inappropriate and consumes a great deal of time in answering questions.
- Teachers also have concerns about the confidentiality and relevance of any comments they make about students if parents can obtain daily student records through some type of Personal Identification Number on a web site.

### Computer Assisted Instruction

- Computer Assisted Instruction (CAI) or Computer Assisted Learning (CAL) uses computers as an adjunct to traditional classroom practices.
- Some CAI applications use computers as nothing more than sophisticated typewriters and encyclopedias.
- Other CAI approaches use computer programs as elaboration of materials covered in class or for various types of drills.
  - Computers are especially good for drills since they can generate a large number of problems at various levels, and the student can work without exposing any errors to a teacher or other students.
  - Students can learn at their own rate without fear of failure.

## The Electronic Classroom

- Some technically literate teachers with visions of a new digital world use computers to produce whole new approaches to education in the classroom.
  - These teachers believe that the big division of the future will be between techno-peasants and technophiles.
- Possibilities of collaboration and communication among many different groups of people are explored. Students can belong to academic and other **listservs** or mass e-mail groups, and connect to **electronic bulletin boards** or sites where people post material that might be of interest to others.
- Students are encouraged to use the new electronic media to research areas of interest and produce multi-media reports for electronic publication.
- Students and teachers work side-by-side rather than the teacher always being the expert.
  - The teacher is a leader of a communications team.
- Links to the community usually are an important part of this approach.
  - These classes often have their own web sites and may even act as servers or web hosts for community groups and individuals.
- Relatively inexpensive digital cameras, scanners, and graphics programs mean that classes can publish their own **zines,** or privately produced electronic magazines, and distribute them widely through sites that host zines and through listservs of different types.

# DISTANCE EDUCATION

## Rationale

- Distance education offers a point of entry to the education system for those students who cannot or do not want to use the traditional school system.
  - Examples include students in isolated conditions, those who are sick, those who have difficulty with the usual classroom, and those whose parents wish to home-school.
  - Other students are travelling, have extensive involvement in arts or sports, experience timetable conflicts, or already have careers of various types.
- Students can work at their own speed and level without having to be concerned about the rest of the class being ahead or behind them.
- Students can work at whatever time they please except in the case of interactive video, discussed below.

## General Operation

- Students register for courses with a distance education provider.
- Usually there is some timeline for completing projects and courses.
- A variety of electronic and paper-based delivery mechanisms are used.

- Students and parents contact their distance education teacher through appointments, e-mail, or phone.

- Evaluation of assignments is done at some central location or by a teacher in a local school.

- Exams may be take-home or involve going to some location where several distance-learning students are writing.

## Manuals and Tapes

- Manuals and video or audiotapes have been the mainstay of distance education for decades.

- In recent years these materials have been supplemented through the use of web sites and e-mail.

- Copyright is a very important consideration in all forms of distance education. Permission must be obtained before copyrighted material can be used in any form of publication or distribution.

- Interactive video sometimes is used to overcome the lack of contact between teacher and student.

## Interactive Video

When interactive video is used, the teacher is in a studio or teaching a class in a classroom and the lesson is simultaneously broadcast to another class or group of individuals. There is some type of connection between the distance students and the teacher including video cameras in the distance classroom, e-mail, phone, and/or fax. There also is the potential for two classes to interact.

- Teachers need technical support at both locations, although they do have to understand enough about how the system works to structure their lesson and teaching materials for maximum impact.
  - It is necessary to spend time telling technical people what you plan to do so they can help.
- Teachers usually have to modify their teaching approach to fit the requirements of the new media.
  - Usually teacher movement is restricted.
  - Broadcast time costs money, so having people working in groups may not be very cost effective.
  - Changes in facial expression have to be used to carry the messages that larger body movements do in the regular classroom.
  - Even clothing has to be considered with care. Stripes are out, for instance.
- Classroom management becomes very difficult for the remote location as all the students there are seeing is a head on a screen, and all the teacher sees is a bunch of people in a room where you cannot recognize anyone without zooming in.

- Students in both host and remote locations have more of a tendency to just sit and take notes.
- Usually technical people on remote locations are not involved in classroom management.
- Teachers have to learn how to present effectively on video.
  - They have to resist the tendency to concentrate on the equipment rather than the students.
  - They have to feel that they are having a pleasant phone conversation rather than acting.
  - Concepts must be clear and graphics of high quality.

## VIRTUAL SCHOOLS

Virtual schools and virtual reality introduce entirely new directions to our concepts of the nature of education. A whole host of factors such as time, distance, and age become irrelevant. Educational institutions can no longer count on students from a particular area being 'their' students. Those organizations and individuals who count a regular crop of students coming through the door may soon find that they have been left behind as students flock to virtual schools, colleges, and universities.

### General Operation

- Virtual schools or education sites operate much the same as traditional distance education programs. The principal difference is a heavy reliance on computer-based technology.
- The computer allows the educational organization to make vast amounts of information available to the student at relatively low cost, except for preparation of the original materials.
- The computer allows a high level of interaction between the students and any teacher involved in the program.
- Students can take courses literally anywhere in the world without having to worry about postage, customs, and perhaps even language if translation programs are involved.
- These new programs are true distance education rather than 'flying suitcase' or travelling instructor programs. Typically they involve easy registration, a completely flexible timetable, prior learning assessment, and interactive web sites.

### Fees for Materials

- Some universities and colleges may decide to place much of their research and other material on web sites and make it freely available to everyone.
- Other educational institutions may decide to charge for lecture notes, research papers, etc.

- While this has an impact for the teachers in these institutions, there is no student registration involved and no issue of student management.

## Open or Restricted Access

- Credit for taking a course will have to involve some type of registration and usually the payment of a fee.
- Virtual schools might have open sites where anyone could have access with only those registered receiving any interaction with teachers or credit for the course.
- Some sites might use regular web sites while others use programs such as WebCT or Blackboard, where class lists and student information are maintained and students are able to interact with each other and with the teacher through e-mail, chat rooms and bulletin boards.
  - Virtual schools using programs such as WebCT and Blackboard usually restrict access to the site to only those students the site manager has enrolled on the program.
  - Teachers who use interactive sites such as these must protect their students from those who might endanger them, or who might use the site to promote views unacceptable to the educational institution.

## Academic Concerns

- Exams are possible with some of the programs, although the instructor has to be sure who is writing the exam and what kind of support is available. A local school may supervise.
- As students download the notes rather than listening in class and writing them by hand, they may not realize that they have no idea what is in the notes.
  - Some students may not be able to study the notes on their computers and will have to print them out.
- Classroom management issues still have to be dealt with.
  - Students fail to complete assignments.
  - Students sometimes respond in a very emotional manner to the teacher, perhaps even more than in a traditional classroom.
  - Students forget their passwords or use bulletin boards or chat rooms inappropriately.

## Administrative Concerns

- Intellectual rights are important as discussed above.
- The amount of time involved in managing one of these sites is very large. Students tend to interact a lot more with a teacher over a web site than they do in a classroom, not to mention the time involved in preparing material for the site.
- Both students and teachers need computer equipment and server support that is sophisticated enough to handle the amount of material being sent and the demands

from students to access the site. A computer server where all access is taken up in the evening is of no use to those offering web-based courses.

## VIRTUAL REALITY

- Virtual reality involves the computer program providing a variety of sensory inputs to the person wearing stimulation devices so that the person has difficulty distinguishing between the simulated situation and a real situation.

- Virtual reality is used in many forms of technical education such as flight training, but has tremendous potential for teaching a broader range of topics. How about visiting Paris to learn French, talking to someone from thousands of years ago, or watching animals behave in a 'real' environment?

| Exercise 20–1 | **Electronic Learning Centre** |
|---|---|

This exercise is meant to help students become more familiar with some of the issues involved in producing materials for computer-based education in either the classroom or for different types of distance and virtual education. Three or four students will work together to develop a computer-based learning centre around a particular concept chosen by the group. A learning centre is a location in the classroom where students can go and work on their own to learn more about a particular topic. The centre could be a physical group of objects and activities where students can view demonstrations and experiment on their own; in this case it is a disk or CD.

Your learning centre should include some text explaining the concepts involved, graphics to demonstrate principles, and activities that students could do with simple equipment usually found in a classroom or home. It is not expected that students will be able to interact with your project on a computer.

## CASE 20-1: THE DISTRICT WEB SITE

The Provincial Ministry of Education was going to provide additional funds to each School District to enhance the use of information processing technologies in the District. Because of budget restrictions, proposals had to be at the Ministry's office within two weeks. Officials in Spring View District felt that a web site for each of the schools in the district would be an excellent use of the additional funds. The sites for each school would be accessed from the main District site. The money would be used to buy more sophisticated equipment for all the schools, and to hire a consultant to do the initial development of the site.

After the site was up and running, teachers at each of the schools could post their lessons for the day or week, any homework assignments required, and suggestions that parents could use to help their children. Class newsletters and notices could be posted on the site rather than being mailed to parents. Perhaps there also was a way that parents could access comments and evaluations about their children using some type of password.

## Discussion Questions

1. What administrative issues should the District officials consider before they go ahead with this project?

2. What would be the advantages and disadvantages for teachers of having such a web site?

3. What are the pros and cons of having parents being able to access comments and evaluations about their children from a web site?

## CASE 20-2: SPICE IT UP A BIT

"The whole second half of the year just to get my notes ready for the production of a CD," thought Anita Holroyd. "I really needed a break from the classroom and this just came along at the right time."

Anita had been teaching for nine years and over that time had developed a sophisticated series of units for her Chemistry classes. She had given several workshops on her approach and had submitted two articles to education journals at their request. Now the Ministry of Education was buying her time for six months to produce an electronic version of her notes for use in the province's schools and distance education programs.

Her first uneasiness occurred when she learned that the Ministry of Education would own the copyright to the material because she was being paid as a teacher when she originally produced the notes and now was being paid to work on the CD. She was assured that her name would be on the CD as the original author.

The next shock occurred when an editor for the project said that Anita would have to change some of her notes to make them jazzier for the electronic format. "Remember you won't be there to keep an eye on things, so the stuff has to keep their attention," he said when he noticed her concern. Over the next couple of months further suggestions came from other members of the production team. Some of the suggestions showed such a poor understanding of both chemistry and teaching that they would have been hilarious in another context. Those offering the suggestions were serious however, and thought their ideas had a lot of merit when considered from a media context. Anita was disappointed but not surprised to find her name listed as the author in small print on an inside page along with members of the production team.

## Discussion Questions

1. What issues should Anita have considered before she even started on the project?

2. What types of changes do you think will be required in the way educational materials are presented if they are going to be used in an electronic format on a stand-alone basis?

3. Is there an inherent conflict between education and the new media?

# REFERENCES

## Electronic and Virtual Schools

Open Learning School: http://www.openschool.bc.ca

Open Learning School is responsible for K-12 distance education courses in British Columbia. Courses are delivered primarily through Distance Education; some school districts have used them as well. Open Learning Schools projects that the number of courses available on-line will grow dramatically over the next few years for all grade levels, with an emphasis on Grade 11 and 12 programs.

Most courses contain four modules with four sections per module. The assignments in each section are typically student-regulated and marked, with various formats of assignments or tests sent to the instructor at the conclusion of each section. If the course is provincially examinable, the student must take the exam in person at a designated location and time just as they would for any other distance education course.

Toronto Virtual School: http://www.intoronto.com/virtualschool

The Toronto Virtual School offers online math and science curricula for Grades 8 to 12. The materials are complementary to what is being taught in the classroom rather than independent courses. There are step-by-step lessons and interactive exercises and tests. This type of site will be very attractive to parents who feel their children need extra help and to parents who wish to monitor their children's progress. Private businesses can be expected to develop many variations of this type of site.

Virtual High School: http://www.virtualhighschool.com

This is a distance education secondary school in Ontario. They claim to be the first secondary school using electronic textbooks (e-text) in the province's distance education program. The courses are fully accredited and are 'go at your own pace', with both computer and teacher-based evaluations. The focus with this company appears to be on e-text development that is designed specifically for the Internet rather than as an adaptation of conventional distance education courses. Credits via the Internet have been available here since 1996.

Listserv Information: http://www.lsoft.com

SCHOOLNET: http://www.schoolnet.ca

Canada was the first country in the world to connect its public schools, including First Nations schools, and all public libraries to the Internet. Schoolnet is the organization mandated by the Federal Government to work with all the groups involved to extend connection to classrooms and First Nations communities, and is one of the most important sites to start looking at issues related to electronic education.

Zines Information: http://www.zinebook.com

# chapter twenty-one

## Advanced Cases

*NOTE TO INSTRUCTORS AND STUDENTS: The cases in this chapter involve concepts discussed in several chapters. Because instructors may want to use them for assessment, they do not have discussion questions.*

### CASE 21-1: HE'LL GROW OUT OF IT

Leigh Urquhart was an emotionally sensitive child; at least that's what the experts had said. His parents remember the pediatrician telling them, "Don't worry, Leigh will be fine. He just needs a warm, loving home. Try not to let things disturb him. This is just a stage; he'll grow out of it."

But Leigh didn't grow out of it. He always was very 'moody'. He didn't like this and he didn't like that. He would only eat certain foods, and then he would change suddenly and only eat completely different foods. He wanted to go someplace, and then he wanted to go home. He would cry to have someone come over and play with him, and then go to his room and ignore his guest. The only time Leigh seemed to be at some type of peace was when he was in his room watching TV. He was attracted to strange shows that had no particular negative characteristics his parents could complain about, but that tended to centre on characters that were isolated and eccentric.

School difficulties started to show up in Grade 7. Until that time teachers said that Leigh was moody or somewhat anti-social. They said he was a little behind the others in reading, but that he "…would grow out of it". His Grade 7 teacher, however, said that Leigh was reading at a Grade 4 level and that his Math was at about the same level. She said that Leigh was going to have trouble in High School unless his reading and math improved. She gave Leigh a fail grade in Language Arts and a C- in Math during the year, but allowed him to continue with his class by giving him a C- in both areas at the end of the year.

These marks caused a great deal of alarm for Leigh's parents. They pressured him to work harder and tried to check that he was doing his homework on a regular basis. "You have to work hard if you want to get ahead," they stated repeatedly. Leigh resented this pressure and became increasingly uncommunicative with his parents. He did appear to be trying, however; he just didn't like anyone checking to see how his was doing. Unfortunately, despite his parents' pressure for him to work harder and even his apparent effort to do so, his Grade 8 marks were similar to those he received in Grade 7. Only the pleading of his parents led to his going on to Grade 9.

Leigh never was physically violent to others and indeed, made every effort to avoid those who are aggressive or into delinquent behaviours such as property destruction. His parents first noticed that he was smoking when he was in Grade 8, however. When he was asked about it, he responded with, "Yeah, so, lots of people smoke." He then went to his room and refused to talk about the issue again.

Last month Leigh's mother found two joints in his coat that she had taken from his room to wash. When his parents confronted him about the drugs, he got very angry and complained about people touching his stuff. He refused to discuss the issue and stormed to his room. Leigh's parents had never been able to discuss anything in depth with him. He would stop talking and sit there with a bored expression. Questions about his friends or his schoolwork were met with an angry silence and his leaving the room or even the house. Even comments like "Good morning" often were met with no response or a grunt.

Leigh entered Grade 9 this year and since about the middle of September, increasingly has complained about not liking school. His first report card for the term showed he had skipped a couple of days. Mr. Simpson, the local busybody, told Mrs. Urquhart about seeing Leigh hanging around the corner store one afternoon. "Probably just had the afternoon off," sniffled Mr. Simpson.

During the past few weeks Leigh has spent more and more time by himself, just sitting in his room watching TV. He has been smoking in his room as well. No one has come to visit him and he usually has left the house without saying where he is going. If confronted about his trip, he mumbled, "Just downtown." He often claims that he is not hungry if called for a meal, although he can be heard late at night opening the refrigerator.

Mr. and Mrs. Urquhart are dismayed by Leigh's behaviour. They believe they both have worked very hard to get a home and establish a family. They also know the importance of having friends and are trying to help Leigh understand the importance of hard work and social contacts. They stress how much they want Leigh to succeed. They are beginning to realize that changes are necessary, however, even though they dread having to examine all of their beliefs and dreams about Leigh.

## CASE 21-2: THE FIRST YEAR

Second week in June and Ilio Pepitone could feel the restless energy in his classroom — it was like being in a cage of large animals just before feeding time. Ilio was amazed at how he could feel the energy and yet not be panicked by it. What a change from last September!

Ilio knew that every September for the rest of his life would bring memories of his first year in teaching. He really hadn't made a careful decision to become a teacher; there just didn't seem to be anything else he wanted to do at the end of university, and so he chose education. His classes had gone well, although he had viewed them as just another set of hurdles to get over. During his practicum he had some difficulty with classroom management. Fortunately his sponsor teacher was a big help and gave him a lot of encouragement. Indeed, it really was her recommendation that led to his being offered a job in the district.

Over the summer Ilio spent a great deal of time and money preparing for his first year as a teacher. He had all his lecture notes, overheads, homework assignments, and quizzes ready when classes started. Everything was planned; he just had to wait for the students to show up.

That first Grade 10 class was like a deluge of cold water. The students entered his room like floodwaters from a broken dam. They swirled and pushed and shoved in their attempts to get favourite seats. One student, who seemed to have some motor difficulty, stood to the side and finally took a chair in the far corner when everyone had settled down. The students then turned and looked at Ilio; he was sure some of them were drooling in anticipation of having a new teacher. After repeated calls for quiet, he finally was able to get the students settled down a bit and to take attendance. There seemed to be many more non-Anglo-Saxon names than he expected. Fortunately there was an Assembly the first day and so he only had the students for about 15 minutes before the buzzer rang.

Two days later the students came in for their first 'real' class and sat in 'their' seats. Ilio was not really happy with the seating arrangement but did not want to antagonize the students by asking them to change. He also didn't like the way some students pulled their chairs out of their row and faced them at angles, but again it didn't seem worth wasting time for such a minor issue.

After a "good morning", Ilio started on the topic he planned to cover that day. His overheads forced him to stay at the front of the class but at least everything was organized. Most students took out their notebooks and started to copy the material from the overheads. Some did this in such a slow, casual manner that everyone else had to wait for them to finish; others looked completely confused as to what they were supposed to do. A few ignored Ilio and slouched in their seats or smiled at their neighbours. Ilio was determined to get through his material however, and was pleased to find that the last overhead went up just before the bell. Perfect timing!

During the second class Ilio had to give one student a lecture about behaving in a respectful manner in the class. The student hung her head and seemed unsure whether to smirk or be embarrassed. Another student got up to sharpen his pencil while Ilio was talking. Ilio told him this was definitely against the rules and the student muttered something about not knowing. As if students could get up and wander around the class whenever they liked!

Over the next couple of weeks the class seemed to settle down. There were minor outbursts that Ilio was able to control with a scowl or by telling the student that the behaviour was not allowed in the class. From time to time a few of the students snickered a bit in the back when Ilio turned to the blackboard but they really were not all that disruptive.

Copying the overheads seemed to keep most of the class on track. There was little response from students when he asked them if they had any questions, however. When he asked specific students a question, they often responded with, "I don't know." Other times their answers were so off the mark that Ilio could not help but frown in frustration.

At the end of the fourth week Ilio held his first quiz, and the results were a complete shock. About 40 percent of the class did pretty well, although only a few were able to answer satisfactorily the questions where students had to apply their knowledge to particular contexts. The other 60 percent of the class did very poorly. Some of these students seemed to have mixed all the concepts together in some unrecognizable hodge-podge; others apparently had not studied because they didn't give any answers to many of the questions. Six or seven students had attempted to answer the questions, but their spelling and grammar were so poor Ilio couldn't really tell what they meant to say. Ilio expressed his disappointment at their performance during the next class, hoping that he could stimulate them to do better. Ilio could almost feel the class drawing away from him as he talked; a couple of students even looked like they might cry. He couldn't think of anything else to do though, so he finished his talk and started on the next concept for the class.

The next time he turned his back, a couple of students started whispering and Wayne, one of the students with the lowest marks, prodded another student in the ribs resulting in an exaggerated scream. Ilio immediately sent Wayne to the office and gave the class another lecture about behaviour in the class. He gave the class an exercise from his university Methods course and walked around the class making sure that all the students knew he was watching them. This seemed to quiet the class. Ilio noticed, though, that some of the students were not doing the assignment. When he asked them about it, they responded with comments about not knowing what they were supposed to do. A couple of students seem to be having trouble understanding him even when he explained what he wanted again. Two or three others seemed to understand what he was saying but still did not know what to do.

Discipline problems increased over the next week. By Friday, Ilio was spending more than 50 percent of the time putting out brush fires. He would just get the class back on track when something else would happen. At that point Ilio knew he needed help and asked his previous sponsor teacher if she was available for coffee. Thanks to her continued suggestions he was able to turn his class around. Now in June he realized he would actually miss these students even though he was looking forward to the end of the year.

## CASE 21-3: THE NEW MUSIC TEACHER

"Tricia, have you got a few minutes to see me after school?" asked the principal in her sometimes maddening professional voice. You never could tell with Ms. Liu. Probably she would use the same tone of voice to announce the end of the world.

"Sure. What's this about?"

"Oh, just a little note from one of the parents that I think we should go over before I reply. About 4:15 would be a good time to come in."

"A note from a parent," thought Tricia. "Why didn't they send it to me? Must be some kind of complaint. Just what I need. As if I didn't have enough problems."

After completing her education program, Tricia had taught English for two years in Korea. It wasn't her teaching area, but she needed the money to pay student debts and being a Teacher-on-Call (TOC) seemed to be the only teaching job available in her province. Last year she returned to Canada and spent a year as a TOC — no long stretches in any one class and not much opportunity to develop her approach to teaching.

The full time job offer last summer had seemed like winning the lottery. The principal had been so positive and in August the school had seemed so bright and full of possibilities. Tricia would have two music classes for students who wanted to complete their graduation requirements in Fine Arts, responsibility for the new junior band, and one social studies class. The music classes were in an annex that had poor acoustics and no risers. The room was not normally used for music; it was used for a variety of other classes. This meant that music stands, instruments, and music had to be put away after each class.

Tricia's homeroom was in the main school building. She kept her class notes and files in this room although she had to leave the desktop clear for other teachers who were coming in and make sure that any sensitive files were locked away. Fortunately she also had her homeroom for social studies. For the music classes and the junior band, though, she had to take everything she needed with her to the annex.

Tricia's training had not prepared her very well for the classes she met in September. The variety of students was first thing that struck her. The principal had told her that she would have classes where the majority of students would not have English as their first language, although most should have some understanding of English. What Tricia really was not prepared for was the variety of behaviours and abilities. Plus the students seemed to be grouping themselves in the classroom according to language and ethnicity. At first it was like having five different communities in the same room.

Tricia thought about her Grade 11 Music classes in particular. While all of the students had some music background, this background was far from consistent. A few had taken piano or singing lessons. Four or five students in each class had some background in guitar, although rock music seemed to be their main interest. Two students from one class and three from another were part of a Caribbean steel drums group that met every Friday night in a local warehouse. The Friday night event seemed to be a big cultural gathering with food and dancing.

In addition to the many language and cultural groups, the music classes had a number of students with different types of disabilities. Most of these disabilities were various types of learning problems, but one class had a student with cerebral palsy who was confined to a wheelchair. This student was able to use her electric wheelchair with sometimes alarming speed, and she did not have an aid. Unfortunately, she was unable to play the guitar. The other Music class had a student with multiple disabilities and a fulltime aid. The student seemed to enjoy the music class but did not participate. His aid sat nearby; sometimes the aid beat a rhythm on the student's chair. Other times he seemed to be bored waiting for the class to end.

Music appreciation and literacy were the two goals that Tricia set for the music classes. The school had class sets of guitars that could be signed out for the term and she planned to use these. A previous teacher had catalogued a series of CDs that the school owned in such a manner that they could be used to demonstrate all aspects of Western music from early Church music to modern jazz. He had even left sheets that could be handed out to students with the details of each type of music. This material was a resource that was just too good to pass up.

Discipline was a real problem in the music classes. A few students practised their music and offered relevant comments on the composers Tricia introduced to the class.

Many of the students did not seem to know for sure what was expected of them. They watched other students for signs as to what they were to do. Many of them seemed to have great difficulty putting the music in any type of context. They were unable to tell one type of music from another and often tried to guess the composer and period. The sheets with information about the composers did not seem to help very much. Some students memorized the sheets but others either didn't or couldn't get anything from them. A few students in each class were always acting out in some manner. There was nothing too abrasive. Dropping music on the floor and knocking over music stands were favourite tricks. Three students had taken to deliberately playing a wrong note during class performances. The other students thought this was quite funny and it often took Tricia five minutes or more to get everyone back on task.

Since it was only the end of September, Tricia did not have a good idea of how individual students were doing. Her one written assignment had been a group project. She was pleased with the work of a few groups; they seemed to understand the underlying concepts she wanted them to explore. Many of the groups handed in short, general papers containing bits of information that might have come from an encyclopedia or the Internet, but showing no real grasp of the principles involved. The rest were quite a bit below the level she expected from a Grade 11 class; the spelling and grammar errors alone were alarming.

Today was over, however — time for the dreaded meeting with Ms. Liu. Tricia entered the principal's office with some trepidation. Ms. Liu greeted Tricia with her usual smile. "I don't trust that smile," thought Tricia. "It seems to make me feel some vague feeling of guilt. It's like being worried that my mother has found out something about me."

"Thanks for coming in, Tricia," said Ms Liu. "I have a letter here from Mrs. Javorski. She is concerned that her son does not seem to be doing very well in school. She thinks he is far behind his peers in reading and that he cannot seem to write even a sentence on a birthday card or note to his grandparents. Mrs. Javorski says that you are his favourite teacher and that you might be willing to help."

Tricia was unprepared for this information; she was expecting some type of difficulty. In addition, she was surprised that Thomas Javorski saw her as his favourite teacher. Thomas was in one of her Music 11 classes. She didn't have a very good idea of his ability in areas other than music, although he seemed to have practiced his music and made an effort to participate in class. The only written assignment he had been involved in was the group project and Tricia did not know how much he had contributed to it. His group had been one of the majority who had submitted short, superficial papers.

"Well, I don't know what to say. I don't know all that much about Thomas. I'm willing to help but I don't know where to begin."

"Great," smiled Ms Liu. "Perhaps you could make up a little report on Thomas so I could get back to Mrs. Javorski."

## CASE 21-4: HARDER THAN EXPECTED

It was Thursday afternoon, last period coming up and almost the end of October. Corinne Vezina's mind drifted away from her class to her next pay cheque and her short career as a teacher. She already had filled in the forms for direct deposit of her cheque; the rent and car payment came directly from her account. Maybe by the Christmas break she would have enough money saved to take a little holiday and fly home to visit her family. She remembered the going-away party in August and her comment when asked how she felt about moving. "I'll finally be able to get out of my parents' house," she had remarked.

Corinne had been a Teacher-on-Call (TOC) for two and a half years in her hometown but hadn't received many calls. In December of last year, she read about a shortage of TOCs in another area of the province and applied for a position. She immediately had been put on the TOC List and so had moved in January of this year. The six months from January to June had been a chaotic jumble of different classrooms, two small suites in different boarding homes, her uncle's 1983 Toyota without a heater, and a haphazard attempt to get to know her new community a bit.

Several full-time jobs came up and she was short-listed a couple of times, but it looked like it was back to TOC next year. In June she packed all her stuff in the Toyota and headed back to her parents' home. Both of her parents were glad to have her back, although her father's new computer had to be moved from her old bedroom and her mother was very concerned about the weight Corinne had lost during the six months she had been away. Her father seemed to be aghast that she had not changed the oil in the Toyota and went around muttering about "grit damaging the cylinder walls". Corinne thought, "Good riddance. It would be better if someone put the poor thing out of its misery."

Summer was very relaxing. Corinne felt that she could leave everything until the middle of August and then return to her new community, find a decent place to live, and start getting a few lesson plans ready in case she was called in for one of those teachers who never left any instructions about what was to be done. On August 10th Corinne received a phone call from the principal of one of the schools where she had been short-listed. A Grade 11/12 Biology teacher in the school was going to take a year off and the principal was wondering if Corinne wanted to work as a replacement teacher for the next year. Corinne responded, "Absolutely. Oh this is so great." The next morning she realized that she didn't know enough about what she would be teaching and had to phone the principal back for the details.

It turned out she would not have exactly the same courses as the teacher she was replacing had been teaching. Other teachers in the school had known about the new vacancy for a week or more and had talked to the principal. They had picked over the former teacher's position a bit and had convinced the principal that it would be better if they taught the Biology 12 classes and Corinne taught other classes since the Grade 12 classes had provincial exams. Corinne's position would involve two of the former teacher's Biology 11 classes plus a Career class, a Grade 10 Math class, and a Communications 12 class. It also was mentioned that one of the PE teachers really could use some help with the large number of females who were coming out for the new rugby program.

Corinne moved back near the school on August 18th and took a year's lease on one of the few apartments available. It was clean but looked like something out of a 1960s edition of *Modern Living*. Her next step was to purchase a 2-year-old car; she was amazed that the bank seemed so happy to give her a loan based on her new job.

On August 21st she went into the school for a meeting with the principal. Her homeroom was a Biology classroom but she had to teach the three other classes in two different rooms while other teachers used her room for Biology. "Why didn't they just let me teach all Biology?" Corinne lamented.

Classes started on September 4th, so Corinne had about two weeks to prepare. She had a few Biology lessons from her Education courses but that was three years ago, and it was quite a stretch to see how she could use them with the new textbook that the school district had adopted. Corinne knew she had a lot of work ahead of her but the students always had liked her when she was a TOC; indeed she often felt more energized at the end of the day than at the beginning.

"No problem," she had thought.

The buzzer brought Corinne back from her revelry. She turned to face Communications 12. "Just what I need for a last class on Thursday," mused Corinne. She thought of Communications 12 as the 'class from hell', a phrase that she indignantly had protested against when another teacher had used it in the staff room last spring. During the first week in September she had tried to get to know the students in all her classes and had spend most of the time telling or listening to details of each other's lives and discussing events in the community and in the school. The students seemed to be enjoying her classes and several mentioned that she seemed like she was going to be much more fun than the teacher they had last year. One student even came up and said, "You're the best teacher I have ever had. Because of you I am thinking of becoming a teacher."

In the second week of classes Corinne started on the lessons she had prepared. She had worked night and day in the little time before class in preparing lectures and homework for each of the classes. She even had rounded up some interesting activities for the Biology classes. The Math seemed quite straightforward, as there were lots of problems for the students to work on in the textbook. Communications 12 was a bit more of a problem until a Physics teacher mentioned that there was no provincial exam and that the marks didn't count for university, so it didn't really matter what the students did. Corinne resented this dismissal of the importance of her class but also felt some relief when she realized that the expectations of other teachers for the class were not very high. There was a whole series of exercises and survey questions available on different web sites and Corinne decided to use them for this year at least.

Corinne noticed the change in all of the classes from the start of the second week. Students in the two Biology 11 classes behaved quite well. They wrote careful notes from her overheads, prepared good reports from the labs she ran, and, for the most part, did well on the weekly quizzes. The one ESL student in the class seemed to be having quite a bit of difficulty but a couple of other students were helping him and Corinne felt that he would pass the course all right. There were a couple of other students who seemed to have trouble grasping the concepts but they worked hard and did not complain.

Corinne wished that there was more enthusiasm from her Biology classes. They never had any questions and seemed to be motivated only by the marks they knew would be used for university entrance. Even the experiments were greeted with the same attitude that most people reserved for dishes the morning after a party. Corinne found teaching the classes very tiring but was not apprehensive about them.

It was the Communications 12 class that Corinne already had come to almost dread. Before her were 28 young people aged 16 to 19 years. There were 17 boys and 11 girls in the class. None of the students were planning on going to university and Corinne was unsure what the future held for them. She knew that two of the girls were teen mothers. She had seen several of the students working in local stores in the evenings or on weekends. Three students were the children of recently arrived refugee families. Four or five different students were away from class every period. Students slouched in their desks and talked to their neighbours; they ignored Corinne.

Corinne called out, "Ladies and gentlemen, can we start now?" No response. Corinne had her usual moment of panic. Her chest got tighter and tighter; a feeling of overwhelming tiredness washed over her. If it hadn't been for a concern about the loss of her job, Corinne would have picked up her briefcase and left them all there. Instead she said, "Raymond, stop talking and face the front."

This quieted the area near the back corner. Three of the girls near the middle of the class continued on with a heated discussion about one of their boyfriends. There always seemed to be some sort of drama with these three. Corinne called, "Judy, perhaps if your story is so interesting you could share it with the rest of the class." Judy and the other two quieted down but gave Corinne a dirty look.

Corinne had tried everything to get this class to behave. She could live with the lack of enthusiasm in the Biology classes but the behavioural problems in this class already were coming to the attention of the principal. In the past week Corinne had sent two of the students down to the office for persistent talking and laughing. The Principal had spoken to them but there was little change in the next class. The principal asked Corinne if she needed any help. Corinne felt that the principal's question had a tone of censure and so had quickly responded with, "No thanks. The class is a little rowdy but everything is OK."

In September Corinne had given each student a list of rules for the class. These rules had been developed during a group project in one of her Methods classes at the university. The rules emphasized respect for others and the need to treat others in a manner that made the classroom a safe place. Corinne deeply supported these principles and had spoken movingly about them at the beginning of the year. Now the students ignored her rules and she overheard one student refer to her class rules as being "like right out of the Brady Bunch." It wasn't that the students really were hostile or that they deliberately set out to hurt each other or Corinne. Rather, they just seemed to behave from some quite different view of life.

Corinne really tried to develop a course content that might appeal to the students. She had them do papers on items in the local news and allowed them to comment on their favourite poem chosen from the *Norton Anthology*. The result for most students was a few short sentences showing an appalling lack of knowledge about grammar and spelling. As a result, she felt she had to spend a least a few classes covering the basics. She remembered her recent class on nouns and verbs.

"Jeremy, can you give me an example of a noun?" she asked. Jeremy focused on her but she could see that the others were waiting for Jeremy to get it wrong as he often did. Jeremy hung his head and didn't respond. Corinne swept her arms over the classroom and said, "Nouns are everywhere." Jeremy looked a bit unsure but suggested "air". Corinne felt a wave of relief, smiled and said, "Great, air is a noun. Thank you Jeremy."

Corinne then asked Jean to use the noun 'air' in a sentence. Jean, a bit of a class clown, responded by saying, "Jeremy is an air head." At this the class broke into hoots of laughter and Corinne hardly could keep from laughing herself.

She reminded the class of the rule about making fun of others and added, "As well as being rude Jean, your answer is incorrect. You all know the rule about respecting others." At this point the atmosphere in the class changed to a kind of sullen silence and Corinne's feelings of anxiety returned. She got through the rest of the period by showing examples of nouns and adjectives on the board and discussing the relationships between them. Finally the bell rang and the students broke into numerous conversations. She heard one excitedly holler something about a new popular CD.

Corinne slumped back into her chair, let out a big sigh, and closed her eyes. She was exhausted and there still was the staff meeting, marking, and preparation of classes for tomorrow. She realized that teaching involved a lot of hard work and but she was more than willing to put in the hours; she really wanted a career as a teacher. What she really feared was that she would be unable to deal with the lack of involvement from students and the continuous classroom management problems.

# Index